A Library of Modern Religious Thought

LIBERAL PROTESTANTISM

A LIBRARY OF
MODERN RELIGIOUS THOUGHT
General Editor: Henry Chadwick, D.D.

S. T. COLERIDGE
CONFESSIONS OF AN INQUIRING SPIRIT
Edited by H. St. J Hart

LESSING'S THEOLOGICAL WRITINGS
Selected and translated by Henry Chadwick

DAVID HUME
THE NATURAL HISTORY OF RELIGION
Edited by H. E. Root

S. KIERKEGAARD
JOHANNES CLIMACUS
Translated and edited by T. H. Croxall

JOHN LOCKE
THE REASONABLENESS OF CHRISTIANITY
Edited and abridged by I. T. Ramsey

THE MIND OF
THE OXFORD MOVEMENT
Edited by Owen Chadwick

LIBERAL PROTESTANTISM
Edited by Bernard M. G. Reardon

LIBERAL PROTESTANTISM

EDITED AND INTRODUCED

BY

BERNARD M. G. REARDON

LECTURER IN CHRISTIAN THEOLOGY IN THE
UNIVERSITY OF NEWCASTLE UPON TYNE

STANFORD UNIVERSITY PRESS
STANFORD, CALIFORNIA

FIRST PUBLISHED 1968
© 1968 A. AND C. BLACK LTD

LIBRARY OF CONGRESS CATALOG CARD NUMBER 68–17139

PRINTED IN GREAT BRITAIN

CONTENTS

CONTENTS

CONTENTS

ACKNOWLEDGEMENTS

Thanks are due to the following for permission to print extracts from the books mentioned: Macmillan & Co. Ltd for H. R. Mackintosh and A. B. Macaulay's translation of Ritschl's *Justification and Reconciliation*; Ernest Benn Ltd for J. S. Stanyon's translation of Herrmann's *Communion of the Christian with God*, T. B. Saunder's translation of Harnack's *What is Christianity?*, the (anonymous) translation of Auguste Sabatier's *Religions of Authority and the Religion of the Spirit*, T. A. Seed's translation of the same author's *Outlines of a Philosophy of Religion*, and for V. Leuliette's translation of Jean Réville's *Liberal Christianity*; T. & T. Clark for G. Ferries's translation of Kaftan's *The Truth of the Christian Religion* and for William Adams Brown's *The Essence of Christianity*; Allen & Unwin for F. C. Conybeare's translation of Lotze's *Outlines of a Philosophy of Religion* and for C. J. Cadoux's *Catholicism and Christianity*; and finally the Syndics of the Cambridge University Press for J. F. Bethune-Baker's *The Way of Modernism*. B.M.G.R.

INTRODUCTION

1. What is Liberal Protestantism?

To define Liberal Protestantism at all concisely is by no means easy. It is nothing like a closed system of doctrine and has never been formulated in a confession. Indeed its attitude to dogma is apt to be detached and critical, and its general approach to Christianity historical rather than schematic. Liberal Protestantism is in fact simply what those who would think of themselves as at once Protestant and liberal conceive the Christian religion essentially to be; a wholly personal estimate, therefore, in which differing interests and emphases are bound to manifest themselves. For the word "liberal" is notoriously vague; it can mean more or less, as the case may be, and when applied to Christianity covers a wide variety of opinion as to the actual truth and value of traditional teachings. Thus one who unquestionably regarded himself as a Liberal Protestant, Jean Réville, wished to distinguish between Liberal Protestantism in the true sense and mere Protestant liberalism. "A moderately orthodox believer," he says, "may practise liberalism; he will not thereby become a Liberal Protestant."[1] On this view Liberal Protestantism implies not only liberalism in the matter of dogma or doctrine—by which presumably is meant a piecemeal adjustment of the received theology to at least the more insistent demands of contemporary thought—but certain positive convictions which, although erosive of the inherited doctrine of all the Protestant churches, is nevertheless held to be not only more responsive to the needs of the present time but also more in keeping with the original spirit of the Reformation and of the gospel itself. Yet for all this it is difficult to draw lines of demarcation. Réville himself was an advanced liberal, like his contemporary, Ernst Troeltsch, in Germany. But the founder of the Liberal Protestant school, Albrecht Ritschl, as too his disciples, Wilhelm Herrmann and Julius Kaftan, claimed to be thoroughly orthodox, seeking not a mere reduction of Christianity to whatever an increasingly secularist age could manage to swallow, but the

[1] *Liberal Christianity* (English translation by V. Leuliette, *1903*), p. *7*.

9

maintenance of Christian truth in its integrity, as testified by nearly four centuries of Protestant faith and piety. Further, Liberal Protestantism has not been a purely European phenomenon, having had a considerable following in this country and in America; and within the Anglo-Saxon religious tradition it similarly discloses variations ranging from moderate to radical. Hence to attempt to classify modernizing types of Protestantism into the Liberal, properly so-called, and the merely "broad" or "progressive", and to confine the designation Liberal Protestant to the former alone would appear arbitrary. It is a question much less of kind than of degree, and in the present selection of authors we have included, besides acknowledged adherents of the Ritschlian school and representatives of the liberal wing of the Reformed Church in France, a Congregationalist, a Presbyterian and an Anglican from the English-speaking world. But all alike are definitely Protestant and would have agreed on the necessity of giving renewed strength and currency to Protestant Christianity by adapting it to the spiritual wants of the modern man, even if much that the past had accepted without demur would have to be discarded.

Liberal Protestantism can, then, best be determined by a study of its historical emergence and progress, a method which liberals like Harnack or Sabatier would have deemed the right one. The movement arose during the last century, of which in obvious respects it is a type product. But its antecedents are older, whilst its later developments supply a potent element in the Christian outlook of our own time, however qualified by the experiences of recent history and the theological reaction which accompanied them.

That Protestantism should have attempted to come to terms with the advance of knowledge was natural and inevitable. The appeal to reason and conscience was inherent in Luther's own protest. Later no doubt it was stifled by the biblicism and dogmatism to which Reformation theology itself succumbed, but the assertion of the right of the individual believer to judge for himself—albeit under the Spirit's guidance—was something which could never be wholly expunged. Granted that the religious revolution of the sixteenth century was also in certain ways reactionary: that it feared and repudiated the Renaissance humanism, that it decried "natural" reason, that it set up a religious authoritarianism of its own choosing in place of that which it had defied, that it suspected secular learning as a needless diversion of the soul from the only truth that saves—all this is undeniable. Yet the Protestant movement was itself an expression of the new forces then bestirring contemporary society, a mark of and in turn a stimulus to the unrest of mind which was bound to follow upon the disintegration of the old order. The promotion of the Bible as a literally infallible authority, an oracular voice of truth every statement of which is a revelation calling for implicit acceptance, might result (as it certainly did result) in a new dogmatism even more rigid than that which it supplanted; more rigid because untempered by a living authority having power to interpret the written word as circumstances might prompt. But the principle that the believer's own inward experience is the final criterion, to which even Scripture is subject, was one that in the course of time could yield some unforeseen consequences. Not that the Bible would cease to command profound respect from the heirs of Luther and Calvin; but in an age for which history rather than dogmatic definitions supplied the measure of truth in human affairs the authority of the Bible, as itself a historical document, was likely to be shifted from the dogmatic to the historical plane. And the difference is all-important: the claims of dogma are absolute, but history speaks only of relativities.

2. Kant and Schleiermacher

The liberal movement in nineteenth century evangelical Christianity was mainly prompted by the advance of the sciences, especially the sciences of nature. So long as no excessive discrepancy showed itself between what religion bade men believe and what an increasingly common knowledge compelled them to recognise as fact—between their aspirations, that is, and their understanding—faith encountered no undue strain. A few sceptical minds might doubt or openly deny, but in a society which still unhesitatingly thought of itself as Christian the great majority were content to take the statements of Scripture relating to earthly conditions as readily as those which pointed to heavenly. But when geology came to tell a different tale from that of Genesis and the unique creation of man was contradicted by theories based on the clear evidence of biology—as, still more, when the investigation of matter seemed to suggest that mind itself might be only a material by-product—what was the believer to do? Shut his ears to science alto-gether and thus exclude himself from the civilization which was his by right? Or ought he simply to abandon religion as a relic of ignorance and superstition? Many, less or more consciously, took the former course, distressing though it often proved. Others chose the latter, finding, it might be, in the new *philosophie positive* of Auguste Comte a rationale of life which, at whatever cost to the hopes and ideals to which traditional Christianity had given assurance, at least afforded the satisfaction of intellectual consistency. But to the Christian who wished to feel at one with his own age and yet retain his confidence in the values to which, at the deepest level, religion alone lent sanction, some middle way of compromise had to be discovered. The very health of the human spirit demanded it. Catholicism, it appeared, was unable to adjust itself: Pius X's *Syllabus of Modern Errors*, issued in *1864*, confronted the modern world with a blank *non possumus*. But Protestantism rested on presuppositions of a kind that could be as liberating to the mind in the nineteenth century as in the sixteenth. As Herrmann confidently put it: "He today who is willing to see, can find the way which, even in a world altered by science, leads those who seek God to Christ." Or, more broadly, and in Ritschl's own words:

> "In every religion what is sought, with the help of the superhuman spiritual power reverenced by man, is a solution of the contradiction in which man finds himself, as both a part of the world of nature and a spiritual personality claiming to dominate nature. For the former rôle he is a part of nature, dependent upon her, subject to and confined by other things; but as spirit he is moved by the impulse to maintain his independence against them. In this juncture, religion springs up as faith in superhuman spiritual powers, by whose help the power which man possesses of himself is in some way supplemented and elevated into a unity of its own kind, which is a match for the pressure of the natural world."[1]

Religion, rightly understood, is the assertion and stay of man's freedom, of his sovereignty over that same inconscient nature to which science, acting on its own principles alone, would rigorously confine him. It is a liberating force, now as ever.

So far as Liberal Protestantism has been of German provenance or come under direct German influence its philosophical inspiration has

---

[1] *Justification and Reconciliation: the Positive Development of Doctrine* (English translation by H. R. Mackintosh and A. B. Macaulay), 2nd ed., p. *199*.

been that of Immanuel Kant, the major part of whose achievement was his critique of rationalism. Kant distinguished indeed between two kinds of philosophy, the dogmatic and the critical, the former of which aims at founding belief upon knowledge, thus making it rationally demonstrable. But the dogmatist soon meets an opponent for whom the proof is inadequate and the belief unwarranted. Deadlock is caused because they share the same presuppositions. A critical philosophy, however, will recognize that knowledge and belief are two different mental activities. The one pertains to the order of natural law, the other to that of morality. Confuse them and the claims of belief quickly appear dubious; distinguish them and a mutual adjustment becomes possible. There is a sense of course in which we allude to the "knowledge" of faith, but it is not knowledge in the strict sense, as with the facts of nature. For faith is not an activity of pure reason, and its object cannot be proved by reason. But neither can pure reason be used to overthrow it. The old antithesis between the material world and the spiritual may in this way, Kant holds, be resolved. The phenomenal world, with its observable data and rationally grounded laws, can neither be the basis of faith nor an effective obstacle to it. Natural science has its proper sphere and validity, but of man's moral life it cannot speak. If we want to know how things are in the realm apprehended by our senses, it can tell us; when we seek to understand their ultimate purposes and significance we turn to it in vain.

For Kant is convinced that life and the world are not purely matters of empirical fact. Man of his very nature recognizes moral good as his supreme goal. But this is not a conclusion of the rational intelligence alone; the *will* also plays its part—or as Kant calls it, the practical reason. The practical reason, in truth, is an expression of the "whole man", intelligence, will and emotion all entering into it. But the will is the paramount factor, since it is to it that the moral imperative is addressed. The pure reason has no immediate concern with the conative side of man's nature, whilst the emotions are usually an impediment to it. In any case, when we talk about good and evil we are talking of "ends", not simply of matters as they are or are not, to be affirmed or denied as true or false. Mere nature does not yield us moral values, and whether the "good" life is or is not worth pursuing is something that strict logic or scientific observation cannot itself decide. The practical reason therefore is all-important for living. It runs a risk because it is unable to prove; but once the venture has been made subsequent experience amply justifies it.

Yet it also must be asked whether and how these two orders of knowledge are related. Kant's reply is that they correspond to two distinct worlds, that of sense and that which is beyond sense, the *transcendental*. The first, the phenomenal world, is affirmed by pure reason *a priori*, not indeed as a thing in itself—for what things are in themselves we can never know—but as it appears to us, and even then only according to its form. Reality, it is to be understood, lies behind appearances, a suprasensible world which Kant calls the noumenal and which is bound always to elude reason's grasp when reason is taken in its exacter connotation. But it is to this same world of noumenal or ultra-phenomenal reality that religious belief refers. Man himself, in his spiritual essence, also belongs to it: it is because he is what he is that he is capable of apprehending it. The transcendental world is a world of spirit, of freedom, and hence of a higher order of being than that merely of nature and necessity. That the language man uses to describe this world lacks scientific precision, that it is figurative or symbolic only, does not imply that it is inappropriate. On the contrary, it is entirely appropriate, since the needs of man's life themselves prompt it.

Kant's analysis of knowledge delivered religious belief from the throttling grip of rationalism. The spirit seemed to regain its freedom, while the universe of nature could continue to be studied in terms of the fixities of law. That the critical philosophy dichotomizes the human understanding and that the noumenal and phenomenal worlds remain in the end uncoordinated might have to be admitted. For the Kantian doctrine was ambiguous at some vital points and pursuit of its implications could take one direction or another, according to the interpretation imposed. But if it inhibited religious dogmatism from a terrain in which it had no competence it also gave the lie to the pretension that science alone has the key to truth. Neither the rationalist nor the dogmatist, therefore, could claim an exclusive authority over man's mind. Science and religion both were strengthened by clear enunciation of their basic principles. What belongs to nature and history has its own criteria of assessment, but the great affirmations of the moral life likewise have theirs, and no better grounds exist for denying the one than for questioning the other.

For all their differences, which were immense, Kant and Luther had this in common, that their thinking was of revolutionary effect. Both men appealed to the facts of human experience which the prevailing dogmatic systems either ignored or overrode. Luther was a man of the heart; his own experience, and the theology in which he expressed it, sprang from the emotions. He craved for assurance and peace, for that sense of acceptance by God to which the consciousness of sin was an intolerable obstacle. His whole life was motivated by an intense religious conviction. Kant, by contrast, was a man of the reason; he had very little religious feeling at all and was unsympathetic towards distinctively religious ideas and attitudes. "Everything," he declared, "outside of a good life by which man supposes he can make himself well-pleasing to God is superstition." He detested what he called *Schwärmerei*; religion's proper sphere was that of the moral will. He believed, however, that the existence of God was a necessary postulate of reason in its practical function. It was not and could not be a scientific conclusion, but its certitude was in its way as great as any to be reached in the empirical realm. Luther freed the spirit from ecclesiastical dogma and the oppressiveness of an institution which had lost sight of its true purposes. Kant freed it from the intellectual straightjacket which, at the end of the eighteenth century, represented Lutheranism itself in its theological decadence.

Kantian epistemology was a reaction against and a criticism of two opposing errors. On the one side, it firmly rejected the crude empiricism which explained knowledge wholly with reference to external stimuli and reduced it in effect to a bare sensationalism. This was a theory that failed to account for the unity of human experience. On the other side, it was equally hostile to the concept of innate ideas, which sought to originate all knowledge in the mind itself. Here the omission was to relate the mind to the outside world—to say indeed how knowledge of the world is ever arrived at. Both arose from the mistake of assuming that knowledge is all of a piece, coming either wholly from without or wholly from within. But the human mind, Kant argued, is neither an empty space waiting to be filled nor a universal creativity sufficient of itself. On the contrary, it has a dual capacity. In one aspect it is receptive, drawing upon what is presented to consciousness but does not spring from it, perception being the gateway to and from the exterior world. In the other it is constructive—what enters consciousness from without is incomprehensible until examined, sifted and coordinated. Only as the mind works on the material which sensation affords it is the latter systematized as knowledge. But this the mind does by virtue of its own constitution, in imposing the patterns or forms of its *categories* (in Kantian language): for example, space, time or cause. These categories are of course essentially formal; for its actual "matter" the mind has always to go outside itself. From this it follows that what things are *out of relation* to the intelligence which apprehends them cannot be said. The *Ding-an-sich*, the thing-in-itself, is a metaphysical quantity of which direct knowledge is impossible. Hence the scepticism of Kant's philosophy when compared with the brash confidence of current rationalisms, such as Wolff's. Yet the Kantian scepticism is far from being merely negative. It is not scepticism for its own sake. Kant's aim, as he himself stated it, was "to deny knowledge, in order to make room for faith". What he seems not to have perceived was that he had thus cleared a path for agnosticism as to the truth of any religious affirmation.

But Kant himself had no doubt that the practical reason is entirely valid for the sphere of action, as conceived in terms of duty. For duty is justifiable only as duty; it must not be presented as an object of desire. To do what is right for any other motive than that of doing right is to transform obligation into self-interest; and this, as it seemed to him, is what religion, at least as popularly understood, so often does. Kant's moral rigorism here clearly reflected his own pessimism concerning human nature. For man in his view was not, as Rousseau preached, naturally good; rather is there within him a radical propensity to evil (*das radicale Böse*), as Reformation theology has insisted. If duty and desire were to coincide it would mean that man's sense of obligation had been undermined by the inclinations of a nature fundamentally base. The categorical imperative, however, must be obeyed regardless of all other satisfactions. Accordingly morality must be independent of religion. Yet for Kant it is the only ground of belief in God. For although we may not do good from the desire of happiness, such desire is inherent in our nature, and it is hardly conceivable that in a rational world moral values should be permanently out of harmony with men's other ends and aspirations. Hence the conclusion that the highest good, the union of virtue and happiness, is attainable only if God exists as moral governor of the universe, dispensing reward and punishment according to man's moral deserts. Religion is thus to be seen as the recognition of all duties as divine commands. It is not the basis of morality, but itself rests on it. The two differ only in their formal structure and terminology, not in substance.

Christianity, although suffering from the inevitable imperfections of an historical institution, nevertheless approaches the ideal of an ethical theology more nearly than any other religion. Its doctrines embody profound moral insights, if in symbolic guise. Especially valuable, Kant thinks, is that of the Kingdom of God, or the Church Invisible, as representing an "ethical commonwealth" or community of those united in reverence for moral law and their determination to treat one another not as means but as ends.

The influence of Kant's ethical idealism, like his rejection of all transcendental reasoning about religion, is abundantly evident in the case of Ritschl and his followers. Kantian also is the Ritschlian distinction between fact and value, nature and spirit, science and moral action. But to the student of Liberal Protestantism the effects of Schleiermacher's teaching are scarcely less apparent. Kant, for all his anticipation of later trends of thought, was very much an eighteenth century figure. The individualistic note of ethical rationalism is persistent in all his work. Schleiermacher, on the other hand, introduced into religious reflexion a different spirit and gave it a new ethos. For him religion is a condition of the heart. Its essence is *feeling*. Without a deep emotional impulse it cannot be sustained in its true character and becomes either rationalism or moralism. Christian doctrine, he urges, must be set forth "in complete independence of each and every philosophical system". Faith, that is, is not as Hegel was teaching, imperfect philosophical understanding. Basically it is a feeling of absolute dependence —in the instance of Christianity a feeling of absolute dependence upon God in Christ—and therefore a matter of individual experience, of a personal intuition. Doctrines and rites are subsequent. The fundamental meaning of all religion is the discovery of the infinite in the midst of the finite. Schleiermacher's thought, especially in his early *Addresses on Religion*, undoubtedly tends to pantheism, but this is offset by a strong sense of individuality. Religious experience he holds to be multiform; it spreads itself into "many provinces", and "no one will have his own true and right religion, if it is the same for all". Nevertheless Schleiermacher does not reduce religion to mere individual sentiment. Like

B

other basal human experiences it is a social concern and propagates itself through contact. The existence of the Christian Church is part of the Christian experience, registering a common consciousness. Salvation, for Kant, as for most of his contemporaries, was almost exclusively an individual matter, and the Church, accordingly, was no more than an aggregation of units. But for Schleiermacher the social aspect of Christianity is of constitutive importance and salvation cannot be achieved except in relation with others. Society is necessary for mediation and communication, and as a corrective to individual eccentricity. Not that he insists on any particular condition or organ of unity—a dogma or rite or hierarchy. What Schleiermacher himself meant by the Church was simply that part of mankind which shares the Christian consciousness. To give too sharp a definition to the determinants of this consciousness would only lead back again to the traditional dogmatism and institutionalism, Protestant no less than Catholic.

Again—and the point is one on which later liberal theology was to lay great emphasis—Schleiermacher insisted that the connexion between the Christian religion and the historicity of its founder was unseverable. For Christ is related to the faith which bears his name in a manner unlike that of the originator of any other, his actual historical character being of the highest significance. His place in revelation is unique, determined by his unparalleled sense of relation to and dependence upon God. Not simply *a* man, he is the very type of mankind, the perfect realization of the human ideal. Eighteenth century theology, with its concern for "natural" religion and universal moral truths, had virtually ceased, in practice, to make the figure of Christ central to Christianity as the constituent factor in Christian experience. This imbalance Schleiermacher was to rectify, and his own emphatic Christocentrism had marked influence on later liberalism. Christianity he saw essentially as a redemptive religion, indeed the redemptive religion *par excellence*. The historic Jesus had been for man the source of a new life of spiritual communion with God, in that the communion he himself knew has become a possibility also for those who are drawn into fellowship with him in his Church. Redemption being deliverance from sin—from that state of heart and mind in which man's higher self-consciousness is darkened and enfeebled into one in which it is rendered strong and clear again—the result is a change in man's entire nature. The power of human self-direction towards the good is restored and life attains fulfilment in the service of others.

All these characteristic positions of Schleiermacher's are re-affirmed in Liberal Protestantism. Individual liberals may be critical on this score or that: Ritschl especially is often distinctly cool in his appraisal of the great Romantic theologian; but Schleiermacher's shadow falls across the whole century. However, after his death in *1834* it was Hegel, rather, who dominated the intellectual scene. And Hegel, who equated the real with the rational and saw all mysteries unravelled in the light of his transcendental metaphysic, had no difficulty in explaining Christianity. To him speculation was the breath of life. The Christian religion he took for a figurative system whose conceptual equivalents found their precise and adequate statement in his own philosophy. For the older and cruder style of rationalism he had indeed nothing but disdain, and his professions of respect for religious orthodoxy were sincerely meant. Yet the metaphysician who read the Christian dogmas only as symbols of the Absolute and for whom the gospel's historical foundations had no intrinsic significance was one from whose hands an account of Christianity that was spiritually satisfying could scarcely be expected. Hegel's initial impact on the mind of his time was overwhelming, but his followers soon split up into different camps. Some on the "right"—Biedermann, for example —stood for a Christianity at least formally orthodox; others, like Feuerbach, far to the "left", channelled the Hegelian principles into a declared atheism. However, Hegel's main influence on theological study was really in the field of historical and biblical criticism, of which F. C. Baur was the acknowledged master. Baur's views on the origin and early development of Christianity and the date and authorship of the New Testament writings explicitly conform to the Hegelian law of historical evolution, the triad of thesis, antithesis and synthesis. But even here the effect of a philosophical apriorism was to impede any proper understanding of what Christianity is, whether in its historical process or in its living character. The Hegelian approach to the problem was in fact a blind turning, and if Protestantism was to meet the demands of the new scientific era and still preserve its religious and moral vitality it would have to look for other and more congenial mentors. And these it found in the thinkers whom absolute idealism had temporarily eclipsed.

3. Albrecht Ritschl

The spearhead of the Liberal Protestant movement may be identified with the Lutheran school of Ritschl and his disciples, which in the second half of the last century replaced the Hegelian in the leadership of progressive Christian thought. In Germany the collapse of Hegel's intellectual *régime* was astonishingly rapid and complete. The spell which his doctrine had cast, whether upon philosophers, theologians, historians or economists, was suddenly broken. In an age in which the mass of coordinated knowledge was steadily increasing the whole grandiose system was seen to rest on an insufficient factual basis. Phenomena, in whatever province of discovery and research, were obviously too multifarious and complex to fit the rigid pattern which the Hegelian doctrine forced upon them. Once more, as in the previous century, the reign of rationalism brought about its own downfall, and again it was the critical philosophy of Kant which, in theology, provided the instrument of demolition. In any event the new phenomenalism and positivism had scant sympathy with the high-flown metaphysic of the Absolute and Infinite manifesting itself under the finite and relative conditions of human history. Such large abstractions were either beyond knowledge or without meaning—which amounted to the same thing. When therefore the pretensions of idealism to a universal understanding began to be questioned the resulting disillusionment was swift and thorough. In the domain of theology the idea that Christianity is simply the historic fulfilment of natural religion, the culminating self-disclosure of immanent Spirit, seemed an outright denial of its claim to any unique status and authority. To uphold this claim, whilst at the same time facing constructively the unavoidable challenge of the natural and historical sciences, was the task, it now seemed, incumbent on the serious Christian thinker. The work of Ritschl was to prove in this respect of epochal importance.

The most influential Protestant theologian of his age, Albrecht Benjamin Ritschl was born in Berlin in *1822*, the son of an Evangelical pastor who later became bishop of Pomerania. Educated at the universities of Bonn, Halle, Heidelberg and Tübingen, he soon became acquainted with the leading theological teachers in Germany: with Nitzsch at Bonn, with Tholuck and Julius Müller at Halle, with Rothe at Heidelberg, but above all with Baur at Tübingen. These were his

Hegelian days, and for a time he was Baur's ardent disciple, as is evidenced by his earliest publication, on the relation of Marcion's gospel to that of Luke.[1] His first academic post was as a *Privatdocent* at Bonn, whither he returned after only a year at Tübingen, his adherence to Tübingen views, however, continuing firm. Thus in *1850* he brought out his book on the origin of the old Catholic Church,[2] which still clearly reflects Baur's opinions. But the Hegelian infatuation was not to prove lasting and in *1856* he decisively broke with the Tübingen master. Meanwhile, in *1852*, he had been appointed extraordinary professor at the same university, acceding seven years later to the ordinary professorship. He was now in process of working out his own doctrine, in which he derived a good deal of stimulus from the philosopher Hermann Lotze at Göttingen, whither he went as professor in *1864*—to remain there indeed, despite offers of chairs at Strassburg and Berlin, for the rest of his life.[3] In *1870* appeared the first volume of his most celebrated work, *The Christian Doctrine of Justification and Reconciliation*, containing an account of the historical development of the doctrine,[4] to be followed four years after by a second and third, the one dealing with the biblical foundations, the other—and much the most important of the three—presenting the author's own system in detail.[5] His later publications comprise an essay on Schleiermacher's *Addresses* (*1874*), the three volumes of his history of pietism (*1880–1886*),[6] and the book called "Theology and Metaphysics" (*1881*),[7] which offers a fuller and more polemical account of his philosophical position. His *Instruction in the Christian Religion* (*1875*),[8] although none too lucid for its avowed purpose, is intended as a summary of evangelical theology for use in schools. His lectures and essays were collected

---

[1] *Das Evangelium Marcions und das kanonische Evangelium Lukas* (*1846*).

[2] *Die Entstehung der altkatholische Kirche.* A second and much revised edition was published in *1857*.

[3] On the influence of Lotze upon Ritschl see Otto Ritschl, *Albrecht Ritschls Leben*, ii, pp. *20*, *244* f., *376*.

[4] *Die christliche Lehre von der Rechtfertigung und Versöhnung.* An English translation by J. S. Black became available in *1872*.

[5] A second edition of the entire work was published in *1882–3*, a third in *1888*, and a fourth in *1895*. This last, however, is simply a reprint of the third. The English translation of the third volume, cited above (p. 12), came out in *1900*.

[6] *Die Geschichte des Pietismus.*

[7] *Theologie und Metaphysik: Zur Verständigung und Abwehr* (2nd ed. *1887*).

[8] *Unterricht in der christlichen Religion.* An English edition, by A. T. Swing, dates from *1901*.

in a couple of posthumous volumes (*1893* and *1896*) respectively),[1] whilst a two-volume biography by his son Otto completed publication in *1896*. Academic pursuits engrossed Ritschl's whole life, and his lecture-room at Göttingen was always thronged, although in his latter years controversial exchanges with his many critics, both conservative and liberal, proved a by no means unwelcome diversion. He died in the spring of *1889*, at the age of *67*.

Fundamentally Ritschl was in agreement with Schleiermacher that the facts of Christian experience are the theologian's proper starting-point, and that no attempt at an *a priori* rational validation of Christian truth is either necessary or possible. Where Ritschl parts company with the earlier teacher is, however, in his account of what the Christian experience essentially is. Schleiermacher's conceptions, with their elevation of the emotions, always seemed to him perilously subjectivist. Not personal feeling but the objective testimony of history was the only bedrock of doctrine. If it were true that religion is primarily an emotional disposition, or even such a personal and private experience as that of the mystic, then there could be no assurance that the believer was in contact with a reality above and beyond himself. What, in fact, could be meant by *belief* at all? It may fairly be asked whether Ritschl's own key-idea of the "value-judgment" is not in its way equally subjectivist.[2] But what Ritschl evidently maintains is, not that Christianity has nothing to do with subjective attitudes, since "experience" is inseparable from them, but that the experience in question is caused by objective data. Thus his examination of the biblical doctrine was undertaken, he tells us, "in order to ascertain what idea of the forgiveness of sins, justification, and reconciliation—together with their relations—had been called into existence by Jesus as the Founder of the Christian Church, and maintained by the apostles as its earliest representatives".[3] In Ritschl's view the theologian should start not merely with the religious consciousness as such, but with the gospel;[4] and the gospel, being grounded in history, must needs become the subject of historical inquiry. This is a task, Ritschl thinks, which the theologian simply cannot shelve if the nature of Christianity is to be

[1] *Gesammelte Aufsätze.*
[2] See, e.g., J. Wendland, *Albrecht Ritschl und seine Schüler* (*1899*), p. *77*.
[3] *Justification and Reconciliation*, p. *1*.
[4] Cf. F. Kattenbusch, *Von Schleiermacher zu Ritschl* (2nd ed., *1893*), pp. *72* f.

understood. Accordingly his own earlier work on the origins of Catholicism seeks to depict the Christianity of the first two centuries as something distinctive and original, incapable of explanation only in terms of its religious and philosophical environment.[1] Further, Ritschl dislikes Schleiermacher's characterization of religion as a feeling of *dependence*, for what acceptance of the gospel really brings is a sense of *freedom*. It is less the emotional than the conative side of man's nature to which Christianity appeals; in the gospel the ethical element is uppermost. Hence Ritschl's great respect for Kant, since it was he who, as Ritschl himself phrases it, first perceived "the supreme importance of ethics for 'the Kingdom of God' as an association of men bound together by the laws of virtue"; although he concedes that Schleiermacher was the first also "to employ the true conception of the teleological nature of the Kingdom of God to determine the idea of Christianity", a service, he judges, which ought not to be forgotten even if Schleiermacher failed to grasp the discovery with a firm hand. For as Ritschl understands it Christianity is above all else a life devoted to action both Godward and manward, in which the ethical imperative is basic.

Thus the nature and function of religion are inherently pragmatic. Religious activity Ritschl defines as an "interpretation of man's relation to God and the world, guided by the thought of the sublime power of God to realize the end of man's blessedness".[2] But this implies that religious knowledge is not theoretical, since religion and mere theory, although they may deal with the same objects, are not even partially coincident but diverge wholly. The special power of religion is to deliver man in his spiritual capacity both from the determinism of his physical environment and the enslaving passions of his own nature. Certainly in his physical being he is a part of the natural order, dependent upon it and ever subject to and confined by external forces; but as a spirit he is moved by the impulse to maintain his independence against them.

"In this juncture, religion springs up as faith in super-human spiritual powers, by whose help the power which man possesses of himself is in some way supplemented and elevated into a unity of its own kind, which is a match for the pressure of the natural world."[3]

[1] Cf. O. Ritschl, *Leben*, i, pp. *292* f.
[2] *Justification and Reconciliation*, p. *194*.   [3] *Op. cit.*, p. *199*.

In other words, religion begins not as speculative curiosity about the world and its constitution, but in the situation in which man actually finds himself. Religious doctrines, therefore, instead of being—as so often supposed—simple statements of fact, are really *Werthurtheile*, value-judgments elicited by man's attitude to the world around him and relating to his spiritual satisfaction or its opposite—according, that is, to whether he "either enjoys the dominion over the world vouchsafed him by God, or feels grievously the lack of God's help to that end".[1] Or to put it in rather different terms, the knowledge of God becomes *religious* only when he is thought of as the agent of man's spiritual liberation. This however does not mean that "value-judgments" are no more than personal and subjective preferences having no necessary correspondence with reality, an idea as we have said, far from Ritschl's intention. Kaftan, for example, believes that he is interpreting Ritschl quite correctly when he states that "the truth of the propositions of faith means nothing else, and can mean nothing else, than that they are *objectively* true".[2] Nevertheless on this issue his critics have accused him of an intolerable dualism.[3] Yet whatever may be thought of the value-judgment as a true explanation of religious cognition, this particular criticism rests on a misconception. Ritschl does indeed distinguish sharply between the scientific and the religious methods of arriving at truth, holding that a religious assertion is intrinsically different from a scientific fact; but he is not a dualist in the sense of teaching that what may be true in religion can be false in science and *vice versa*. What he is affirming is that the idea of God is not simply a philosophical concept, towards which a man may be morally neutral. God is known to us as a personal activity in a manner beyond the purview of metaphysics or the traditional natural theology, which,

---

[1] *Ibid.*, p. *205*.

[2] *Das Wesen der christlichen Religion* (*1881*), p. *102*.

[3] See, e.g., J. Orr, *The Ritschlian Theology* (*1897*), p. *242*; and J. Denney, *Studies in Theology* (*1894*), p. *14*: "Though Jesus has for the Christian consciousness the religious value of God, He has for the scientific consciousness only the common real value of man. He is, in truth and reality, to the neutral consideration of science, mere man like any other; it is only the *Werthurtheil*, the subjective estimate of the pious Christian, that gives him the value of God." H. Schoen, in his *Origines historiques de la théologie de Ritschl* (*1893*) considers that this dualism runs through all Ritschl's teaching: "We have two kinds of judgments, two kinds of truths, and two ways of knowing these and those" (p. *33*).

like Luther, he rejects out of hand.[1] Thus the scholastic "proofs" of
divine existence, appealing as they do to nothing more than a sense of
rational consistency, lead not to the object of Christian faith and worship but merely to theories of world-unity which have nothing whatever to do with the religious impulse.[2] Such a use of metaphysics must
therefore, Ritschl urges, be entirely excluded from theology if the
latter's authentic character is to be preserved. The verification of faith
is experience, not abstract logic. *Whosoever willeth to do the will of God
shall know that the doctrine of Christ is true.*[3] Hence Ritschl's antagonism
towards the whole Hegelian doctrine of a monistic Absolute.[4] A like
objection applies also to the sundry metaphysical attributes—infinity,
eternity, aseity, impassibility and so on—which scholasticism, Catholic
or Protestant, so liberally assigns to God. For whatever God may or
may not be "in himself", as a transcendent being, the significant truth
for the religious consciousness is that he *reveals* himself as a loving
Father and a merciful Redeemer. The essence of the value-judgment
concept is the distinction it draws between the pure "factualness"
established by the critical reason and that necessary *interpretation* of fact
which assesses its meaning and use for life. To see truth in terms of
value is no more than to relate it to practical ends.[5] It should be noted
that Kaftan himself holds that while value-judgments are the basis of
religious doctrines the latter, as such, are none the less theoretical

[1] "If any one builds Christian theology on a substructure of pretended natural
theology he merely takes his stand outside the sphere of regeneration, *which is
coterminous with the community of believers*" (*Justification and Reconciliation*, p. *8*)
(Italics ours).
[2] The cosmological and teleological arguments, he points out, do not take us
beyond the limits of the world, and in any case "their pretended results, even if
they were correct, differ from the Christian conception of God in that they fail to
express his worth for men, and in particular his worth for men as sinners". Only
the moral argument, as propounded by Kant, has any validity. It shows that while
Christianity is in harmony with reason "it is always with the reservation that
knowledge of God embodies itself in judgments which differ in kind from those
of theoretical science". See *Justification and Reconciliation*, p. *225*.
[3] John vii, *17*.
[4] See *Theologie und Metaphysik*, pp. *17* f. Although systems of monistic idealism
have, he says, asserted their agreement with Christianity, whose leading ideas
have been worked up into a general philosophic view, the only result has been to
demonstrate once more the utter disparity between all such systems and the
Christian faith.
[5] See O. Ritschl's further explanation of his father's views in *Über Werthurtheile*
(*1895*), pp. *9–12*.

propositions, although he believes that here his difference from Ritschl is one of expression rather than principle.

The importance which Ritschl attaches to the value-judgment as the mode of religious knowledge can be rightly appreciated only when we realize that his entire view of religion is dominated by his ethical concern. The religious life is a life essentially of moral goodness. But moral goodness can be achieved only in society: the godly life is a social life, in which the individual fulfils his responsibilities to his fellowmen. "An interest in salvation, in the Christian sense, is incompatible with egoism." Any attempt to separate faith in God from public spirit and recognition of one's duty to the community is, from the Christian standpoint, a profound error. "In Christianity the religious motive of ethical action lies here, that the Kingdom of God, which it is our task to realize, also represents the highest good which God destines for us as our supramundane goal." This is the end to which religion serves as means: it is by religion that we can realize the potential of our moral being. Hence its rôle in promoting *this*-worldly activity and enabling man to exercise his God-given dominion. Justification itself involves this:

> "The sinner who in his previous distrust of God shows himself dependent on the world, can, in his confidence in God's forgiveness of his sins, be proved to be changed only inasmuch as the new dominion over the world through confidence in God's universal providence is combined with it."

Ritschl always resented the charge that, like Kant, he makes religion a subordinate appendix to morals, and claimed that his actual teaching (as distinct from its common misinterpretation) showed the very opposite.[1] Yet Kantian echoes are undoubtedly there. Ritschl—to be fair to him—is stating his belief in Christian terms, but Kant's idea of religion as the practical postulate of the ethical life at once springs to mind.

It follows from Ritschl's overall view of Christianity that his account of redemption should receive a strongly moralistic colouring, and he complains that traditional Protestantism, in its stress on personal salvation, has failed to do justice to the ethical understanding of faith

[1] See *Justification and Reconciliation*, p. *226* n.

implied by the doctrine of the Kingdom of God. The Christian religion, he thinks, "resembles not a circle described from a single centre, but an ellipse which is determined by two *foci*"—as Catholicism has in its own way recognized.[1] Moreover, in this respect Christianity provides the key to the meaning of all religion. For the former is not to be seen, as Hegel and Schleiermacher saw it, simply as an instance of a wider phenomenon and, to that extent, with a predetermined character. Rather, if a definition of religion is to be framed at all it must be upon the basis of the Christian experience as the criterion of every other.[2] An attitude of mere neutrality towards Christianity with a view to deducing its meaning from a consideration of the religious phenomenon as a whole will only result in undermining Christian conviction. Any general conception of religion, that is to say, will be of no more than regulative use. The distinctiveness of Christianity among the great religions lies, Ritschl characteristically maintains, in its offer of mastery over the world through dependence upon God: "The knowledge of God can be demonstrated as religious knowledge only when God is conceived as securing to the believer such a position in the world as more than counter-balances its restrictions."[3]

Ritschl's own comprehensive definition of Christianity is that of

"... the monotheistic, completely spiritual and ethical religion, which, based on the life of its Author as Redeemer and Founder of the Kingdom of God, consists in the freedom of the children of God, involves the impulse to conduct which, from the motive of love, aims at the moral organisation of mankind, and grounds blessedness on the relation of sonship to God as well as on his Kingdom."[4]

It is the culmination of the monotheistic and teleological religion of the Bible, and is dominated by *both* a redemptive and an ethical motive, mutually conditioning:

"Christ made the universal moral Kingdom of God his end, and thus he came to know and decide for that kind of redemption which

[1] *Ibid.*, p. *11*.
[2] *Ibid.*, p. *194*. But Ritschl does allow that some illumination of Christianity itself may be derived from the study of religious history in general, although in making comparisons its uniqueness must never be overlooked. See *Justification and Reconciliation*, p. *8*.
[3] *Ibid.*, p. *212*.   [4] *Ibid.*, p. *13*.

he achieved through the maintenance of fidelity in his calling and of his blessed fellowship with God through suffering and death."[1]

Ritschl's emphasis on the Kingdom should be noted as (in fact) the outstanding feature of his doctrine. As he sees it the Kingdom must be understood as the gospel's final objective; yet it is a truth, he thinks, which Protestantism had neglected and he blames the Reformers of the sixteenth century—with the sole exception of Zwingli—for having represented the Kingdom as a purely inward union, wrought by grace, between Christ and the believer. Kant was the first to perceive the signal importance of the idea for ethics, and his insight was further developed by Schleiermacher, if not very fully. Modern Protestantism must realize that the Kingdom as a moral goal is central to the teaching of Jesus and that the necessary means to its attainment is the religious fellowship which he founded; for "Christ did not describe this moral task, to be carried out by the human race, in the form of a philosophical doctrine and propagate it in a school: he entrusted it to his disciples."[2] Salvation accordingly is not directed to the individual alone. Freedom in God is of course the *private* end of each individual Christian, but the ultimate end is the divine Kingdom as such. It transcends the natural limits of nationality to become the moral society of nations.[3] Schleiermacher, although assigning to the Church a clear place within the Christian scheme, looked first of all to the individual—misled in this, Ritschl supposes, by his "mystical" notion of the soul's absolute and isolated dependence on God: "Only in a secondary way is the world brought into relation with the religious faculty." Consequently for the Romantic theologian a church is merely an aggregate of individual believers; the religious society is approached *through* the individual and its organization for an overall moral end is never really envisaged by him. That Ritschl should have begun his own systematic theology with the doctrine of justification ought not therefore to be allowed to obscure the fact that for him the *Church* is of primary significance and the only proper context for the salvation of the individual. His words indeed could not be plainer:

---

[1] *Ibid.*, p. *10*.
[2] P. *12*.
[3] Cf. *Unterricht*, sect. *5*: "Das Reich Gottes ist das von der Gott gewährleistete höchste Gut der durch seine Offenbarung in Christus gestifteten Gemeinde."

"Justification, or reconciliation, as positively connected with the historical manifestation and activity of Christ, is related in the first instance to the religious community founded by Christ as a whole, which maintains the Gospel of God's grace in Christ as the direct means of its existence, and to individuals only as they attach themselves, by faith in the Gospel, to this community."[1]

It is to the Church in its corporate identity that God's promises are made, as it is in the Church alone that justification and forgiveness, freedom and sonship can be obtained.

The central and presiding theme of Ritschl's work is, as its title indicates, man's redemption, and all other doctrines are arranged around it. In this it is typically Lutheran and in the original tradition of Luther himself. But by a long-standing convention systematic theology had followed the "logical" scheme of starting with the being of God as he is "in himself" and apart from any special revelation to mankind. The doctrines of man, sin and redemption came afterwards, so that the specific content of Christian experience made its appearance only by degrees. Ritschl however reverses this order and begins with the moral and religious life: sin, consciousness of forgiveness, the recovery of the moral will, freedom and the gift of divine love—the entire process, in short, of justification and reconciliation. The facts appealed to being psychologically and historically significant, the method of theology thus can justly be claimed to be empirical and scientific, as much as in any other field of study. Schleiermacher also had based his system on religious experience, but for him the essential form of such experience was the feeling of dependence, of which redemption is a particular, not the universal, expression. His own scheme, for example, is founded upon man's primal dependence on God as revealed in nature; and only after treating of this does he go on to consider the effects of sin and the knowledge of God's saving acts, approaching them moreover on the plane of the individual. But to Ritschl the redemptive experience on its broadest ground is fundamental, since without it Christianity would not exist; as without Christianity there likewise could be no religion in the real meaning of the word. Hence the respective accounts of Christian

---

[1] P. *139*. Elsewhere (p. *30*) he says that "the religious conceptions of justification and reconciliation, to be explained, must not be applied in isolation to the individual subject, but to the subject as a member of the community of believers."

experience which the two greatest systematic theologians of the nineteenth century have to offer diverge from the outset. Schleiermacher's thinking is mystical, quasi-pantheistic, and concerning human nature essentially optimistic: at least, evil is felt to be a relative and transient condition, a temporary impediment to man's native awareness of his dependence on God. Ritschl, on the other hand, is like Luther, deeply conscious of man's sin and need of forgiveness, and reconciliation he sees as a moral goal yet to be attained, with the atoning work of Christ as the one road thereto.

Not that for Schleiermacher also Christ's work is anything but the necessary condition of redemption: Christianity rests on Christ, beyond all question. But in Ritschl the uniqueness of Christ and of what he accomplished for the human race has clearer recognition. For the older theologian Jesus represents a stage, albeit the highest and most complete, in a process of divine self-disclosure assuming many forms. To the younger he stands absolutely alone, an innovating force entering and renewing history.

Christ's significance for the Christian is threefold. First, he only, says Ritschl, was qualified for the special vocation of inaugurating the Kingdom of God. Jesus' consciousness of this is evident from what he tells us in the gospel of his knowledge of the Father, a claim consistent with his entire conduct and in particular his patience and steadfastness under suffering. Next, his work in founding the Kingdom was a fulfilment of God's purpose for the world. "The integral unity between Christ and God, which Jesus accordingly claims for himself, refers to the whole extent of his activity in his calling, and thus consists in the reciprocal relation between God's love and Jesus' vocational obedience."[1] Hence for Christian faith he is "alone of his kind", all possibility of obedience to the divine will being dependent upon him as the one mediator. Thirdly, Christ exercizes lordship by virtue of both his oneness with God and the suffering and death by which he overcame the world. So strong indeed is Ritschl's emphasis on Christ's utter uniqueness that even the attempt to write his life implies "the surrender of the conviction that, as the Founder of the perfect moral and spiritual religion, Jesus belongs to a higher order than all other men".[2] It is for this reason also that the significance of Christ cannot be

[1] *Unterricht*, sect. 22.
[2] *Justification and Reconciliation*, p. 3.

established on a biographical assessment alone. The full compass of his historical actuality can be discovered only from the belief of the Christian community. At the same time Ritschl will have nothing to do with the Chalcedonian Definition as a statement of Christ's divinity in that it offers no adequate account of the relation of the two natures. Luther he criticizes for sticking in theory to the old orthodoxy, but commends him for his own more dynamic view in seeking the Godhead in the manhood. "While the Church formula is retained"— Ritschl is referring expressly to the *Longer Catechism*—"it really is in Christ's human achievements that his Godhead becomes for his people manifest, conspicuous, intelligible, winning our faith, not in the form of an assent to an unintelligible dogma, but of personal trust for our own salvation."[1]

Ritschl's detachment of the revelation given in Christ from all other types of religious experience and his denial of any *praeparatio evangelica* apart from the Old Testament is of course a salient feature of his teaching and one for which he has been a good deal criticized.[2] But the fact that Christianity is *sui generis* should not blind us, he holds, to the evident truth that in its historical development it has been conjoined with elements wholly foreign to its nature. Of these Greek philosophy is the predominant, and under its influence the God of biblical revelation has been transformed into a metaphysical Absolute, and the Jesus of the gospels correspondingly reduced to the personalized Logos of the Alexandrian Platonists. The history of ecclesiastical dogma is indeed its own sufficient condemnation. Living religion has became a quasi-philosophical system and personal faith the intellectual acceptance of formal propositions. No doubt the process, under the prevailing cultural conditions, was inevitable; but it is none the less deplorable for all that and must be recognized for the corruption that it is. A main aim of the liberal movement in Protestantism thus must be to separate the authentic substance of Christianity from its alien accretions—a task more deliberately assumed by Ritschl's followers, Kaftan and Harnack

---

[1] *Ibid.*, p. *394*.

[2] Ritschl is careful to explain that the uniqueness of Christianity does not exclude the Old Testament, which is the historical foundation of the New. Christianity and Judaism are in fact but two parts of a single whole. See *Justification and Reconciliation*, p. *10*. The original sources of the Hebrew religion in the Old Testament are related to those of Christianity in the New "as indispensable auxiliaries for their understanding". See *Unterricht*, sect. *2*.

—and to show that religion is primarily a life and not a set of dogmatic formularies.

Yet although the Ritschlian theology is a "new" theology in that it frankly discards many traditional concepts it advocates no clean break with the past and in Ritschl's own teaching at least attaches surprisingly high importance to the Church as the continuous embodiment and expression of Christian experience. This Ritschl makes plain at the very outset. It is not sufficient, he says, simply to repeat Jesus' own statements about the forgiveness of sins; for although these may seem clear their meaning becomes really intelligible only when reflected in the consciousness of those who believe in him. The content of the doctrine of forgiveness, justification and reconciliation is to be sought not so much directly in the recorded words of Christ "as in the correlative representations of the original consciousness of the community". Hence the rôle of the apostolic teaching. Only a mistaken purism will prefer the less developed statements of Jesus to the apostles' doctrine, including the Pauline in its richest elaboration. To understand Christianity's founder, not simply as a historical figure but in his significance for Christian life and thought down the ages, we need more than the gospel story. The actual *experience* of Christ, that is, belongs to the Christian community, and on this presupposition alone is there any hope of constructing a theological system worthy of the name.[1] But of course the New Testament is strictly normative and a true idea of what Christianity is can be arrived at by no other route than a careful reconstruction of the thinking that lies behind it—confirmed moreover "by being compared with other species and stages of religion".[2]

The doctrine of the incarnation Ritschl interprets of course in terms of the *Werthurtheil*. In Jesus Christ the Christian sees God, and in particular God in his essential nature as love.[3] "Whoever, therefore, has a part in the religion of Christ in the way Christ himself intended, cannot do other than regard him as the Bearer of the final revelation of God."[4] Christ, that is to say, has inherently and uniquely the *value* of God, the use of the word "value" being meant to indicate a fact of concrete experience: forgiveness of and deliverance from sin and participation in a divinely conferred freedom. Thus Jesus is not simply an example but a saviour, having done what only God can do. His

[1] *Justification and Reconciliation*, p. 4.   [2] *Unterricht*, sect. 3.
[3] *Justification and Reconciliation*, pp. 296 f.   [4] *Ibid.*, p. 388.

divinity is a truth not in any "objective" metaphysical sense, as the traditional Christology has tried to make out, but a value-judgment conveyed in the dogmatic teaching of the Church and realized in the personal experience of the individual believer, who feels himself to have been translated into a new world of peace and strength, even if he cannot explain exactly how or why. Because of this doctrine of Christ, although springing from a historical context which scientific criticism has every right to investigate, is in the final resort beyond such criticism. Its truth is bound to no "evidence" but that of the inner testimony of the religious life itself.

Yet though the "proof" of faith is thus internal—a view which exposed him to repeated charges of subjectivism—Ritschl was temperamentally antipathetic to mysticism. He unsparingly denounces the Neoplatonic doctrine of an immediate contact of the soul with God, in which the former appears to transcend finite limitations. Religious experience cannot be divorced from the historic Christ and the common faith and life of the Christian community. Besides, mysticism has psychological and spiritual perils:

> "The mystics claim to enjoy the blessedness of the future in moments of ecstasy in the present life. They have, however, to suffer for their elevation of spirit at such moments through subsequent lassitude, aridity and barrenness of the feelings, and the sense of desertion by God."

The Reformers, on the other hand, live in the faith that eternal life and the joy which attaches to it are present gifts, a consequence of the forgiveness of sins. The mystical view is entirely out of harmony with the doctrine of justification, as Luther saw clearly.[1]

Of Ritschl as a philosopher little need be said. In this domain he had no power of original thought. After Kant his debt is chiefly to Lotze, but his ideas are so ambiguous as to suggest that he had never really worked them out. To some critics he was a subjective idealist, to others a crude realist. His epistemology is basically phenomenalist. He does not deny the reality of noumena; on the contrary, he regards them as apprehended *in* phenomena. But he will not pass from the empirical apprehension (*Vorstellung*) of reality to a rational conception (*Begriff*)

---

[1] *Justification and Reconciliation*, pp. *98* f.

C

of it. This principle prevents any advance from the phenomenal to the noumenal on the theological plane, where, as he insists, speculative interest is illegitimate and must be suppressed. Hence although the theologian may, for example, discuss the *work* of Christ—the phenomenon, that is—his *person*, the noumenon, eludes all rational grasp.[1]

Altogether outstanding though Ritschl was among the Protestant theologians of his age, he is not easy to classify, doubtless for that very reason. He inclines to follow a mediating course between conservatives like Frank and more thorough-going liberals such as Pfleiderer and Lipsius. Further, he is a dogmatist and even something of a reactionary against the anti-dogmatic trends of the time. He wished to defend Christianity intellectually whilst abjuring any overtly apologetic intent; and he always urged the point of its complete originality against views which would assimilate it in greater or less degree to environmental conditions, religious, philosophical or social. On the other hand he was often enough ready to cut loose from traditional positions in order to impart to Christian theology a new aspect, suited to the age. It is not surprising therefore that even his professed disciples should have differed among themselves, some stressing one side of his doctrine, some another. To certain leading representatives of Ritschl's school we must now turn.

4. The Ritschlian School: Herrmann, Kaftan, Harnack

The historian of Ritschlianism, G. Ecke, marked out three periods in its development: first, from *1874* to *1880*, when Ritschl's original teaching was still being closely followed; secondly, from *1880* to *1889*, when Kaftan emerges as its principal exponent, although with certain characteristic emphases of his own; and thirdly, from *1889* onwards, when Harnack became its most prominent figure, but also when its influence was more diffuse and less easily identifiable.[2] Ecke's survey is confined to the religious situation in his own country, but in the final decade of the century the Ritschlian theology was gaining increasing

---

[1] But it has been said that Ritschl did not follow his own principle consistently. Otto Pfleiderer's conjecture, that he "did not make (his) theory of cognition the basis of his theology from the first, but rather propounded it subsequently, in its defence", is probably justified. See *The Development of Theology in Germany since Kant (1890)*, p. *183*.

[2] See *Die theologische Schule Albrecht Ritschls (2 vols., 1897–1904.)*

attention beyond Germany, in France, Britain and America. The movement to which Ritschl gave the impetus continued, in fact, to be the
main intellectual force in evangelical Christianity until the appearance
of the earlier work of Karl Barth, when the whole situation in Protestant theology underwent an important change.

Nearest to Ritschl's own standpoint are Wilhelm Herrmann (*1846–
1922*) and Julius Kaftan (*1848–1926*). Harnack likewise may be regarded
as standing in line of succession. But Ernst Troeltsch, a decided "left-
winger" among liberals, seems to have owed little to him directly. In
Britain, although interest in the movement was considerable, Ritschlianism found critics rather than avowed adherents.[1]

Herrmann, who held a chair at Marburg, was if anything even more
anxious than his Göttingen master that the break between theology and
metaphysics should be complete. In his first published work, a brochure
on "Metaphysics in Theology",[2] he declares it a matter of indifference
to the theologian whether philosophy is deistic, pantheistic or theistic.
Metaphysics poses the question of the universal forms in which, without contradiction, all being and all events can be represented. "For the
correctness of these representations it in no way matters in what
relation to our volitional aims, to our weal or woe, things stand."[3]
Philosophy is concerned only with the world of fact, whereas religion
asks how the world must be judged if the highest good is to be realized:
its interest is in *ends*. Philosophy is the completion of science inasmuch
as it purports to offer a uniform description of reality as a whole.
Religion gives assurance that man's spiritual ideals have a divine source
and are not merely his own invention. Between the "feeling of the
value of goodness and the knowledge of facts" there is "an irreducible
difference", for what religion and philosophy each call the real are
essentially different things. Herrmann also goes farther than Ritschl in
assimilating religion to ethics. "The Christian idea of God is a function
of the moral spirit, which seeks and experiences in that idea freedom
from guilt and evil"; for whilst metaphysics signifies "the creative
reality by which we make the possibility of all being and becoming

---

[1] See, in addition to the studies of Orr and Denney, A. E. Garvie, *The Ritschlian
Theology* (*1899*), J. K. Mozley, *Ritschlianism* (*1909*), E. A. Edghill, *Fact and Faith: a
Study of Ritschlianism* (*1910*), and O. C. Quick, *Liberalism, Modernism and Tradition*
(*1922*).
[2] *Der Metaphysik in der Theologie* (*1876*).   [3] *Op. cit.*, p. *8*.

intelligible to ourselves", Christianity is concerned with "the incommunicable experience of the work of Christian goodness". Any attempt therefore to confuse the two conceptions negates the truth that "the ethical fact in which the world-view has its roots is a separate thing, wholly neutral in regard to the general forms of being and becoming, and one with which metaphysics cannot at all deal".[1]

In his "Relation of Religion to our Knowledge of the World and Morality", published a few years later,[2] Herrmann returns to the same problem, treating it more fully. Now he inclines to regard metaphysics itself as having a practical concern, attributable to man's deeply rooted desire to see the world in its totality. But the philosopher's conclusions do not possess the same high degree of certainty as the scientist's, for the latter relate only to selected areas of research and employ methods perfected to that end. It is not then surprising that the fate of the various metaphysical systems is to no small extent determined by the progress of scientific knowledge: as science advances philosophy likewise is bound to change.[3] Religion too takes in reality as a whole, as the scene of the human drama, but its procedure is far different and gives it greater independence and permanence. Hence the final mistake of trying to ally theology to metaphysics, since the former is actually better equipped for their common task than is philosophy itself. In any case metaphysical criteria cannot be those of religion. A classic illustration is the effective and disastrous substitution by the scholastic philosophy of the Aristotelian conception of God for the biblical. What the modern theologian must do is to avoid the metaphysical by-path altogether and confine himself to the contents of the Christian consciousness. His proper interest is the interpretation of faith, not its rationalization in terms of categories alien to it.

But Herrmann's best-known work and his most constructive is *The Communion of the Christian with God*.[4] In this he endeavours to point a way for those who in an age of science "seek God in Christ". Essentially, Christianity requires a transformation of a man's inner life. Doctrines play a part in this transforming process, but to insist on doctrinal unity among Christians is idle and unnecessary. Such notions are "worthless

---

[1] *Ibid.*, p. 17.
[2] *Die Religion in Verhältniss zum Welterkennen und zur Sittlichkeit* (*1879*).
[3] *Op. cit.*, p. 78.
[4] *Der Verkehr der Christen mit Gott* (*1886*). English trans. by J. S. Stanyon, *1895*.

dreams which arouse useless strife" and impede the true path to unity. Indeed to sever doctrines from the stem of real life and frame them into a system is the last thing, Herrmann thinks, which the Christian Church should wish to undertake. "If, on the other hand, we keep our attention fastened on what God is producing in the Christian's inner life, then the manifoldness of the thoughts which spring from faith will not confuse us, but give us cause for joy."[1] Does this mean, however, that Christianity is to be resolved into purely subjective experiences? Herrmann denies the suggestion and states firmly that "the knowledge of the objective Christian realities is the only nourishment on which faith is fed." But the objective realities are nevertheless grasped inwardly and by faith, so that the nature of religious belief itself is a question the theologian must carefully probe. First, however, such inwardness must be distinguished from mysticism, which Herrmann dislikes no less than does Ritschl himself. Mysticism, he says, is present

> "when the influence of God upon the soul is sought and found solely in an inward experience of the individual; that is, in an excitement of the emotions, taken, with no further question, as evidence that the soul is possessed by God, without, at the same time, anything external to the soul being consciously and clearly perceived and firmly grasped as the positive content of any soul-dominating idea giving rise to thoughts that elevate the spiritual life."[2]

In short, it is a type of piety which regards the *historical* element in faith only as a burden. Even in Protestantism this tendency will continue, he fears, so long as history is retained under dogmatic forms, as "something unintelligible". In the final resort the inner life is, admittedly, secret and incommunicable; but for the Christian the basis of certainty must be the historical fact of the person of Jesus, in whom, once and for all, he is vouchsafed a positive view of God. Divine revelation, that is, occurs within the concrete order of reality to which the believer himself belongs.

> "We are Christians because, in the human Jesus, we have met with a fact whose content is immeasurably richer than that of any feelings which arise within ourselves; a fact, moreover, which makes us so

---

[1] *The Communion of the Christian with God*, pp. 15 f.
[2] *Op. cit.*, pp. 22 f.

certain of God that our conviction of being in communion with him can justify itself at the bar of reason and conscience."[1]

Communion with God becomes possible through the *man* Jesus, who after all is an undoubted reality.[2] The tradition *concerning* Jesus, however, is for Herrmann merely the medium through which the historical reality of Christ is conveyed to us; it is not itself a constitutive factor in our experience. Nevertheless he flatly rejects the criticism that the Christian thus clings only to the memory of a life once lived and that Christ cannot be a *present* reality; and in all fairness to him it must be said that while the source of the Christian's experience and the actual means of his communion with God is Jesus' earthly life as shown to us in the gospels, Herrmann's estimate of Christ is certainly not a merely humanitarian one, as of a good man living and dying simply for the truth of his convictions. Christ is a living reality with whom the Christian here and now is in spiritual communion. Yet it is the historical life which is revelatory, and apart from it we should have only "mysticism" and subjective emotions.

With revelation as personal experience Herrmann deals expressly and very impressively in his Giessen lecture on "The Concept of Revelation".[3] Revelation, he there tells us, is not an external publication of truth but a personal address which touches man at the point of his sinfulness and spiritual need. To know what it is we must look within ourselves, at our own struggle with temptation and the misery of heart which it brings, along with the judgment of conscience and the remorse of guilt. Revelation is what lifts a man out of this "state of death". It is a passing "from darkness into God's heavenly light". Further, as the *personal* disclosure of God's Son to the sinner it is not a matter of believing doctrines, or of moral striving, or even of imbibing the words of Scripture.[4] The spirit of Jesus may reach out to us from the pages of the gospel or show itself in the lives of other Christians, but in either case revelation occurs only when the Christ of God becomes real to us as a personal influence for good, creating trust and peace of mind.

---

[1] *Ibid.*, pp. *36* f.   [2] P. *52*.   [3] *Der Begriff der Offenbarung (1887)*.

[4] "Woe to the Christian who imagines that the sum of those scriptural ideas composes the revelation which could make all things new for him." Scriptural ideas do not form the content of revelation, but they are the thoughts which enable a man to take hold of divine revelation. See *Der Begriff der Offenbarung*, pp. *7* f.

Yet Herrmann is not concerned with the individual alone, even if *The Communion of the Christian with God*, taken by itself, may give this impression. In *Religion and Morality* he turns to the doctrine of the Kingdom, or universal moral community, as "the aspect under which humanity is included in God's purpose for himself". The reality of God's Kingdom, he says, must in some way or other have seized a man and positively influenced his whole thinking if he is to be capable of trusting God in the Christian sense of the word. This, Herrmann thinks, is the starting-point of dogmatics, which must examine the question of how it is possible that man, sinful as he is and ever subject to the forces of nature, can yet with assurance seek blessedness in a personal life expressed in terms of the moral law or in the moral community of the Kingdom. But in answering it much of the traditional dogmatics will have to be dropped, since theology's only profitable concern is with the practical issue of how a man may be saved. The Bible itself is relevant but to this one end. Yet Herrmann indicates all too sparingly what the positive content of a new dogmatics should be. Faith is personal conviction taking shape in a moral re-orientation, and beyond this he scarcely ever looks. Certainly he envisages no large edifice of doctrine in which to frame the Christian experience intellectually. Like Ritschl he makes the understanding of Christ's person depend upon his work, and he distinguishes his own position from both the humanitarian rationalist's and the orthodox believer's. "For the first, it is enough to see in Jesus the man who proclaims a divine truth; for the second, to conceive of a distinct divine being united with Jesus." The third alternative is a matter of experience, "when we look at God himself in the historic Christ".[1] Of the Virgin Birth, however, there can in the nature of the case be no witness. All one may say of it is that it forms part of the Christian tradition, "and he who has found Christ will find the right attitude to this also". What can be testified—and it is sufficient—is that Jesus did not proceed merely from a race of sinners.[2]

Although Ritschl discusses the idea of the Kingdom at length, and in the light of it, as we have noted, attaches high importance to the Church, yet his actual doctrine of the Church is no more than sketchy. Herrmann here is more explicit. As he sees it the Church is not only the

---

[1] *The Communion of the Christian with God*, p. 240.
[2] See Herrmann's pamphlet, *Worum handelt es sich in dem Streit um das Apostolicum*, p. 13.

fellowship of believers but the medium of communion between God and the soul; for when, he says, we live in the midst of Christian people the sense is naturally awakened "by which we may see God in Christ, and the germ of understanding is nourished". When we ourselves have found God and so become new men we are linked with our fellow-Christians not only by feelings of joy but by the spiritual life which the fellowship of faith itself generates. For the Church, as Luther said, is the "mother" of believers, who if they are to remain in communion with God must be in communion with one another. A Church which fails to direct its whole effort at developing such a fellowship of moral intercourse is spiritually dead. This happens when the Christian community ceases to be looked on as the instrument of the saving gospel and becomes instead—as in the hierarchical polity and sacerdotalist theology of Catholicism—a "shell containing certain mysterious redemptive powers" which are effective in so far as we submit to their operation. But as soon as the Church makes the divine act of revelation in the historic Christ an element of our present life, "then all the events we pass through begin to utter the speech of God".[1]

With the name of Herrmann we at once associate that of Kaftan, who became professor of the philosophy of religion at Berlin in *1883*, as representing the authentic Ritschlian standpoint. His literary contribution to modern Protestantism is mainly in two works—"The Essence of the Christian Religion"[2] and *The Truth of the Christian Religion*[3]—which together constitute what is perhaps one of the most impressive attempts ever made to investigate historic Christianity in its essential nature and meaning.[4] Like Ritschl, Kaftan finds its determining elements in the twin ideas of the Kingdom of God and redemption. The Kingdom, as Jesus himself proclaimed it, will be seen by the believer as his "eternal end, lying above the world in God", to which the only road is that of moral development, made possible, however, by "the reconciliation with God which Jesus Christ has brought about". It is upon these truths that the Christian experience rests.[5] But although Kaftan is so far at one with Ritschl, in the interpretation of these

---

[1] *The Communion of the Christian with God*, pp. *190–4*.

[2] *Das Wesen der christlichen Religion (1881*; 2nd ed. *1888*).

[3] *Die Wahrheit der christlichen Religion (1888*. English trans. by G. Ferries, *2* vols., *1897*).

[4] See also his *Dogmatik*, published in *1897*.

[5] Cf. *Dogmatik*, p. *8*.

principles he follows more traditionalist lines, notably in his emphasis on *transcendence*. Thus in the final resort the Kingdom, as our supreme ideal, lies beyond this world, "in God". It is a heavenly and not simply an earthly good, dependent though it is on man's moral endeavour. Again, whilst adopting Ritschl's concept of the value-judgment, Kaftan does not assign it so large a part in the definition of religious knowledge, maintaining that in religion as in science there is a proper place for factual or theoretical judgments, even though ultimately based on value-judgments:

> "Nowhere have I affirmed (he says) that the religious judgments *are* value-judgments, but I hold this expression itself to be at least open to misunderstanding; nay, value-judgments are their basis, but they themselves are theoretical propositions; so essentially indeed that even the judging of the worth of the world in connexion with religious faith, while it is attached to the idea of God, is constituted by theoretical propositions of objective validity, which are derived or demonstrated from the conception of God."[1]

All the same, theoretical propositions based on value-judgments are to be distinguished from the theoretical judgments of science or philosophy. They arise in a different way in that the conviction of their truth is founded *subjectively*. Moreover, even objectively they have "another measure of truth". In other words, whereas Ritschl sees religious doctrines as belonging exclusively to the realm of faith, Kaftan would advance them to that of knowledge, although they originate in faith. The personal factor is always basic, but faith itself yields a *kind* of knowledge, having a truth-value independent of personal interest and commitment.[2] The idea of God, for example, although for the believer it has its roots in personal experience, passes over from a subjective assurance to an objective certainty. God, we feel bound to say, *exists*. We even may think of him in intellectual terms as the Absolute,[3] a concept as valid, Kaftan judges, for the Christian as for the non-Christian. But the Absolute must be understood as a moral reality and not merely as a logical principle.

---

[1] *Das Wesen der christlichen Religion*, p. 49.
[2] *Seinsurtheil*: "judgment of being". See *Dogmatik*, p. 29.
[3] *Ibid.*, p. 161.

Although Kaftan's attitude towards philosophy is thus decidedly more affirmative than Ritschl's or Herrmann's, he too insists on the uniqueness of Christianity as a "supernatural" agency, conveying a special revelation of God's purposes for man. This, he says, is no dogmatic assumption, but is founded on facts: no other religion can compare with the Christian in either its character or its claims.[1] The study of comparative religion, he contends (as against Troeltsch's position), has done nothing to render Christianity more easily classifiable by reference to other types of faith and piety. To choose for or against it is therefore a matter of the utmost moment. "He who cannot allow himself to despair of the highest ideals of humanity and of the reason in history will have to decide for faith in the revelation of God in Christ."[2] Christianity's disappearance would mean for the human race the loss of its richest possession and make an immeasurable difference to its moral outlook.

As for Ritschl and Herrmann so for Kaftan revelation is an historically mediated fact:

> "Conformably with the ethical character of Christianity, the revelation of God should be sought in history, which is the sphere of moral growth and development. The belief that God himself, through Jesus Christ, has interposed in the history of men and offers himself to men for fellowship with them, is the consummation of our faith in revelation. Revelation is a real self-revelation of God; while on the other hand, inasmuch as it is given in history, it has, relatively to the individual and his faith, objective ground and authoritative signific[3]ance."

But the truth communicated is in the shape of broad principles, not of specific doctrines. So the question is raised of the place of dogma in Christianity, and in meeting it Kaftan has to admit that a dogmatic religion scarcely suits the modern temper and that the Church's formal

---

[1] See his articles, "Die Selbständigkeit des Christenthums" and "Erwiderung", *Zeitschrift für Theologie und Kirche*, vols. vi and viii, in reply to Ernst Troeltsch.

[2] *The Truth of the Christian Religion*, ii, p. *407*.

[3] *Op. cit.*, ii, p. *96*. He adds that "there is also implied in it, owing to the spiritual character of the Christian religion, *a real communication of supernatural truths*" (italics ours).

teaching has for many become a hindrance.[1] Yet dogma itself was in origin an attempt to answer the demands of reason, being simply the Church's definition, in terms more or less abstract, of the basic Christian convictions. Faith seems naturally to seek coherent expression—since belief moves towards knowledge—and sound doctrine has proved in fact a need of the Church's corporate life. Theologically the intellectualization of religion is defensible on the ground that although the divine transcends human reason it is not alien to it. Moreover, dogma is especially necessary for Protestants, who rely less than do Catholics on a cultus and ecclesiastical organization. In another pamphlet, "Do we need a new Dogma?",[2] Kaftan indicates the kind of dogmatic he would himself wish to see developed. Certain things ought firmly to be underlined, particularly the truth that as the Christian life is a life "hid with Christ in God" so Christian knowledge is essentially "the obedience of faith". It would also re-affirm the fundamental Reformation principles of the authority of Scripture and the sufficiency of personal faith. Lastly, it would have once more to face the problem of the meaning of Christ. Not only has the traditional doctrine, at least according to its ancient formulation, ceased to be intelligible, it has no organic connexion with evangelical belief. In fact the Protestant and Catholic traditions differ here as elsewhere, for whereas the latter stresses Christ's special relation to God in a way that lifts him above the rest of mankind the former so relates him to men as to bring home to them the possibility of knowing God *through* him. Such knowledge is primarily given by the testimony of the gospel: "We must make the spiritual content of his exalted divine life meaningful by the picture of his historical life." Yet it is still vital to any real belief in Christ's divinity that his origin should not be thought of only "as of men":

"If we believe in the Lord's Godhead, we believe also in his origin from above, out of God. He was a man—truly, for thereon depends our salvation. But he was *the man*, in whom God's eternal will was to unite humanity with itself, the divine Head of humanity made one with God; for thereon equally depends our salvation. And so this unity of God with the one man, Jesus Christ, is a fact which cannot be done away with in the harmony of faith."[3]

[1] See his *Glaube und Dogma* (1889).   [2] *Brauchen wir ein neues Dogma?* (1890).
[3] *Op. Cit.*, p. 59.

Any formula, however, which attempts to *explain* this truth is no more than speculation, not a matter of faith.

Like his fellow-Ritschlians Kaftan is firmly opposed to mysticism, which he deems typical of Catholic piety. When, he says, "the world of expiring antiquity appropriated Christianity with the intellectual means at its disposal" a fusion took place between it and the mystical natural religion of its environment. Something of the sort indeed was bound to occur, but Catholicism was the outcome.

> "The Christian idea of the Highest Good, in which the unity of religion and ethics is secured, is so far displaced that mystical union with the Godhead and world-renouncing asceticism are now sought as man's chief end, and moral activity is thought of only as the condition, indispensable certainly, but yet no more than *external*, of future blessedness."[1]

However, taking mysticism in a wider sense, Kaftan is less critical of it than are Ritschl and Herrmann, and he quotes St Paul's words, "Your life is hid with Christ in God",[2] as expressing a necessary aspect of Christian truth, its Godward as distinct from its manward.[3] This is in keeping with his general concern for the transcendence of the religious ideal; although he is careful to say that the latter can be rightly understood only by way of the counter-truth of "the moral idea of the Kingdom of God *in the world*".

Objection not only to Catholic mysticism but to the whole Catholic tradition of dogma and hierarchy comes to the forefront with Adolf Harnack (*1851–1930*), who in this country at any rate has remained the best-known representative of the Ritschlian school, largely on the strength of his popular lectures entitled *What is Christianity?*, first published in English in *1901*.[4] These were delivered informally to a concourse of students at the university of Berlin numbering several hundreds, one of whom, happily, took them down in shorthand. When printed their success was immediate. Harnack was not indeed primarily a theologian at all, but a New Testament scholar and a

---

[1] See *The Truth of Christianity*, i, pp. *61* f.
[2] Col. iii. *3*.
[3] *Das Wesen der christlichen Religion*, p. *263*.
[4] *Das Wesen des Christenthums* (*1900*). The English version is by T. B. Saunders. Translations of the work were brought out in many languages.

historian whose *magnum opus*, a *History of Dogma*, is a highly detailed account of the evolution of Christian doctrine from its beginnings to the Reformation embodying the thesis that primitive Christian belief was transformed under Hellenistic influences.[1] Ritschlian though he is Harnack's adherence to the school is not unqualified—his Ritschlian sympathies are perhaps most evident in his treatment of Luther—but in the English-speaking world he came to be regarded as typical of Liberal Protestantism.

For Harnack the essence of Christianity is Jesus' own message, a message at once simple and rich: "so simple as to be exhausted in each of the leading thoughts which he uttered, so rich that everyone of these thoughts seems to be inexhaustible and the full meaning of the sayings and parables beyond our reach." His words speak to us across the centuries with the freshness of the present.[2] Although Jesus was the historical founder of Christianity, to be a Christian is to know him *here and now*; and for this no erudition is necessary, but only spiritual feeling and insight. The gospel is immediately recognizable, that is to say, as "eternal life in the midst of time, in the strength and before the eyes of God". More specifically, it is "divine sonship spread out over the whole of life, an inner harmony with God's Kingdom, and a joyful certainty in the possession of eternal goods, and in confidence of protection from evil".[3] This, Harnack avers, is not simply speculation, mere theological theorizing, but a matter of actual experience, realized first by Jesus himself and afterwards by all who, through him, have come to see themselves as sons of God and servants of their fellow-men. There may have been nothing especially new in Jesus' teaching; but, says Harnack, take the people of Israel and search the whole history of their religion: take history generally, and where will you find any message about God and the good that was ever so pure and strong as what we hear and read of in the gospels? Jesus' utterances may be

---

[1] *Lehrbuch der Dogmengeschichte* (*1886–1890*; 6th ed., *1923*, reprinted *1963*. The English translation appeared in *1899*.) Among Harnack's many other works of historical scholarship are his *Geschichte der altchristlichen Literatur* (*1893–1904*; 2nd ed. by K. Aland, *1958*); *Die Mission und Ausbreitung des Christenthums in der drei ersten Jahrhunderten* (*1902*; 4th ed. *1924*, English trans. *1904–1905*); and *Beiträge zur Einleitung in der Neue Testament* (*1906–1911*), which includes the well-known *Luke the Physician* (*1907*).
[2] *What is Christianity?*, p. *46*.
[3] *Op. cit.*, p. *65*.

paralleled in Pharisaic doctrine, but words alone effect nothing—"it is the power of the personality that stands behind them".

The Christian message is not, then, simply the personal belief of Jesus the man. "Either the gospel is in all points identical with its first form, in which case it is a transient phenomenon, appearing in time only to pass away again, or else it presents eternal truth in historically changing forms."[1] The latter alternative is surely the true view. The *Wesen* of Christianity is not to be found only in the Lord's recorded teaching, nor in the experience of the apostles. It must be extracted from the total history of the Christian religion over the ages, and it is as a historian that Harnack himself approaches the question:

> "It is true that Christianity has had its classical epoch; nay more, it had a founder who himself was what he taught—to steep ourselves in him is still the chief matter; but to restrict ourselves to him means to take a point of view too low for his significance."[2]

Only in this way shall we discover the abiding principle which gives unity to change and can therefore be identified as Christianity's determinative element. "What is common to all the forms which it has assumed, corrected by reference to the Gospel, and, conversely, the chief features of the Gospel, corrected by reference to history, will, we may be allowed to hope, bring us to the kernel of the matter."[3] This procedure of Harnack's is worth stressing. Too often is it supposed that Liberal Protestantism—and Harnack himself in particular—looks no farther than the synoptic gospels.

Nevertheless it is with the teaching of Jesus that inquiry must begin. It may, Harnack contends, be reduced to two heads: God as Father, and the human soul so ennobled that it can and does unite with him.[4] Thus his message is essentially one for individuals: "Individual religious life was what he wanted to kindle and what he did kindle." Indeed, "he never had anyone but the individual in mind, and the abiding disposition of the heart in love". But Harnack does not overlook, much less deny, the centrality of the idea of the Kingdom in Jesus' preaching; and he clearly recognizes that its presentation by the synoptists is strongly coloured by apocalyptic imagery. But this last is mere husk. It was something Jesus grew up with and naturally retained. What was

[1] *Ibid.*, pp. *13* f.   [2] P. *11*.   [3] P. *15*.   [4] See p. *63*.

his own was the very different and far more spiritual idea that the Kingdom cometh not with observation, but only by entering into the soul of the believer and laying hold of it.

The question of Jesus' personal place in the gospel is not difficult to assess, once the metaphysical disguise in which dogma has clothed him has been removed. That he thought of himself as the Son of God in the messianic sense then commonly accepted is scarcely open to doubt, but his own idea was really fashioned by his personal consciousness of a unique knowledge of God. It was this conviction which led him to the further belief that he was himself the promised Messiah. But the root of it all was his profound faith in God as a heavenly Father. The whole subsequent theological development must therefore be judged an irrelevance, or worse. The gospel is not a theoretical scheme of doctrine or philosophy of the universe. It is not in fact doctrine at all except in so far as it proclaims the reality of God as Father. Hence the moral challenge of Christ cannot be evaded by the subterfuge of saying that because a man can make nothing of the Church's "Christology" the message is not for him.

> "Jesus directed men's attention on to great questions; he promised them God's grace and mercy; he required them to decide whether they would have God or Mammon, an eternal or an earthly life, the soul or the body, humility or self-righteousness, love or selfishness, the truth or a lie. The sphere which these questions occupy is all-embracing; the individual is called upon to listen to the glad message of mercy and the Fatherhood of God, and to make up his mind whether he will be on God's side and the Eternal's, or on the side of the world and time."[1]

But with the transformation of this simple, elemental message into historic Catholicism—for such was its fate from the second century onwards—"the religion of strong feeling and of the heart passes into the religion of custom and therefore of form and of time". The whole outward and visible institution of a Church claiming divine dignity thus has no foundation whatever in the gospel.

Protestantism, by contrast, is a return to Christianity as it originally was. Its historical advent, however, was revolutionary. Religion was

[1] Pp. *143* f.

taken out of the "vast and monstrous fabric" which had previously been called by its name and reduced to its essential factors, the Word of God and faith. This achievement was Luther's, but it still was incomplete, in that the Reformation was incapable of perceiving all the conclusions which its new ideas implied. Countless problems have since arisen which the Reformers could not have foreseen. Further, they had no means of distinguishing between kernel and husk, original deposit and alien growth, and scholasticism remained ascendant in Protestant orthodoxy. What now is needed is a return to the liberty of the gospel in all its simplicity and vital humanity.

5. French Liberal Protestantism

Ritschlianism was unmistakably an expression of the spirit of German Lutheranism, but Protestant Christianity in France also came under its direct influence. Thus Harnack's position finds a close parallel in that of Auguste Sabatier (1839–1901), professor in the Protestant faculty at Strasbourg and subsequently director of the department of religions at the École des Hautes Études in Paris. Sabatier's numerous publications include, besides the well-known *Outlines of a Philosophy of Religion*,[1] a history of the canon of the New Testament (1877), an address to the Paris Société de Théologie on "The Spirit of Theology" (1878), a notable volume on St Paul,[2] a series of lectures delivered at Stockholm on "Religion and Culture" (1897), and a treatise on the atonement.[3] This last, along with his *Religions of Authority and the Religion of the Spirit*,[4] in which his idea of a thoroughly liberalized Protestantism attains its fullest expression, were both published post-humously, in 1903.[5]

Sabatier, upon whom the influence of Schleiermacher is apparent, was a man of deep religious feeling. Religion, he confessed in the opening paragraph of his *Outlines*, "is a moral necessity of my being". And he adds:

---

[1] *Esquisse d'une philosophie de la religion* (1897. English trans. by T. A. Seed.)

[2] *L'Apôtre Paul: Esquisse d'une histoire de sa pensée* (1870). Originally his doctoral thesis, a third and entirely new edition came out in 1896. The English version dates from 1891.

[3] *La doctrine de l'expiation et son évolution historique.*

[4] *Les religions d'autorité et la religion de l'Esprit.*

[5] An English version of the latter appeared the following year.

"The necessity which I experience in my individual life I find to be still more invincible in the collective life of humanity. Humanity is not less incurably religious than I am. The cults it has espoused and abandoned have deceived it in vain; in vain has the criticism of savants and philosophers shattered its dogmas and mythologies; in vain has religion left such tracts of blood and fire throughout the annals of humanity; it has survived all change, all revolution, all stages of culture and progress. Cut down a thousand times, the ancient stem has always sent new branches forth."

But the validity of the religious impulse cannot hide the fact that religious belief finds ever greater difficulty in sustaining itself in an increasingly secularist environment. The nineteenth century was an age of science, not of faith; but Sabatier was convinced that neither faith nor science may be omitted from the life of rational man. The origin of religion he believed to lie in the struggle between man's empirical and his ideal self:

"Man cannot know himself without knowing himself to be limited. But he cannot feel these fatal limitations without going beyond them in thought and by desire, so that he is never satisfied with what he possesses, and cannot be happy except with what he cannot attain."[1]

Religion thus is like "the rent in the rock through which the living and life-giving waters flow". It is an error however to suppose that it can offer any theoretical solution to human problems. "It does not save us by adding to our knowledge, but by a return to the very principle on which our being depends, and by a moral act of confidence in the origin and aim of life." It is, in a way, the spiritual aspect of the instinct of conservation in the physical world.

In the actual religious evolution of mankind Sabatier observes three stages: the mythological, of which the paganism of antiquity is typical; the dogmatic, represented by Catholicism and orthodox Protestantism; and the psychological, in which divine revelation is realized to be at once interior, evident ("the veil is withdrawn"), and progressive— manifested, that is, in the progress of "the moral and religious life which

---

[1] *Op. cit.*, p. *15*.

D

God begets and nourishes in the bosom of humanity". Only a psychological religion will satisfy the needs of both instinct and reason in the kind of world which man has created for himself today.

Like Harnack Sabatier distinguishes sharply between the "purely moral" essence of Christianity and its positive expression in history. To discover the former we must look to the religious consciousness of Jesus, the animating principle of which was his sense of filial relationship with God and fraternal relationship with men. A sharing of this same consciousness is alone what makes a man a Christian. Beside it ecclesiastical institutions, dogmas and rites are at best of merely transient and symbolic significance. The monumental error of Catholicism is in having elevated such things to a place of prime importance. Dogma may serve as a law and a visible bond of the Church, but it is neither the principle nor the foundation of spiritual religion. Constant reform of the dogmatic heritage is therefore a necessity for both the religious life itself and humanity's moral development. Moreover, a Christianity identified with its essential principle need fear nothing from science, natural or historical. The release of religion from alien forces will be achieved, Sabatier believes, only "when piety and science shall have become so mutually interpenetrated as to be thoroughly united in a single entity; inward piety the conscience of science, and science the legitimate expression of piety".[1] Hence the need of a truly scientific theology—one having a positive and definite object of study whilst at the same time abandoning mere appeal to authority and adopting the method of observation and experiment. Religion, that is to say, should be seen as a body of factual data belonging to the domain of the subjective consciousness and to be grasped, verified and described only through the investigations of religious psychology and the exegesis of the historical documents in which the religious consciousness of the past has left its imprint.

This replacement of dogmatic theology proper by the historical and psychological study of Christianity became increasingly characteristic of Liberal Protestantism at the turn of the century. Thus Troeltsch in Germany completely rejected the Ritschlian supernaturalism, preferring to see the Christian religion in its "natural" setting among the world's faiths generally. Only comparative religion, he held, could

---

[1] *Religions of Authority and the Religion of the Spirit*, p. *349*.

rightly show wherein the uniqueness of Christianity lies.[1] This viewpoint was taken also by another prominent member of the French liberal school, Jean Réville (*1854–1907*), son of Albert Réville, who held a professorship at the Collège de France from *1881* until succeeded there by Jean himself in *1907*. The latter's lectures on Liberal Protestantism, given at Geneva in *1902*,[2] are a forthright statement of the liberal position, at once apologetic and polemical. The author's starting-point is not, as with Harnack, the New Testament, but the Reformation, his concern being to show that modern Liberal Protestantism applies the Reformers' own principles of freedom of inquiry and the supremacy of the individual conscience, only with a greater consistency. Further although orthodox Protestantism has been vitiated by a mechanical biblicism, resort to the Scriptures for authentic documentation of the teaching of Jesus and the apostles was absolutely sound. The Bible, that is, is a unique *historical* authority; the error of the past was to turn a personal witness into an infallible oracle. But the basic Reformation insights were better than the dogmatism which overtook them, for however much Reformation theology may have denigrated man's reason in theory, in practice it asserted and used it freely. And these insights were to be increasingly validated by the advance of human knowledge. Modern Protestantism will respect the authority of the Bible for the content of faith, but is bound also to maintain that of reason and conscience, whose dictates are final:

> "It is not because they are in the Bible that we meditate upon the exhortations of the prophets or the appeals of Christ; we do so because they are supremely beautiful and beneficent."

Liberals, says Réville, are free-thinkers; not professed unbelievers but men who "in the realm of the moral life and the vast domain beyond the ken of positive science, found their beliefs on free inquiry and moral experience".

6. *Theological Liberalism in Britain and America*

In the English-speaking world Liberal Protestantism did not form a

---

[1] See his article, "Die Selbständigkeit der Religion", in *Zeitschrift für Theologie und Kirche* (*1895*), pp. *361* f. "Die christliche Idee (he writes) erscheint als die einfache, von allen nationalen Besonderheit und aller Naturreligion befreite Konsequenz der religiösen Grundenlage überhaupt."

[2] An English translation appeared in the following year. See above, p. *9*.

movement, although it unquestionably has had its representatives. Even among these, however, it is difficult to distinguish clearly between Liberal Protestants in Réville's meaning of the term and theological liberals in a broader sense. One point of view merges with another; different denominational traditions result in different emphases; personal idiosyncrasies, especially in England, count for much. Accordingly, when one attempts to survey the theological scene both here and across the Atlantic (where in any case the religious spectrum is more varied and colourful) the intellectual landmarks always visible on the European continent are found to be lacking and a coherent picture difficult to present. For fear of being lost amid a throng of individual opinions—the Anglo-Saxon has ever been adept at inventing religious variations of his own—as also for reasons of space, we must confine ourselves to such a general outline as can fairly be drawn.

In England during the last century radical views, outside Unitarianism, were seldom voiced. The sort of position taken up by a man like F. W. Newman (the Cardinal's brother) was very unusual, not to say eccentric.[1] The national Church was for the most part set in staunchly conservative ways. John Henry Newman and his followers at Oxford were in principle defiantly opposed to the spirit of liberalism—"the anti-dogmatic principle", as Newman himself dubbed it. The Evangelical party evinced little interest in intellectual issues at all until towards the end of the century when the challenge of secular thought could no longer be ignored. The earliest approximation to a liberal school can be traced back to the twenties, with the so-called Noetics at Oriel College, Oxford, of whom Thomas Arnold, headmaster of Rugby School from 1828 to 1842, is best remembered. The Broad Churchmen of the next generation included the contributors to the then sensational volume, *Essays and Reviews* (1860),[2] and A. P. Stanley, dean of Westminster and Arnold's pupil and biographer. On the whole, however,

---

[1] See in particular his *Phases of Faith* (1850), in which he states that "to set up any fixed creed as a test of spiritual character is a most unjust, oppressive, and mischievous superstition" (Preface, p. iv). *The Soul, its Sorrows and its Aspirations*, which he published a year earlier, was however widely read and achieved considerable popularity.

[2] The most considerable of the essays was that by Benjamin Jowett, then Regius professor of Greek at Oxford, "On the Interpretation of Scripture", in which he made a plea that the Bible should be read like any other book and therefore judged, as to its form, in accord with the established principles of literary criticism.

these groups, heirs to the latitudinarianism of an older day, were liberal as not wishing to insist on the letter of dogma—"In theology the less we define", said Jowett, "the better"—and in favour of heightening the traditionally comprehensive character of the Church of England— Arnold desiderated an all-round Protestant union under its aegis— would have done nothing to undermine an essential orthodoxy, and "Germanizing" tendencies were generally regarded with suspicion. In Scotland religious conservatism was even more deeply entrenched, although occasionally under fire from the philosophers, in whom the temper of David Hume was not quite extinct.[1] Among more liberal thinkers Thomas Erskine of Linlathen, a layman and friend of F. D. Maurice's,[2] must certainly be mentioned;[3] and with him John Macleod Campbell whose book, *The Nature of the Atonement* (*1856*) has been described as "the most important English contribution to dogmatic theology made in the first sixty years of the nineteenth century",[4] but for which its author incurred ecclesiastical censure and deprivation of office. Among the English Nonconformists, in whom the ingrained biblicism of English Protestantism was especially powerful, little or

---

Jowett, who had studied Kant and Hegel, was a man of broad, even nebulous, convictions, of whom Pusey—no unbiased witness—remarked that the only belief the two seemed to have in common was "that somehow Jesus came from God, which the Mohammedans believe too".

[1] Hence the Church's strong opposition to the appointment of Sir John Leslie to the chair of mathematics at Edinburgh in *1805*. *The Christian Instructor*, organ of Scottish evangelicalism, often constantly lamented the prevalence of "heresies".

[2] The Coleridgean tradition perpetuated by Maurice was in the best sense "broad", but Maurice himself was no less a believer in dogma than was Newman, and rebutted the suggestion that he himself was a liberal: "The Liberals ... feel and I feel that we are not a step nearer to each other in *1870* than we were in *1835*. They have acquired a new name. They are called Broad Churchmen now, and delight to be called so. But their breadth seems to me to be narrowness. They include all kinds of opinions. But what message have they for the people who do not live upon opinions or care for opinions?" (Frederick Maurice, *The Life of Frederick Denison Maurice*, 3rd edition, *1884*, i, p. *184*.)

[3] "The reasonableness of a religion", he wrote in the earliest of his books (*Remarks on the Internal Evidence for the Truth of Revealed Religion*, *1820*), "seems to me to consist in there being a direct and natural connection between a believing of the doctrines which it inculcates, and a being formed by these to the character which it recommends. ... What is the history of another world to me, unless it have some intelligible relation to my duties or happiness?" (p. *58*).

[4] V. F. Storr, *The Development of English Theology in the Nineteenth Century* (*1913*), p. *424*.

nothing by way of theological innovation was even envisaged, let alone welcome.

In the second half of the century, however, theological isolationism perforce came to an end. The progress of the natural and historical sciences and its effect upon public opinion had to be reckoned with. The adjustment was not easy. Conservative churchmen deplored what genuinely appeared to them a selling of the orthodox pass by their more liberally-minded colleagues, as in the case of H. P. Liddon and *Lux Mundi*; but their influence had become a waning force. Not only did German scholarship enjoy a higher prestige, the philosophy which once had given it impetus, although now largely abandoned in its own land, made its way here also. In fact the most striking thing about the liberal movement in British theology, and especially so in the writings of the brothers John and Edward Caird, was its neo-Hegelian immanentism, in contrast with the Ritschlian rejection of all idealist metaphysics. Even the Catholic school in the Church of England was affected by it, as *Lux Mundi* plainly showed. To the liberal Christian in this country, particularly if he were an admirer of Matthew Arnold, God could more readily be conceived as a "stream of tendency" than as the transcendent Law-giver of old-fashioned Bible Protestantism.[1] Immanent deity is thus the presupposition of R. J. Cambell's somewhat superficial *New Theology* (*1907*), in which the writer (*1867–1956*), at the time minister of the Methodist City Temple in London, criticizes orthodox doctrine for its "practical dualism" in making men "think of God as above and apart from His world instead of expressing Himself through His world".[2] Campbell's own position stressed the inward unity of God, man and the universe, virtually to the extent of pantheism:

---

[1] Arnold's theological writings comprise *St Paul and Protestantism* (*1870*), *Literature and Dogma* (*1873*)—the best of them—*God and the Bible* (*1875*) and *Last Essays on Church and Religion* (*1877*). The criticism that these are the work only of an amateur in theology would not have ruffled their author, who believed that the age-old attempt to compel the religious imagination into the strait-jacket of a stereotyped theology had been disastrous. To treat religion as though it were science was simply to render it incredible. What was needed was the sympathy and tact of a *literary* approach. Arnold himself was a man of deep religious feeling, even if he found the language of conventional piety repugnant.

[2] *The New Theology*, p. 4.

"When I say God, I mean the mysterious Power which is finding expression in the universe, and which is present in every tiniest atom of the wondrous whole. . . .

"Ultimately your being and mine are one and we shall come to know it. . . .

"My God is my deeper Self and yours too; He is the Self of the Universe and knows all about it . . . the whole cosmic process is one long incarnation and uprising of the being of God from itself to itself."[1]

The Hegelian tone is here obvious. No Ritschlian could possibly have spoken thus, and the viewpoint was extreme for any theology wishing to retain the name of Christian. Not only was it sharply criticized by Bishop Gore,[2] it met with little response from other liberals, Anglican or Free Church.

In the Church of England liberal opinions had been gaining ground, however, mainly under the impulsion of biblical criticism and the historical study of Christian origins. In this field Lightfoot and Westcott, both of them impressively learned, had been cautious, although another scholar, Edwin Hatch (1835–1889) of Oxford, was acknowledged by Harnack himself as having anticipated his own theory that the original gospel had been overlaid and distorted by Hellenism.[3] At the turn of the century the leader of Anglican liberalism was Hastings Rashdall (1858–1924), a Fellow of New College, Oxford, afterwards dean of Carlisle, whose Bampton lectures on *The Idea of Atonement in Christian Theology* (1919) are a forthright re-statement of the Abelardian theory as against any kind of expiatory or substitutionary views, which he rejected as immoral and sub-personal. Other prominent figures were J. F. Bethune-Baker (1861–1951), Lady Margaret's professor of divinity at Cambridge and an authority on early Christian doctrine; W. R. Inge (1860–1954), dean of St Paul's, a Platonist and author of an important study of Plotinus,[4] but also a popular journalist sharply critical of his own times; Percy Gardner (1846–1937), a layman and professor of classical archaeology at

---

[1] *Op. cit.*, pp. *18, 33, 35.*

[2] In *The New Theology and the Old Religion* (*1907*).

[3] See the former's posthumous *The Influence of Greek Ideas and Usages upon the Christian Church* (*1891*).

[4] *The Philosophy of Plotinus* (*1918*).

Oxford, himself much influenced by European Liberal Christianity;[1]
B. H. Streeter (1874–1937), a Fellow, later Provost, of The Queen's
College, Oxford, a noted New Testament scholar whose study of *The
Four Gospels* (1924) must be counted among the very best work in its
field; H. D. A. Major (1871–1961), principal of Ripon Hall, Oxford,
and a doughty controversialist; and E. W. Barnes (1874–1953), bishop
of Birmingham. All were associated with the Modern Churchmen's
Union—Gardner earlier and Major subsequently were for many years
its presidents—but Anglican "Modernism", as it was called, had little
doctrinal coherence. Thus Inge was a right-wing liberal, even in some
respects a conservative, with no liking whatever for theological
immanentism. No more had Hastings Rashdall, temperamentally a
rationalist, who in turn had scant sympathy with Inge's mystical
propensities. Bethune-Baker's views were the most markedly im-
manentist, as may be inferred from his address to the 1923 meeting at
Girton College, Cambridge, of the Modern Churchmen's Union.[2] God
and man are "indissolubly interrelated: neither is complete without the
other. God is being actualized, fulfilled in Man. Man comes to the
fulfilment of his potentiality in God." "The historic process of human
experience is God's own experience,"—words which were, probably,
the last echo of Hegelianism to be heard in English theology. Bishop
Barnes, a Fellow of the Royal Society, was by training a mathematician
—mathematics he had taught at Trinity College, Cambridge—and an
amateur in both philosophy and New Testament study—a fact which
did not prevent him from writing provocatively in either.[3]

Anglican Modernism was in truth a distinctively Anglican growth—
individualistic and sometimes eccentric, but on the whole compromising. It was Protestant in that it was always more or less openly
hostile to Catholicism, but its liberalism tended to follow traditional

[1] See in particular his *Exploratio Evangelica* (1899) and *Modernity and the Churches*
(1910).
[2] "Jesus as Human and Divine", published in *The Way of Modernism* (1928).
See below, pp. 205–17.
[3] His Gifford lectures on *Scientific Theory and Religion* were published in 1933.
The conclusion reached in them is optimistic: "An increased recognition of the
important place which mental constructs occupy in physical theory, coupled with
an understanding that thought, will and feeling cannot be wholly sundered from
one another, has produced a widespread conviction that theism and science will
in the end form a harmonious unity" (pp. 393 f.). *The Rise of Christianity*, in which
the influence of critics like Loisy and Guignebert is evident, appeared in 1947.

"Broad Church" lines. Its chief defect was a certain academicism: for all its intent of reaching the "modern man" it lacked popular appeal. Rarely does it generate anything like the religious warmth of Harnack's *What is Christianity?* or the writings of the famous Roman Catholic Modernist, George Tyrrell.[1] Theologically its interest centred on Christology, in an attempt to combine insistence on Jesus' natural manhood with a credible doctrine of his divinity. A critical view of Christian beginnings required the first, traditional religion—which the Modernists were loath to repudiate—the second. Accordingly it was said that we cannot intelligibly claim God to have dwelt in Christ, "unless we have already recognized that in a sense God dwells in and reveals Himself in Humanity at large, and in each particular human soul. ... If God can only be known as revealed in Humanity, and Christ is the highest representative of Humanity, we can very significantly say 'Christ is the Son of God, very God of very God, of one substance with the Father', though the phrase undoubtedly belongs to a philosophical dialect which we do not habitually use."[2] Streeter's essay on "The Historic Christ" was likewise the contribution to the liberal symposium, *Foundations: a Statement of Christian Belief in Terms of Modern Thought* (1912), which attracted greatest attention, especially his account of the Resurrection-appearances as "objective visions". William Temple, then in his early, liberal period, spoke of the formula of Chalcedon as "a confession of the bankruptcy of Greek Patristic Theology" in that it explained nothing, and criticized that theology's substance-doctrine for its neglect of the moral aspect of the incarnation. But he acknowledged that the "central point—the unique value of the appearance of the Divine in human form in the person of Jesus of Nazareth—has never been more powerfully emphasized than by the Greek Fathers".[3]

However, the more conscious and deliberate type of Liberal Protestantism was to be found outside the established churches of England

---

[1] On English Modernism generally see P. Gardner, *Modernism in the English Church* (1926), H. D. A. Major, *English Modernism: its Origin, Method and Aims* (1927) and A. M. Ramsey, *From Gore to Temple* (1960).

[2] Hastings Rashdall, *Philosophy and Religion* (1909), pp. 180 f. See also the same writer's paper, "Christ as the Logos and as Son of God" (1921), reprinted in *God and Man* (edd. H. D. A. Major and F. L. Cross, 1930, pp. 68–78).

[3] *Foundations*, pp. 232 f.

and Scotland.[1] In the main, indeed, Free Church divines, of whom P. T. Forsyth and A. E. Garvie—the latter a close student of Ritschlianism—are recalled as among the most distinguished, were less inclined to theological innovation than were some of their Anglican contemporaries. Campbell, as we have seen, was a particular exception; others were T. R. Glover (*1869–1943*), a Cambridge classical scholar and author of the popular *Jesus of History* (*1917*), the thesis of which is much the same as Harnack's, and the Congregationalist, C. J. Cadoux (*1883–1947*), whose *Catholicism and Christianity* (*1928*) is a vigorous, not to say aggressive, assertion of radical opinions. The Unitarian tradition, maintained with such high repute throughout the previous century by James Martineau (*1805–1900*)—he was, in truth, the one great English Liberal Protestant of his age[2]—was also well represented, if in a somewhat journalistic style, by L. P. Jacks (*1860–1955*), whose own position, as an admirer of Bergson and William James, was generally that of a pragmatist. "Logical machinery", he said, "cannot follow the movement of the live spirit, nor arrest it even for a moment's inspection,"[3] an attitude which involved him in a certain contempt for all theologizing simply as such. It was sufficient to believe that

"There is that in the world, call it what you will, which responds to the confidence of those who trust it, declaring itself, to them, as a fellow-worker in the pursuit of the Eternal Values, meeting their loyalty to it with reciprocal loyalty to them, and coming in at critical moments when the need of its sympathy is greatest. . . . If (one) chose to call it Christ, or more simply 'the Spirit', I should not quarrel with him."[4]

In America the liberal movement in religious thought may be said to have begun with William Ellery Channing, who himself was

[1] Scottish theology, always solid and cautious, is seen at its best in the work of men like John Oman and H. R. Mackintosh, both of them liberal, but hardly Liberal Protestant.

[2] Martineau was remarkable, in addition to qualities of personal character, for the breadth of his theological sympathies and the balance of his judgment. His early *Rationale of Religious Inquiry* was warmly praised on its appearance in *1836*, but the principal fruits of his thinking were *Studies of Christianity* (*1858*), *A Study of Spinoza* (*1882*), *Types of Ethical Theory* (*1885*), and *The Seat of Authority in Religion* (*1890*).

[3] *Religious Perplexities*, p. *19*.

[4] *Op. cit.*, pp. *58, 60*.

brought up in the strict ways of New England Protestantism. A contemporary of Schleiermacher—Channing died in *1847*—his own initiatives as a liberal—despite America's then almost total intellectual isolation—antedated those of the Oriel school, Thomas Erskine or McLeod Campbell. In his day he came to be considered a unitarian, but although critical of the traditional trinitarianism, as also of the prevailing atonement-theology, he believed Christ to have been at once the perfect revelation of God and the living ideal of humanity—the revelation occurring in the ideal, and to be judged therefore by the conscience. Against the Calvinism of his youth he set a confident faith in man's freedom and inherent capacity for good as a child of God. For any whittling down of man's responsibility as a moral agent, as too for the merely arbitrary and magical in religion, Channing could find no place or justification, a point of view reasserted and emphasized in more literary style by Ralph Waldo Emerson (*1803–1882*), the most prominent American religious teacher of his century. It was he whom Matthew Arnold described, in addressing an American audience, as "your Newman, your man of soul and genius". The comparison may seem less apt to us today—the American writer was (to be frank) something of a wind-bag, a Boston Carlyle—but as the leader of the New England transcendentalist movement he gained nation-wide reputation and influence. His best book is *Nature* (*1836*), the best-known the two volumes of *Essays*—a collection of secular sermons.[1] The basis of Emerson's religious position was his faith in the essential divinity of man. Redemption was to be sought in the individual's possession of his own soul by original thought and effort. Originality was of first importance: "Refuse the good models", he urged, "even those which are sacred in the imagination of men." Jesus was best honoured by men themselves living as he lived, by intuition, the guidance of conscience and trust in the value of the human soul. Yet for all his humanism and disillusion with institutional Christianity Emerson saw the futility of mere negation in theology. But he was not himself a systematic thinker and has no constructive account of Christianity to offer.

A liberal who nonetheless stood firm for orthodoxy was Horace Bushnell (*1802–1876*). Bushnell was trained for the law, graduating at

---

[1] The first series was published in *1841*, the second two years later.

Yale in *1827*, but he chose the Presbyterian ministry and in *1833* became pastor of the North Church at Hartford, Connecticut, a benefice he held for the remainder of his life. From the start he was antagonistic towards the old, stiff orthodoxy, with its preoccupation with original sin and depravity. In a volume entitled *Discourses on Christian Nature*, published in *1847*, he took a mediating line, stressing both the moral inwardness and the corporate character of the religious life, as well as factors which must be held to mitigate individual sinfulness. *God in Christ (1849)* again applies the moral criterion to dogma: conscience must ever be the judge, whilst even in Scripture the "body" has to be distinguished from the "soul". The three addresses of the previous year, *1848*, to the divinity schools at Harvard, Andover and Yale dealt respectively with the atonement, the divinity of Christ and the relation of dogma and the Spirit. In the first of these he urges the vicariousness of Christ's sacrifice as opposed to the substitutionary doctrine of traditional theology; in the second he criticizes the usual statements of trinitarianism on grounds of tritheism, suggesting a doctrine of a more revelational or "economic" type; in the third he pleads for an end to theological factiousness. As the exponent of a moderate, "Catholic-minded" liberalism—his mother was an episcopalian and he himself was brought up in the Arminian persuasion—Bushnell is winning some attention today.[1]

By the end of the century, however, the provincialism of the American theological scene had largely disappeared. European influences were flooding in, although never to the detriment of the stubbornly activist character of transatlantic Christianity. It was indeed this activist propensity which gained a ready hearing for Ritschlianism. The name that at once comes to mind in this connexion is that of H. C. King (*1858–1934*), president of Oberlin College, Ohio, and a convinced disciple of both Lotze and Ritschl. King's concern was for a genuinely "personalist" interpretation of Christian doctrine, giving rise to a theology of "value" in place of the ontological categories of its classical formularies. This is the guiding motive of his books on *The Ethics of Jesus (1910)* and *Reconstruction in Theology (1902)*. The question of Christ's divinity is thus to be understood primarily in ethical terms, although it is fitting enough to speak of unity of essence where essence

[1] A volume of selections from Bushnell's writings, edited by H. Shelton Smith, was published in *1965* by the Oxford University Press.

is taken in a teleological sense. The same principle may and should be extended to the whole scheme of received belief: its significance is moral and practical, as must be demonstrated if it is to be intelligible and relevant to modern life.

Also in sympathy with the Ritschlian doctrine was a slightly younger contemporary of King's, William Adams Brown (*1865–1943*), from *1898* until *1930* Roosevelt professor of systematic theology at Union Theological Seminary, New York. Brown's best work, on *The Essence of Christianity*, published in *1902*,[1] takes the form of an historical inquiry, but his personal view emerges clearly enough. He seeks to adopt a mediating position between the orthodox principle of emphasizing the supernatural character of Christianity and hence of magnifying the contrast between it and other religions, and the broader approach which, since Schleiermacher at least, stresses the resemblances between it and the ethnic religions, grounding the former's primacy in its realizing a universal ideal. In fact the problem of the definition of Christianity is at bottom, he thinks, simply that of reconciling these two divergent assessments. Further,

"the attempt to destroy dogmatic Christianity is giving place to the more fruitful effort to understand it. We see the good which it contains as well as the evil, and recognize that in this development of Christian thought even those parts which seem to us less honourable have a necessary part to play. Ideas in themselves indifferent or even hostile may be so transformed by the spirit of Christ as to serve for generations as the vehicle of the Gospel. What is needed is not denunciation, but insight; not polemic but sympathy."[2]

The same desire to *understand* historic Christianity is again evidenced in the work of A. C. McGiffert (*1861–1933*), who as professor of Church history at Union Seminary from *1893* was himself a colleague of Adams Brown. McGiffert was a liberal who believed religious certitude to be, in the last resort, independent of historical events, a conviction which enabled him to treat doctrinal history with a remarkable degree of candour and tact. His writing in this field, and especially his two-volume *History of Christian*

---

[1] See too his *Christian Theology in Outline* (*1906*) and *Modern Theology and the Preaching of the Gospel* (*1914*).   [2] *The Essence of Christianity*, pp. *304* f.

Thought (*1932–1933*), being models of lucidity and fairness.[1]

Adams Brown was a professional theologian, and McGiffert a historian, both addressing a more restricted audience. Some mention therefore is due here to a popular liberal writer whose books have also found many readers in this country, H. E. Fosdick (born *1878*). Fosdick's *The Modern Use of the Bible* adopts the familiar "evolutionary" standpoint which sees the Jewish and Christian scriptures as a documentation of a continuous and progressive religious experience; and the orientation of his thought generally has been empiricist and pragmatist. Religion, he believes, even in its non-Christian forms — Buddhism especially—is necessary for the soul of man, representing as it does a dimension of life in which personal values receive their highest expression. It is always the subjective aspect of religious conviction which concerns him, as a power to be valued and used for its spiritually therapeutic qualities. Hence the importance of prayer, on which Fosdick has written extensively; for prayer has the reflex effect of heightening the devotee's spiritual sensitivity and receptivity and of conferring the moral benefits of stability of temper, self-control and peace of mind.

From Fosdick to Ritschl may be a far cry, but as in Britain so too in America—there perhaps even more—theological liberalism has had a widely diffused influence, disclosing itself in a variety of kinds and degrees. Nowhere has Protestant Christianity been untouched by it, except on the "fundamentalist" fringe—although this last represents a by no means inconsiderable quantity in American religious life. Even those who have consciously reacted against it, like the Niebuhrs, have obviously imbibed much of its spirit. Their position, like that of Donald and John Baillie, or H. H. Farmer, or Austin Farrer, can best be described as post- rather than anti-liberal. The waters have abated somewhat, but the tide-mark remains.

7. The Aftermath of Liberalism

If it is difficult to arrive at an exact definition of Liberal Protestantism doctrinally it is no more easy to do so chronologically. Its origins we

[1] Others of McGiffert's publications include his study of *The Apostles' Creed* (*1902*), in which he argues that the phraseology of the creed is mainly directed against the heresies of Marcion, the volume on *Protestant Thought before Kant* (*1911*; reprinted in *1962* in an edition by J. Pelikan), and *The Rise of Modern Religious Ideas* (*1915*).

have indicated, broadly at least, but its termination as a movement still cannot clearly be discerned. Indeed it may not have terminated: do not Bultmann and Buri stand firmly within the liberal tradition? Yet it is extremely doubtful whether any living theologian, at once Protestant and liberal, would wish to describe himself as a Liberal Protestant in the way that Harnack, say, would have done, or Jean Réville. The reason for this is that over the greater part of the last half-century Protestant liberalism, once so self-confident, has had to withstand devastating counter-attack from a revived orthodoxy. The spearhead of this counter-attack has of course been the *crisis*-theology of Karl Barth, whose challenge of the basic liberal presuppositions has brought about a renewed valuation of essential Protestant doctrine. Thus a theology of transcendence has replaced philosophical immanentism, divine revelation the speculative reason, the sense of sin that of pride in moral as well as material progress. The inspiration of Calvinism, as against Lutheran subjectivism, has been strong; but the Barthian teaching is Calvinism with a difference, as, for example, in the discarding of the traditional predestinarianism for the doctrine of one and one only predestinated being, Christ. But whatever may be said about neo-orthodoxy in detail there can be no question but that its impact upon the generation following the First World War has been deep and that for many years liberalism was in a trough. Liberal talk about "religious experience", its concern for the rights of critical reason, its belief in human civilization as itself an expression of the divine purpose—in a word, its all-pervading anthropocentrism: all this was impugned or derided. Faith now came to be seen less as a rationally motivated act than, in Barth's own phrases, "a leap in the void", possible for all men "only because it is equally impossible for all". The burden of the neo-orthodox case against liberalism has been that it has evacuated the gospel of its necessary *offence*. "A God without wrath brought men without sin into a kingdom without judgement through the ministrations of a Christ without a cross."[1] For the failure of liberalism, religiously speaking, was, as the post-liberals see it, its inability to contemplate either the actual condition of man or the doctrine of God which the remedy for such a condition inherently demands. The danger to which it was exposed, and in certain instances succumbed,

[1] H. Richard Niebuhr, *The Kingdom of God in America*, p. *193* (Harper Torchbooks edition).

was that of transforming Christianity into a high-minded ethical humanism, a point of view admirable indeed for those—the few— with the moral resources to sustain it, but unavailing for the masses helplessly caught up in the fearful travail of the present century.

Liberal Protestantism has, then, been severely criticized. Objection to it can be summarized by saying that it presents only a *reduced* Christianity; and in some writers it certainly did appear to offer little more than a set of ethical principles. It tended also to be both academic and bourgeois. Further, in its otherwise laudable desire not to separate the "sacred" from the "secular" it too readily identified the secular with the sacred. And in general it was over-complacent about the feasibility of rendering an ancient religion in a form acceptable to the modern Western mind, towards which it was apt to be apologetic and obsequious. Such faults and shortcomings have been noted time and again. Nevertheless, very much of the criticism directed against Liberal Protestantism is undiscriminating and unfair to its more worthy exponents, especially Ritschl himself, who were all of them deeply imbued with the Christian spirit whilst being keenly alive to the difficulty of adhering to the thought-forms and language of traditional Christian belief. They knew that this difficulty must be faced if the religion itself is finally to survive. They realized also that there are elements in the Christian creed which cannot be preserved in anything like their original sense and hence must be relinquished, however regretfully. How far this process of intellectual pruning and reinterpretation need be carried was of course a matter of individual judgment. No two liberal thinkers are ever quite in agreement. But such personal freedom in choosing the way of faith is of the liberal ethos, and liberals would firmly deny that the constraint of a precise dogmatic system in religious belief is something that the modern world is likely ever again to find tolerable.

The selection of excerpts from Liberal Protestant writers which follows is designed to show their teaching alike in its range and variety. Hermann Lotze is represented at the start, both for the direct influence which he exerted upon Ritschl and for the affinity, well brought out in his *Outlines of a Philosophy of Religion*, which his own views bear to the liberal theology of his time and later. As much space as possible has been assigned to Ritschl himself, and a number of passages will be found, all from *Justification and Reconciliation*, illustrating his conception of the scope and purpose of systematic theology, of justification, of the nature of religious knowledge and of the person of Jesus Christ. Herrmann, Kaftan and Harnack are introduced in turn as the leading representatives of the Ritschlian school in Germany. Auguste Sabatier and Jean Réville then appear as the outstanding figures among French liberal theologians, the chapter from Réville's *Liberal Christianity* being as clear and candid a statement of the more "advanced" standpoint as could be cited. The anthology concludes with certain instances of Anglo-Saxon liberal opinion. A choice of suitable excerpts, in view of the necessary limitation of space, has not been easy. Nothing from Troeltsch or Reischle or Lobstein has been included, nor from Hastings Rashdall or Percy Gardner or R. J. Campbell or H. C. King. The editor regrets such omissions as, doubtless, will some of his readers. But enough, it is hoped, has been provided to exemplify, in a little detail, one of the most important phases of modern Christian thought. If the present selection succeeds in inducing the student to investigate these older authors in the original volumes—not, unfortunately, always easy to come by nowadays—it will fully have justified its publication.

E

PART I

HERMANN LOTZE

RELIGION AND MORALITY

If there is no theoretic demonstration forthcoming for religious conviction, yet there must be a motive for retaining this conviction. This is furnished by an appeal to direct and inner experience, which asserts the truth of these religious intuitions just as directly and without the intervention of logic, as the perceptions of the senses attest the reality of outward objects. But as we said above in the introduction, there is no one inner experience, recognised by all, of this divine order of the world not perceptible by the senses; the only feeling common to all men, to which we could appeal as the foundation of religion, consists in the dictates of conscience, which yet only assert directly what should be, though indirectly sanctioning an inference from this about that which is.

There are various conceptions of the office of conscience. We must allow that conscience is not a consistent revelation, anterior to all experience, of commands which our future action has to follow. It resembles rather our faculty of cognition. The highest principles to which our judgment of things leads us back are no original and ready-made possession of our consciousness; our particular perceptions lead us at first in the way of immediate reaction to connect them in a definite order and sense. Later reflection on many single cases shows us on what principles our previously only instinctive action proceeded; and then they become conscious principles which we henceforth follow in our further knowledge. In the same way conscience is moved to single verdicts of approval or disapproval by the contemplation of single fixed cases. The reflective comparison of these single verdicts forms from them those general moral prescriptions which we then term the direct voice of conscience.

Upon the psychological evolution of our conscience, which we must perforce allow, is apt to be based a view which destroys the binding value and the true majesty of moral commands.

The soul approves or disapproves of an action in virtue of its susceptibility to an immediate feeling of pleasure or pain which it experiences therefrom. Later on when it comes to frame general propositions, it only sets store by those maxims, by steadily following which it has learned from experience that it is certain on the average to reach the highest degree and the most enduring length of the pleasure or self-satisfaction which is all it can attain to. All moral precepts are thus made to appear to be maxims of prudence, general formulae of the best way to get on; and they only seem to be universal laws, because our experience of the past, present, and future is too limited to allow of our finding rules and modes of conduct specially adapted for the attainment in every single case of the highest possible good.

This much of truth must be conceded to this way of regarding morality: namely that the experience of human intercourse can alone supply a concrete and definite filling in of those general precepts, in following which moral conduct consists. It is vain to try, as the opponents of utilitarianism do, to derive those specialised precepts from the universal notions of what is good, holy, moral, or right. These universal notions express nothing more than the peculiar impression which particular kinds of action, when we first become aware of them, make upon our soul; on the other hand they do not teach us to know the forms of action to which this impression attaches.

The disposition to regard moral rules simply as prudential maxims won by experience and to attribute all conduct to selfish motives cannot be combated by theory. Only this much is clear, that such an interpretation of moral commands is arbitrary. For even if we do assume that these commands have an intrinsic value and holiness, nothing is changed. I mean to say that they would still actually be the maxims, by following which the greatest sum of happiness is secured. Still, as before, the particular actions which they enjoin would have to be learned by experience, as was stated above. And for that very reason it would still be always possible to represent these moral commands as if they were nothing more than empirical doctrines of what is useful. But, as a fact, we place in direct contrast to that mode of action which only follows these maxims of prudence, another mode as alone of intrinsic value, that, namely, which follows the same rules, but in another spirit, a spirit which considers and desires the establishment of good in the same unselfish manner, in which, for instance, we admire beauty as something objectively of worth without any idea of its usefulness to us, or in a spirit which, in so far as it strives after the production of happiness, finds this happiness only in acts of benevolence towards others and not in egotism. This too may be denied; but then we deny an inner experience on the acknowledgment of which every further religious aspiration is based. Conversely those who are conscious of this inner experience are no less incapable of refutation.

But neither does the recognition of the intrinsic worth and holiness of moral commands lead straight to a religious point of view; on the contrary, alike in ancient and modern times it has been bluntly opposed to religious ideas as to something false and unnecessary. Practically this stoicism or rationalism which despises all religious connection may, by its mere submission to the general laws of morality and of the universe, form the foundation for a very worthy and elevated conduct of life. None the less there is in such a position a peculiar theoretical contradiction.

For, in the first place, it would push aside all speculations as to the origin, whatever it may be, or the final goal of moral laws, on the ground that such speculation must impair the conception of the intrinsic holiness and unconditional obligatoriness of these laws. It is a lofty disposition which so utters itself, yet one which reposes on a theory of morals which is not altogether true or useful. We can think of laws which are utterly unconditioned, in the sense that they govern all reality like laws of nature, and are consequently the expression of a *must* which knows of no exceptions. On the other hand we cannot intelligibly think of an unconditioned *should be*, that is to say, of a law to which reality of itself in no way corresponds.

That which should be or ought to be, must have a reality distinct from that which should not be; and this distinction cannot merely consist in our withholding one or the other of these opposed predicates. More than this, that the one should be and the other should not must have practical force and validity. In other words and simpler, we may put it thus: an unconditioned *should* or *ought to* be is unthinkable; and

only a conditioned *should be* is possible, because it alone holds out
advantages and disadvantages to those who follow or disregard a
precept. These results, however, themselves can ultimately only consist
in pleasure or unhappiness; and in this alone consists the absolute worth
which is possessed by the ideals pointed out by moral laws. A value
appreciated by no one and consisting in pleasure and pain for no one is,
as we saw above, something which contradicts itself.

The stoics put forward as the ideal of life for the wise an immobility
of character, in Greek phrase *ataraxy*, which they associated indissolubly
with the absolute and unconditional obligatoriness of moral precept,
and which is supposed to be an advantage. We answer that, even if this
be a praiseworthy type of character in itself, still its consequences are
not at all praiseworthy; for it excludes a lively enthusiasm for the good
and beautiful, and by suppressing the feelings, sinks the spirit into the
mere manifestation of an impersonal substance. Lastly, so far as we
reached this ataraxy by following the moral laws, the latter would be
really maxims of utility, by following which an egoistic well-being is to
be attained.

Nevertheless, not only the repose of soul, but also the self-respect
engendered by following out the moral laws is in a vague way preferred
as a last aim and final good. This of itself almost points to conclusions
which are religious. If we consider the single person as a mere natural
product, appearing and vanishing, there seems no cause why we should
insist that what we honour as good and holy should be realised in this *I*.
Self-respect can only be understood as a final aim, if it forms part of
what gives us pleasure egoistically, like any satisfaction of the senses. It
can only have another meaning, if we change our conception of our
personality and its position in the world.

The above reflections have not of course the force of demonstrative
proofs, but can merely serve to bring home to our minds the connection
in which alone the particular thoughts sketched out become quite
satisfactory. They point to three propositions which we may regard as
the characteristic convictions of every religious mind, in contrast with a
merely theoretical understanding of things. These propositions are as
follows:

1. Moral laws embody the will of God.

2. Individual finite spirits are not products of nature, but are children of God.

3. Reality is more and other than the mere course of nature, it is a kingdom of God.

We must explain these three propositions and examine their consequences.

Objections have been raised to the first of these propositions, which admit of being reduced to the well-known scholastic alternative: is the good good, because God wills it, or does he will it, because it is good? We had to decide similar questions in regard to the validity of the eternal truths and by the light of their analogy let us look at the question now before us.

If we answer the first clause of the antithesis with a yes, it may be asked: What is meant by the God who in this case is said to will? Is he more than an infinite power without any qualities or attributes? The assertion, moreover, that he willed the good, whether we mean that he resolved upon it in time or that his will is eternal and without beginning, only amounts to our saying that the good should be once and for all, and that this *should be* rests on an act of affirmation or on a positing which had no origin at all. Moreover, it is clear that such an act is merely a display of power and so capable of investing the moral law with the character of necessity, but not with any moral worth at all. The other half of the anithesis is equally useless: that God wills the moral law because it is good in itself. Not only is this way of speaking presumptuous, but it must be pointed out that a spirit does not recognise a precept or body of precepts as being of this binding character, unless it already has for his nature the very truth and worth to be accorded to it by his assent thereto.

We may feel sure, therefore, that these alternatives cut asunder thoughts which have no meaning apart, and embody a single truth, and that we must needs fall into absurdities when we make one of them the condition of the other.

We must, therefore, pronounce as follows: God is nothing else than that will whose purport and mode of action can be conceived of in our reflection as that which is good in itself—as a will which can only be separated by abstraction from the living form in which it exists in the real God. But, in truth, it as little follows after, or precedes the Divine nature, as in a movement direction can be later or earlier than velocity.

It is, therefore, a mistake to object that the true majesty of moral laws is infringed, if they be regarded as the will of God. We make this reflection, not with the purpose of establishing the dignity of those laws by showing where they came from, for their worth is immediately realised by us, so that they win our homage from the first; we make it, rather, because this worth or dignity of the moral law is not to be satisfactorily accounted for in any theory, and so demands some such reflections as the above, not, indeed, in order to be allowed and accepted, but simply in order to be understood and harmonised with the rest of our conception of the world.

We must not be rendered insensible by the somewhat sentimental terms in which the second proposition is couched to the importance of the truth it contains.

Its meaning is twofold. In the first place, it is an acknowledgment of the finite character and of the subjection of the personal spirit to the power and wisdom of God. And here we see the difference between Christianity and the prouder moral systems which pursue as their ideal the self-sufficiency and self-respect of the wise man. On the other hand, this truth fortifies us against that depreciation of personality which consists in regarding it as a passing product of the processes of nature. It asserts that there is a relation of piety between God and man, that this relation is ever a living one, and that through it alone the finite spirit ceases to be a mere dependent natural product.

And, in the place of mere self-satisfaction as the highest good, there comes the hope of being loved by God. And this approval by the supreme spirit takes the place of the pride which claims to find a sufficient good in self-esteem.

As regards the third proposition, we have already seen that we do not know the purport and plan of the Divine government of the world. As a consequence of this, religion must exclude from its province all natural philosophy and consideration of external reality. Science must be left to itself to frame its own methods, and religion must not interfere or try to influence its decisions.

This also distinguishes Christianity from other religions. The heathen religions have mythologies which give extensive explanations and interpretations of reality. The Christian religion has no cosmology of its own, and bases all its reflections on considerations of the spiritual world, of which we have an inner experience.

Outlines of a Philosophy of Religion
(trans. by F. C. Conybeare), pp. *151–64*

DOGMAS AND CONFESSIONS

More than these three tenets is not revealed by the Christian religion. To be penetrated by them, and to submit willingly to the Divine will, this is religion as a living faith, as a condition of the soul.

For all that, it is impossible to get rid of attempts to transform these felt convictions into a succession of formulated and communicable tenets. Experience of life drives men to make such attempts, when, instead of answering the doubts of others by trying to bring them into their own religious tone and temper, they confront them with ready-made convictions, specially dealing with the doubt in question. All such attempts we may term religious mysticism. They are exclusively based on our own inner religious experience and have no force but for, and claim no acceptance but from, the personal subject alone, which seeks in the depths of its soul an answer to its doubts.

This first impulse generated a second. One is involved in contradictions if one tries to stand alone in religious convictions, in which, after all, we are bound up with the entire world. Religion is not only a union of the individual with God, but is through this union also a union with all other men.

This is the one respectable root of religious fanaticism. For, what we ourselves recognise as the highest would not be so, unless it were recognised as such by all. This does not really justify us in thrusting upon others our subjective beliefs, but, it does rightly engender in us all the need of a religious communion within which we may each find again, if not the fulness of our private beliefs and mystical knowledge, at least the outlines of convictions, which may be shared by all its members in common. And herein lies the necessity for dogmas and creeds of general recognition and force.

Without doubt, the historical development of such thoughts will more fully represent the religious feelings than the experience of a single life; although anything which we have once experienced is thereby borne in upon our minds with a greater intensity than tenets merely inherited from the past can ever possess.

Universally received dogmas, therefore, have a double purpose. On the one hand, they embody solutions of doubts won in the course of the past. On the other hand, they are clear outlines of belief outside of which the fancy of the individual may not wander without falling into error.

Our earlier considerations showed that none of these dogmas must be regarded as a theoretically or scientifically sufficient answer to the questions before us; rather they are symbols acknowledging the existence of a riddle and marking out in a figurative and unsatisfactory manner the sphere of thought outside of which the elements of a solution must not even be looked for. Thus to us it would seem erroneous to demand agreement with the literal contents of these dogmas from any one who would join a religious communion. Even in their literal form they cannot be objects of knowledge or the reverse. Before even a question of this can be raised they need some interpretation to be given of the meaning which in a figurative or symbolic way they express. But no interpretation can be given which would meet with general acceptance and appeal to all alike, but every individual must find it in the workings of his own soul.

Of one, therefore, who would belong to a particular communion, it should only be asked: does he feel and acknowledge in his inner nature a religious truth which can be entertained as the meaning of the objectively formulated dogma, and which deserves to be put forward as a public tenet?

It may be objected that there is a kind of dishonesty involved in so partial an assent to the tenets of one's communion. There would be, if we meant that the religion and its dogmas are only to be regarded as binding for the uneducated. But on the contrary we contend that religious truth is absolutely valid for all alike, only that the theoretical expressions which men devise for it are altogether inadequate. And that is why it is permissible for a man to agree upon formulae, bearing the same theoretical sense for all, through which he thinks that the essential meaning is best grasped and comprehended.

It is the same in other parts of our life. There, too, we often find ourselves obliged to look at the world in ways which we, from the standpoint of philosophy, know to be inadequate. The presence of a spacial world outside us, material atoms and forces—these are all ideas, without using which, not only the common, but the philosophic understanding which denies their validity would not be able to rightly observe and handle the external world. In all these cases we do not get at the truth, but only at a picture or figurative appearance, by means of which we can make clear to ourselves the true relations of the real world, which in themselves cannot be expressed.

In the same way it is of no consequence for religion that theoretically objectionable phrases should be provided to express what is in itself superfluous; it *is* important that we should have picturesque or figurative expressions to which the spirit may attach the same feelings as appertain to the true content.

Now, we must allow that we could only speak so simply as this, if these dogmatic formulae were about to be established for the first time. But, in fact, we have them as a legacy of the past, and what is more, have them too often in a form which admits of a great deal of misunderstanding of their true sense. But that is no reason why we should, in a self-willed way, separate ourselves from the circles which recognise them; it only entails upon us that we should not erect these dogmas into objects of theoretical knowledge, and that we should, as a matter of honesty and concern for the spiritual well-being of others, combat the evil of a false interpretation of them.

The attempts at a theory fall into three parts, of which the first alone —theology in the narrower sense—is thoroughly accessible to philosophy.

In the foregoing we have tried to show, firstly, of what, in the way of a definite characterisation of the Divine being, philosophy admits; secondly, what it rejects; lastly, what it insists upon, though unable to exhibit it adequately in theory. The general results of our investigations we may sum up thus: the belief in a personal God conflicts with none of the metaphysical convictions to which we must hold fast. On the other hand, there is nothing to be said for the views of those who, while rejecting all religious beliefs, in a facile manner swallow any kind of physical theories, and pretend that spiritual life arose out of the forces of mere matter. Lastly, the reproach of anthropomorphism is unjust, because the distinction between finite and infinite spirit is by no means overlooked. It is the height of perversity to set up as the principle of the world an unconscious and blind substrate, the idea of which is strictly dark and impenetrable to us.

Further speculations, for example, about the Trinity would have no importance for the religious life, except for their bearing on the position which, through the establishment or revelation of religion, the human race has assumed towards God. These form a second and large branch of religious theory. We have shown reasons for believing that God is ever active in the world and upon individual spirits, and as we admittedly know nothing about the plan after which God governs the world, there is nothing in the way of our believing that at particular moments and in particular persons God has stood nearer to humanity and revealed himself more fully than in others.

When, therefore, as a title of honour, the founder of our religion is called the Son of God, no serious objection can be raised; we are certainly justified in holding that the relation in which He stood to God was not only different in degree to that in which we stand, but also unique in kind.

But no adequate expression can be found for that which we mean in this case. In a literal sense Christ cannot possibly be the Son of God; it is a figurative expression and admits of no literal interpretation. There is, therefore, no room in this case for a theoretical dogma, and in affirming that Christ is the Son of God, we merely express our conviction of the unique importance which Christ and his relation to God have for mankind; we cannot define either the one or the other.

Any one who impartially lets the teaching and history of Christ's life work upon his soul, without analysing the impression, cannot but feel that therein an infinitely valuable and unique act of healing has been performed for mankind. But to try to fix in rigid theory the exact value and import of the act is to take away from it rather than to add to it.

We cannot say that the honour of God is wounded by man's sin and that it is satisfied by the sacrifice of an individual. Apart from the crude conception of God involved in this view, it rests on the impossible assumption of such a solidarity between all men that the blame and punishment of all can be thrown on one person, who can bear it for all.

The more human ideas of an expiation or redemption, the latter especially, leave it undecided from whom or what humanity is really set free by this ransom. It can hardly be God; it must therefore be the order of natural law which has bound up with our finite nature sin, and with sin, condemnation.

We know, however, that we are not freed either from physical evil or from the possibility of sin. There remains therefore as the practical result of our redemption no more than the faith revealed, and that frees us from the fear and misgiving of the creature, so far as it teaches us that all our ills are a Divine probation, and also that our entire earthly life is neither meaningless nor an irrevocable last, but an epoch of preparation, of the sins committed during which we are by the Divine grace absolved in a manner which, as a matter of theory, we can not in the least define.

All further speculations than this about the origin of sin and its consequences are for the religious life utterly useless.

The third section of these speculations comprises what is called eschatology and admits not of any theoretical treatment. The earthly future of the human race, the manner of our immortality, and the requital which the world's assize will bring to each of us, these cannot be depicted in any concrete fashion. And indeed the humanity of this age has quite outgrown the old coarse imagery, and is content to retain the general idea of a continued life, in which we shall be gradually perfected, as well as receive some requital for the past. And this is good evidence that for a really religious life there is not wanted that intimate acquaintance with the future life to which a perverse and blundering dogmatic system pretended.

We pointed out above of what importance it is that in our religious convictions we should not stand alone. It is the more important, because the very gist and marrow of these convictions lies in the faith that all men are bound up with one another and with God in an eternal communion into which every one may enter of his own free will. This communion we call the invisible Church. The visible Church is only a human institution of the community of the faithful, partly for common worship, partly for the ordaining of their earthly affairs in accordance with the commands of their faith. Hence the folly of any Church which claims to be the only way of salvation, claims not only to teach and lead us along it, but to open or close it to us of its own power. For the rest, the Church, like any other institution, should not stand in opposition to the State; though their proper relations to one another are scarcely well described by saying that the Church ought to be subject to the State in everything but certain unessential externals. On the contrary it is the misfortune of the present time, and a mere historical accident, that the State must exist without any religious foundation, and thinks that it does not want any.

But perfect unity of the State in religious as well as in secular matters presupposes that two parties, now inimical, should be reconciled to each other. Neither theological learning nor irreligious natural science should continue to assert that they both know so much that they do not and cannot know; in the recognition of Divine mysteries which are left to the interpretation of every single faithful soul and of general moral precepts—about which, indeed, there exists no controversy—religious life should develop according to this motto: *in necessariis unitas, in dubiis libertas, in omnibus caritas.*   *Ibid.*, pp. *165–76*

PART II

ALBRECHT RITSCHL

THE TASK OF THEOLOGY

Christianity ... is the monotheistic, completely spiritual, and ethical religion, which, based on the life of its Author as Redeemer and as Founder of the Kingdom of God, consists in the freedom of the children of God, involves the impulse to conduct from the motive of love, which aims at the moral organisation of mankind, and grounds blessedness on the relation of sonship to God, as well as on the Kingdom of God.

This conception is indispensable for systematic theology if the material correctly obtained from Biblical ideas is to be fully used. The history of theology affords only too many examples of the construction of what is either marely a doctrine of redemption or merely a system of morality. But it must also be observed that we are not to base theology proper on the idea of redemption, and ethics upon the idea of the Kingdom of God. On the contrary, so far as theology falls into these two sections, each must be kept under the constitutive influence of both. Dogmatics, that is, comprises all the presuppositions of Christianity under the form of *Divine operation*; ethics, presupposing the former discipline, comprises the province of personal and social Christian life under the form of *personal activity*. Now since the revelation of God is directed not only to the goal of redemption, but also to the final end of the kingdom which he realises in fellowship with the redeemed, dogmatics cannot dispense with the latter guiding idea. And as the spiritual activity of those who are called to the Kingdom of God and redeemed does not manifest itself merely in their moral influence on others, but also in the peculiar functions of Divine sonship, ethics must be conditional likewise by the idea of redemption.

Theology has performed its task when, guided by the Christian idea of God and the conception of man's blessedness in the Kingdom of God, it exhibits completely and clearly, both as a whole and in particular, the Christian view of the world and human life, together with the necessity which belongs to the interdependent relations between its component elements. It is incompetent for it to enter upon either a direct or an indirect proof of the truth of the Christian Revelation by seeking to show that it agrees with some philosophical or juridical view of the world; for to such Christianity simply stands opposed. And as often as systems even of monistic Idealism have asserted their agreement with Christianity, and its leading ideas have been worked up into a general philosophic view, the result has only been to demonstrate over again the opposition between even such systems and Christianity. The scientific proof for the truth of Christianity ought only to be sought in the line of thought . . .: "Whosoever willeth to do the will of God, will know that the doctrine of Christ is true" (John vii. *17*). Here it is indicated that Christianity can be verified, not when our aim is to understand the domain of spiritual life and of social human action by means of universal grounds of speculation, but only when we mark off the knowledge of that domain from the knowledge of nature and her laws. To subordinate the ethical to the idea of the cosmical is always characteristic of a heathen view of the world, and to its jurisdiction Christianity is not amenable; before it Christianity will never succeed in justifying itself. Even when such an explanation of the world starts from an idea of God, if offers no guarantee that it can prove the truth of Christianity. Christianity includes as one of its elements the distinction of the ethical from the world of nature in respect of worth, inasmuch as it attaches blessedness for man, as the highest and all-dominating notion of worth, to participation in the Kingdom of God and lordship over the world. The theological exposition of Christianity, therefore, is complete when it has been demonstrated that the Christian ideal of life, and no other, satisfies the claims of the human spirit to a general knowledge of things.

Justification and Reconciliation
(trans. by H. R. Mackintosh and A. B. Macaulay), pp. *13* f., *24* f.

JUSTIFICATION

1. *Justification and the Forgiveness of Sins*

Justification, as understood by the Evangelical Church, signifies in general the act of God which gives to believers in Christ their religious peculiarity of character. The Divine operation on the believer, indicated in this conception, is a positive one. Yet not only does Paul, to whom we owe this terminology, interchange at will the positive term—justification—with one which has a negative ring—*the forgiveness of sins*; but in the discourses of Christ (with the exception of Luke xviii. *14*) we meet with the latter form alone. This is due to the fact that it rests directly on Old Testament modes of thought, while the conception coined by Paul is designed to oppose the Pharisaic perversion of the idea of active righteousness. It was possible for Jesus, like the men of the Old Testament, to rest satisfied with the negative term, inasmuch as they alike employed it in estimating sinful phenomena in the life of the people of Israel. For however much the sins of the Israelites, for which forgiveness is either expected or bestowed, are regarded as *ipso facto* disturbing their proper fellowship with God, yet the actual continuance of that fellowship for the people of Israel, according to the terms of the Old Covenant, is taken for granted both by Old Testament witnesses and by Christ. On the other hand, Paul was directly led to construct the positive conception of justification; for he opposes it to his view of the total sin of humanity, in which he on principle disregards the fact that, in the community constituted by the Mosaic law, the Jews possessed a form (though inferior) of fellowship with Divine grace. For while, in particular cases, he can hardly divest his mind of the impression he had of the advantages possessed by the Israelites over the heathen in virtue of their having the law (Rom. ii. *17–20*, iii. *1, 2*, ix. *4, 5*), yet these advantages are ignored in his decisive utterances about the sin of the human race, and about the function of the law in multiplying sin. Since Paul, therefore, finds justification through Christ foreshadowed, not in the legal community of Israel, but only in the promise connected with Abraham and in the sayings of later prophets, and since he sees in justification a saving operation of God on the totality of mankind which is counteractive of universal sin, he prefers the conception which is unquestionably positive, and only employs the term "forgiveness of sins", which he borrows from the Old Testament, to clear up the meaning of his own.

Now the fact that the Reformers used these two conceptions by turns, and expressly ascribed to them complete equivalence and identical scope, is explained by the influence of their situation within the Church as the sphere of positive fellowship with Divine grace

F

When contrasted with this organisation of grace, even the sinfulness of men within the Church, however severely he judged it, appeared to Luther exceptional, so that he found the negative expression clear enough for describing the counteractive force. Yet the positive expression "justification" was recommended, not merely by Paul's usage of it, but also by its antithetical relation to universal sin; and so the Reformers did not scruple to treat both terms as synonymous even in this connection. For while, to begin with, they steadfastly kept the positive grace of God in sight as the basis of the whole saving dispensation, and asserted in consequence that the relation established by grace constitutes the acknowledged standing of Christians before God, it seemed to them all one whether grace, in the form of justification, stood opposed to man's general state of unrighteousness, or, in the form of the forgiveness of sins, served to remove the derangement of Christians' gracious fellowship with God. The attempt to distinguish the two conceptions appeared in Dogmatics for the first time after there had been elaborated the idea of the justice of God and of the law as the original dispensation determining the relation between men and God; and thereupon grace retired into the position of a Divine dispensation which is merely relative. Not until the circumstances had thus changed do we find the forgiveness of sins discriminated as the negative, and justification as the positive effect. Nevertheless, side by side with this later view, there reasserted itself from time to time the contention of the Reformers, that the two expressions differ only *verbaliter*, while in respect of the fact which they denote they are identical. Historical reasons therefore demand that our definition of the idea of justification should base itself on the assumption that justification is synonymous with forgiveness of sins.   *Ibid.*, pp. *38–40*

2. Justification as Adoption by God

Our task is to ascertain in general the attribute of God through which the positively Christian conception of the forgiveness of sins is to be understood. Now it is almost inconceivable that the orthodox theologians, in spite of their endeavours to reproduce the ideas of Holy Scripture, have been entirely oblivious of the fact that Jesus explicitly connected this operation of God with *his attribute as Father*. He directed his disciples to invoke God as Father when they prayed to him for forgiveness of their sins; and, to bring home to them the necessity of their forgiving their fellow-men, he promised them that their Father in heaven would also forgive them their sins (Luke xi. *2-4*; Mark xi. *25*; Matt. vi. *9-15*). In so far, too, as the forgiveness of sins is mediated through the expiatory death of Christ, the apostles recognise the love, or the grace, or the righteousness, that is, the self-consistent saving purpose, of God as the ground of that scheme (Rom. iii. *25, 26*, v. *8*; Heb. ii. *9*). Moreover, the Old Testament idea of sacrifice, through which this whole circle of conceptions must be understood, contains nothing analogous to the judicial procedure of vicarious punishment; the sacrifices of the law are rather the symbols of a Divinely-ordered scheme for the appropriation of the Covenant-grace. It is true that the God whom we invoke as Father, has also inherent in his nature the attribute of impartial Judge (*1* Pet. i. *7*); but he acts as Judge only in vindicating the rights of his people. The title of Judge as applied to God has therefore for Christians no real place alongside of, or over, the relation in which he stands to them as Father. It is only, therefore, when the love of God, regarded as Father, is conceived as the will which works toward the destined end, that the real equivalence of forgiveness and justification, which is represented in the religious conception of things, can be made good. If, however, God be preconceived as Judge in the forensic sense, the two ideas come into direct antagonism with one another, as was indeed explicitly maintained by the leading representatives of the older theology. The man who has gone through the punishment he has merited can, of course, be no more looked upon as a criminal, but he cannot by any means yet be regarded as an active and successful member of the moral community; in order to attain this place, the discharged culprit must give special evidence of his fitness for membership in the community. If, therefore, a judicial procedure on the part of God is recognised in this, that he regards sinners as free from punishment and guilt on account of the satisfaction which Christ has made, he must also, in order to judge them as positively righteous, impute to them the merit of Christ. It has been shown that this train of thoughts carries us beyond the limits of the conceptions derived from the analogy of the human judge. But the forgiveness extended by a father to his child combines in one act the judgment that a fault committed by the child ought to bring about no alienation between father and child, and the expression of the purpose to admit the child, as a right and gracious action, to the unfettered intercourse of love.

The attribute of father stands in relation to the peculiar moral and legal fellowship of the family. Therefore all the preceding arguments regarding the attitude of God to the forgiveness of sins, which have been derived from the analogy of the head of the State, that is, the legal and only relatively moral society of the people, are found to be incongruous with the Christian idea of God. The representation of God under the attribute of Father corresponds exactly to the transference to the whole of mankind of his relative moral and legal Lordship over the people of Israel for the bringing about of the highest moral end. Now, not only does this universal destination of the Kingdom of God exclude comparison with the form of government of any definite people, but the designation of God as our Father shows expressly that the real analogy for the Kingdom of God should be sought, not in the national State, but in the family. The consequences which this principle involves for the representation of the Christian view of the world cannot yet be brought out. One result, however, is the confirmation of a formerly established position, namely, that the forgiveness of sins by God as Father finds no real standard of comparison in the right of pardon which belongs to the head of the State. The difference between the two is seen in this, that the right of pardon is only exercised in individual instances of legal condemnation, which as such stand in no connection with one another and always form exceptions to the recognised legal order, while the forgiveness of sins by God as Father is a universal, though not unconditioned, fundamental law, established in the interest of the community of the Kingdom of God. . . .

If, therefore, the Divine υἱοθεσία in the Christian sense is understood in reference to the closest conceivable spiritual fellowship between man and God, then the form of the resolution . . . is in exact harmony with that of the analogous resolution in the relationship of the human family, which we have taken as our standard of comparison. Seeing, however, that the resolution to admit children to moral fellowship applies not only, as a general rule, to children of the blood, but also, in extraordinary cases, to alien children, and that the resolution can extend in these cases only to the transmission of property rights, the idea of the Divine υἱοθεσία cannot be held to be completely harmonious in these essential respects with its human analogue. For those who are admitted to the rank of children of God are all, by virtue of their innate moral destiny, "of Divine race", but all in reality, because of sin, "as alien children" to God. Through the paramount influence of this fact, therefore, the Divine υἱοθεσία appears as most closely analogous to the human legal form of adoption. If, now, justification is an operation in which God appears under the attribute of Father, then the adoption of men as God's children is a substantially equivalent idea. The latter modifies the former only in this respect, that the fellowship with God to which sinners are admitted, is conceived to be as close as that which exists between the head and the members of a family. Therefore the functions in which the believing make manifest their justification and reconciliation must also be conceived as the functions of sonship to God.

3. Justification and the Mystical Union

The union (Gleichheit) with God, which must be included among the privileges which the justified enjoy as the children of God, finds expression in the formula, that justification brings the believing into possession of *eternal life*. In Luther's proposition, "Where the forgiveness of sins is, there is life and blessedness", this attribute is conceived as a present possession. ... As contrasted with the Catholic view, the possession of eternal life is brought from the sphere of the future and the world-to-come into the present state of the earthly life of the believing. By this interpretation of justification we also rise beyond the mystical standpoint. The mystics claim to enjoy the blessedness of the future in moments of ecstasy in the present life. They have, however, to suffer for their elevation of spirit at such moments through subsequent lassitude, aridity and barrenness of the feelings, and the sense of desertion by God. The Reformers, on the other hand, live in the faith that eternal life, and the joy which attaches to it, namely, blessedness, are present gifts, continually enjoyed as the result of the forgiveness of sins. But yet this thought, although presented in a series of proof-passages, has not been made quite clear by them. From the Catholic use of the formula, which was familiar to the Reformers, we must conclude that "eternal life", in their view, denotes a peculiar union and fellowship with God. In the Greek Church, indeed, "deification" is used as an expression equivalent to "eternal life". This usage has extended also to the Western Church. Bernard, for example, started from this idea in his exposition of the doctrine. The mediaeval mystics, although they strove to attain blessedness in the ecstatic knowledge of God, or the annihilation of their own wills, were yet led through their Neoplatonic conception of God as the only Reality beyond the idea of blessedness as consisting in union with God, to that of blessedness as consisting in the losing of self in the Divine essence. But Luther had no such idea in his mind. This is evident from the fact that ever since *1518* he set himself in deliberate antagonism to all mysticism. Moreover, the re-acceptance of the mystical view is out of harmony with the doctrine of justification. Therefore the original Lutheran sense of eternal life cannot be ascertained through the notion of the *unio mystica*.

4. Faith as a Condition of Justification

As an operation of God upon men, justification is correlative to *faith*. This is the condition which prevents justification, or the forgiveness of sins, being represented as a contradiction to the presupposed estimate of sin. Up to this point, in our definition of justification, man has been treated in his peculiar character as sinner, and the subject of the consciousness of guilt. It was presupposed that with sin a state of alienation between God and men was brought about through the existence of real moral opposition between them. Justification, then, signifies the bringing back of the sinner into nearness with God, the removal of the alienating effect of the existent opposition to God and the accompanying consciousness of guilt. If, however, man in his relation to justification were to be represented only as sinner, his alienation from God, both in the objective and in the subjective respect, would continue, and the opposite status, that, namely, of justification, could not even be conceived. The sinner must therefore be thought of likewise as the subject of faith. Here, it is true, a new difficulty may be found. For if the condition must be fulfilled before the result can be reached, the faith of the sinner really appears to precede his justification. The question then will be whether and how the sinner can fulfil this condition. This difficulty may, however, be waived in the meantime, if we take into account the opposite fact that the idea of reconciliation, in which justification is represented inclusive of its result, makes the faith of the sinner to appear precisely as the result of justification. justification effects a change in the consciousness of guilt in this respect, that the feeling of mistrust towards God which is bound up with that consciousness, and the shrinking from him which results therefrom, are replaced by a consenting movement of the will towards God. This new direction of the will to God which is evoked by reconciliation is, in the Evangelical view, faith; and, in so far as it expects to be determined solely by God, it belongs as a special class to the general idea of obedience.

The meaning of the idea of faith, and the relation in which it stands to justification, have indeed been accurately determined in Evangelical theology. From various passages in Melanchthon we ascertain that faith means neither the acknowledgment of the correctness of traditional facts, nor the acceptance of orthodox propositions, but trust in God's grace. Calvin has elucidated the idea of faith with still greater care than Melanchthon. He emphasizes the fact that the knowledge which is included in faith, having for its object the goodness of God, is of quite a different nature from our knowledge of the world, which consists in the explanation of phenomena and perceptions. Faith is emotional conviction of the harmony between the Divine purposes and the most intimate interests of man. A certain interest, it is true, attaches to our ordinary knowledge of the world, as is shown in the act of attention. But the interest which expresses itself in emotion—that is, interest not in the discovery of truth for itself, but in the feeling of moral pleasure and in the satisfaction of our own spirit—is of quite a different nature, inasmuch as it connects the maintenance of our whole personality with the highest standard of our life, the Divine goodwill and our own blessedness.

5. Justification and the Community of Believers

The ground of justification, or the forgiveness of sins, is the benevolent, gracious, merciful purpose of God to vouchsafe to sinful men the privilege of access to himself. The form in which sinners appropriate this gift is faith, that is, the emotional trust in God, accompanied by the conviction of the value of this gift for one's blessedness, which, called forth by God's grace, takes the place of the former mistrust which was bound up with the feeling of guilt. Through trust in God's grace the alienation of sinners from God, which was essentially connected with the unrelieved feeling of guilt, is removed. This is evidence that the guilt, so far as it prevents access to God, is forgiven by God. The purpose of God to forgive sinners is represented by the Reformers, under the notions of *promissio* and *evangelium*, not only as an openly revealed volition, but also as one which lays the foundation of a *fellowship* among men. In the gradation of the bearers of this Revelation, Christ, as the Mediator of the Gospel, is reckoned first. The next place after him is accorded to the community which he founded, every member of which has authority to proclaim the justifying grace of God, especially the official representatives of the Church, whose function is to transmit the *promissio remissionis peccatorum propter Christum*. Besides these human organs, who by their word make the revelation of God in Christ efficacious for the community which he founded, the sacraments are channels of the same sin-forgiving grace, inasmuch as they contain the Word or Gospel of God as their essence, and apply the Gospel in a peculiar way to the members of the community. Therefore the unity of the Church is essentially bound up with the pure preaching of the Gospel and the proper administration of the two sacraments, and in the same degree with nothing else. Now the pure Gospel is defined in the Augsburg Confession, chap. vii., as the preaching of justification in the above-represented sense, namely, as depending on the merit of Christ, and thus excluding the idea of human merits. This preaching of the Gospel is the distinctive mark of the existence of a community of believers; for, according to the same Confession, chap. v., it is only through the Word of God, in preaching and sacraments, that faith is called into existence. It follows, then, that, through the operation of the Holy Spirit, faith is identical in each individual case, and common to all the members of the community. Against this representation, however, the objection has been made that faith may be awakened in men through their own efforts, without the regular instrumentality of the publicly preached Word.

But these fundamental views of the Reformation are not disproved by the fact that very many hear the preaching of the Word without being led through any mechanical compulsion to the point of faith, and the contrary fact that very many attain to faith without being directly led thereto through the hearing of a preached sermon. The principle was not arrived at from the consideration of such instances. Therefore it ought not to stand in the way of a full investigation of the manifold experiences of life. The recognition of the principle, in reality, only involves the proviso, that one cannot arrive at and maintain individual conviction of faith in isolation from the already existing community of faith, and that that community is coextensive with the spread of the Gospel, that is, the public preaching of the forgiveness of sins. . . . The maintenance of this principle is necessary for the welfare of the Church, in order that the individual's own struggle for faith may not be esteemed as independent of, or opposed to, the public preaching of the Word. The effect of such individualistic ideas would be, as seen, for example, in the history of the Anabaptists, that the Church would be given over to the conflicts of sectarianism, and that the faith itself would be falsified. The connection of faith with the revelation of grace through the Word was also plainly recognised by Calvin. If, therefore, the community of believers is coextensive with the influence of the Gospel, and if the Gospel has no other sphere for the proclamation of its glad tidings of God's readiness to forgive sins, then those striking statements of Luther are intelligible, namely, that "the Church is full of the forgiveness of sins"; that "within the fold of the Christian Church God daily and richly forgives me, the individual, all my sins"; and that "the Church, as a mother, bears and nurtures every individual through the Word". Calvin repeats the latter statement (*Inst.* iv. *1. 4*). Finally, Luther pursues the same thought in a characteristic way. He loves, namely, to represent the Church as the Bride of Christ, with whom, in accordance with marriage right, Christ joins in a mutual exchange of benefits, he taking upon himself the sins of the believing, and himself imparting his righteousness to them. In this representation of the process of justification by faith, however, Luther insists on the fact that the blessings which accrue to the individual are only imparted to him in common with all the others with whom he is bound up, through the same salvation, in the unity of the Church.

This idea, that the benefit of justification accrues to individuals as constituting the community of believers, corresponds to the significant expressions used in the New Testament regarding the sacrifice of Christ. For the conception of Christ's sacrifice through the types of the covenant sacrifice and the yearly sin-offering of the Israelites brings the forgiveness of sins which results from Christ's sacrifice into direct relation to the community founded by him. The individual can therefore appropriate the forgiveness of sins by faith only when he unites in his faith at once trust in God and Christ, and the intention to connect himself with the community of believers. For the individual who is led to faith always finds the domain of human life which is determined and governed by the forgiveness of sins already marked out for him; and, moreover, he has to attach himself to the community of believers all the more decisively that he is indebted to that community for the knowledge of salvation and for stimuli of incalculable strength urging him to appropriate salvation.   *Ibid.*, pp. *93–111*

6. *Faith as Personal Assurance of Salvation*

Justification or reconciliation denotes the status before God into which sinners are brought through the mediation of Christ within his community. We belong to God as a child does to his father, in spite of the abiding consciousness that, in virtue of the previously dominant tendency of self-will, we used to stand in contradiction to him as sinners. We know ourselves to be, in our present relation to God, entirely dependent on his purpose of grace openly made known; for the abiding recollection of the pain of the consciousness of guilt excludes not merely every legal claim to the Divine pardon, but also any possibility of our having earned it by any meritorious actions whatsoever. Now, as this status before God comprises none save purely spiritual relations, so also the form of its appropriation, faith, is a purely spiritual function which, as such, can be exercised without any sensible actions whatever being essential to it. Nevertheless the fact still remains, that the opposition between man and God which is solved by justification is not altogether eliminated from the experience of the believer. If in Christianity the range of forgiveness included merely the sins of our past years, or, in addition to that, merely individual transgressions of the Christian life, the felt opposition between the sense of guilt and what God claims from men would no longer normally hold a place among the experiences of a Christian. From this point of view the Socinians assign forgiveness, as remission of punishment, to the accidental side of Christianity. The Evangelical Confessions, on the contrary, in so far as they find in justification the fundamental precondition of Christianity whether personal or social, reckon on the regular continuance of the consciousness of guilt in those who profess adherence to them. If one were to say, as a Christian, that he had no sin, he would make God a liar; for through his promise of the forgiveness of sins, which forms the fundamental characteristic of the Christian community, God affirms the presence of sin in its members (1 John i. 8-10). From this point of view, according to Luther and Melanchthon, our knowledge of our own sin is to be drawn directly from the Gospel. That fact makes daily prayer for forgiveness of sin a fitting thing. Such prayer is no more inconsistent with the general assurance of this blessing which has been given to the Christian community, than prayer for Divine gifts is barred by the knowledge we have that God is willing to bestow them. On the other hand, if we did not daily perceive occasion to pray for it, we should lose sight of the importance of forgiveness as the foundation-stone of the Christian religion. Thus the value we set upon this blessing demands the continual confession that every one needs it. The consciousness of this need, however, will in the Christian life normally extend to nothing which is not forthwith covered by the certainty of forgiveness bestowed by God. Now the traditional form of systematic theology leads to the contention that in his daily life every Christian must pass through the whole interval between the need of redemption and the acceptance of grace—an interval the magnitude of which finds expression in the unconnectedness of the doctrine of sin, as traditionally developed, with the doctrine of redemption. Such teaching gives special support to the demand of Pietism, that we should compel ourselves to such a comprehensive estimate of our own sin, and should impress upon ourselves our own inborn hatefulness and worthlessness or nothingness to such a degree, that we cannot consistently attach thereto any well-founded assurance of grace, but must wait for some incalculable deliverance from this state of feeling. This monkish method of self-abasement is proved false by 1 John iii. 19-21. Nor can dogmatic theology concern itself with such movements of sentiment: they belong to the province of pastoral theology. For Dogmatics, which has to interpret the normal course of the elements of the Christian life, can affirm man's permanent need of redemption in no other way than by recognising that the forgiveness of sins is the necessary basis of the Christian religion, both as a whole and in detail. But that is to assert, not to deny, that the need of redemption must be presupposed.

Faith, which, as related to the promise attached to the work of Christ, appropriates forgiveness, is to be understood as trust in God and Christ, characterised by peace of mind, inward satisfaction, and comfort. The

pain arising from one's state as a whole, which formed an element of
the presupposed sense of guilt, is thereby removed. This pain, however,
is an expression of that opposition to God and to the purpose of our
being which forms the essence of sin—and that as a personal certainty
for the individual mind. Trust in the justification imparted in Christ,
therefore, is attended by certainty of an opposite kind. The pain of the
sense of guilt is a matter of feeling; the certainty which accompanies
trust in the justification assured by Christ can therefore only be interpreted as a feeling of pleasure. From the nature of this connection
between Divine act and promise and human trust, it follows that the
subjective *certainty of justification* springs only from a vision of the object
of faith. But although this object of believing and peace-bringing trust
is clearly outlined, and fitted by its Divine origin to call forth and to
sustain the subjective function of faith, yet experience shows that what
we have here is not a mechanically regular process of cause and effect.
The certainty of justification, without which faith does not fully satisfy
the conception of it as trust, is a characteristic which in many cases is
liable to change in quantity; it may increase, just as it is liable to inter-
ruptions of uncertainty. Now it is worth noticing that Melanchthon,
when forming a judgment on the latter case, does not take the view
that the fact of justification is rendered inoperative and invalid by the
want of continuous subjective certainty. No doubt, as his whole mode
of thought moves within the limits of the individual life, it strikes one
as contradictory when, on the one hand, justification as a permanent
status is brought into relation to believing trust, and conceived as
operating only in response to trust; while, on the other hand, justification is held to be valid even when the subjective certainty of it varies.
Nor was Melanchthon able altogether to remove this appearance of
contradiction in the argument on which I am now commenting. The
remark of Luther, indeed, might have been recalled, that in this struggle
of repentance the very feeling of being at an infinite distance from God
is a product of his grace; but what is wanted here is that this conviction, felt by an impartial observer of the soul that is passing through
repentance, should be appropriated by the latter, and thus his conscience
be calmed. Only, this view of the matter taken above offers no ground
for this. Therefore the admission that within the domain of justification
faith may be uncertain, always depends on the presupposition that the
struggle for assurance of Divine grace is only a transition stage, leading

in all probability to the goal of that certainty which belongs ideally to actual justification. But as this conclusion is anything but self-evident, a kind of categorical imperative lays on us the task of gaining assurance of justification by faith.   *Ibid.*, pp. *140–4*

THE KNOWLEDGE OF GOD

1. *What Religion Is*

The endeavour to construct *theology* in the Gentile–Christian Church arose from the belief that the positive conception of God as the Father of Christ, and of Christ as the Son of God, must be demonstrated as a universal truth of reason, in relation to the knowledge of the world which men had then attained. This belief has been, not confirmed, but rather shaken to the very foundation, by the manifold turns which the history of theology and philosophy has taken. For one thing, we can no longer conceal from ourselves the fact that the Greek Fathers carried the thought of God and Christ out into notions of the ultimate and the mediate ground of the world, which are peculiar to the later eclectic philosophy of Greece, and neither cover nor exhaust the original sense of the former conceptions. On the other hand, Gentile–Christian theology always insists on the reservation that the Christian religion presents an element which transcends all merely secular knowledge, namely, the end and the means of the blessedness of man. Whatever content may have been ascribed to this word *blessedness*, it expressly denotes a goal, the knowledge of which is unattainable by philosophy, and the realisation of which cannot be secured by the natural means at the command of men, but depends upon the positive character of Christianity. Consequently, the theology of the Greek Fathers is not merely cosmology, but, above all, a doctrine of redemption; the cosmology upon which the doctrine of redemption is built, however, is developed by means of ideas borrowed from Plato and the Stoics. The Scholastics carry on this method, and Thomas Aquinas makes a statement on the point which harmonises with the foregoing criticism of Greek theology. For, in the assurance of blessedness given by Christianity, he sees a destiny for men which was not provided for in their creation by God, nor included in their natural constitution, and which cannot be understood merely by the use of their reason. But he does not make this special feature of Christianity the key to his view of the world as a whole; rather, it is underpropped by a thoroughly rational theology, the material of which has no relation to Christianity, and which is unmistakably derived from Greek Philosophy. The same procedure is still adhered to by the traditional theology among ourselves. Nevertheless the division of the material of theology into propositions given by reason and propositions given by revelation is a method whose validity can no longer be maintained. In opposition thereto there has gradually come into force the contrary principle, that religion and theoretical knowledge are different functions of spirit, which, when they deal with the same objects, are not even partially coincident, but wholly diverge. This heterogeneity must be accurately established ere it can be decided what use is to be made of general theoretical knowledge in the scientific exposition of Christianity.

If religion in every case is an interpretation of man's relation to God and the world, guided by the thought of the sublime power of God to realise the end of this blessedness of man, advancing insight into the history of religions has forced on us the task of formulating a universal *conception of religion*, under which all the particular species of religion might find their peculiar features determined. But this task involves no slight difficulties, and contributes less to the understanding of Christianity than is often expected. The formula by which this very thing, religion in general, has just been described, makes no claim to be a definition proper of the generic conception of religion. It is too definite for that. The ideas which is employs—God, world, blessedness—have so directly Christian a stamp, that they apply to other religions only in a comparative degree, *i.e.* in order to indicate the general idea of religion, we should have to specify at the same time the different modifications which they undergo in different religions. For, besides belief in the One God, there falls to be considered the ascription to the Godhead of multiplicity, or duplicity, or difference in sex, and there is, further, the recognition of superhuman power in the spirits of the dead. Again, the relation of the Godhead to the world undergoes modification according as the world is conceived as a unity, or this point is left obscure, or the immediate surroundings of a particular wild tribe are taken as its world. It is modified, further, according as the Divine beings are identified with the forces and phenomena of nature, or distinguished from nature and creation, or, in the latter case, occupy a more negative or more positive relation to the world. Lastly, as regards blessedness, we have to consider the different cases in which what is sought through adoration or adjuration of the superhuman powers is merely some chance benefit, or the idea of a supreme good is formed, and this again is sought in the world, or apart from the world, or in a combination of both forms. As, therefore, the historical religions offer, under each of these heads, a rich supply of specific and sub-specific characteristics, which have no place in the general conception of religion, language can furnish no terms sufficiently neutral and indeterminate to express the general conception of religion desired. But, besides, it would be impossible to state in their proper place the above-discussed modifications of the several parts of the definition, without making obscure the very point which is professedly of importance.

If, however, we have once arrived at a general conception of religion more or less distinct in outline, it serves, as do all general ideas, as a clue by which to determine the chief characteristics of the various species of religion. Now we have no difficulty in ascertaining by an examination of all other religions, that the secular knowledge which they involve is not disinterestedly theoretical, but guided by practical ends. This circumstance, therefore, when given a place provisionally in the general conception, suggests, first, that objection may justly be taken to the exactly contrary use of theoretical knowledge which has made its way into the Christian Church; and next, that the later should be expelled, as something accidental, from the idea of the Christian religion. In the investigation of Christianity the general conception of religion should be used *regulatively*. I desire to distinguish myself very precisely in this respect from those who, in interpreting Christianity, make a *constitutive* use of the general conception. For when this method is employed, no longer as Scholasticism employs it, but in such a way that the influence of the general conception of religion makes one even for a moment neutral towards the Christian religion itself, in order to be able to deduce its meaning from the conditions of the general conception, then the only effect of this is to undermine Christian conviction. Christian conviction, however, is necessarily left intact when, as a theologian, one forms a general conception of religion, whatever the nature of that conception may be, for regulative use. For the observation and comparison of the various historical religions from which the general conception is abstracted, likewise shows that they stand to one another not merely in the relation of species, but also in the relation of stages. They exhibit an ever more rich and determinate manifestation of the chief features of religion; their connection is always more close, their aims more worthy of man. Such a way of looking at them opens up more fruitful vistas than are offered by the abstraction of a general conception of religion, followed by the comparison of the historical religions as species of this genus. For in this case the various religions are treated merely as natural phenomena; in the other case they are viewed as elements in the spiritual history of humanity. To prove that religions are related to one another as stages, is a scientific problem which still awaits an impartial and unprejudiced solution. Consequently we have to consider that several religions, such as Christianity and Islam, claim to occupy the highest stage above all others; and that Buddhists and Hindus who have become acquainted with Christianity put forward reasons which are meant to demonstrate the superiority of their faiths over the Christian. When, therefore, as Christians, in reviewing the series of stages presented by the religions of the world, we judge them by the principle that Christianity transcends them all, and that in Christianity the tendency of all the others finds its perfect consummation, the claim of the science of religion to universal validity may seem to be sacrificed to the prejudice arising from our own personal convictions. But it is aimless and impracticable to attempt to prove the universal validity of the view that religions can be arranged in an ascending series. Do people expect to discover thus a way of demonstrating scientifically to a Mohammedan or a Buddhist that the Christian religion, and not theirs, occupies the highest rank? In carrying out the task we have indicated, we have no such aim. It were indeed a desirable result, in the case of people who have been born Christians, and now, e.g., declare the verdict of their scientific knowledge to be the inferiority of Christianity to Buddhism, if we could detach them from their error. But it is impossible for us, when arranging religions in a series of stages, to shut our eyes to the claim of Christianity to occupy the highest place. For those qualities in other religions by which they *are* religions are intelligible to us chiefly as measured by the perfection which they assume in Christianity, and by the clearness which distinguishes the perfect religion from the imperfect. The arrangement of religions in stages, consequently, amounts to no more than a scientific attempt to promote mutual understanding among Christians; and assent to the statement that Christianity is the highest and most perfect religion is therefore no obstacle to the scientific character of the theory.

Here, therefore, our task is not to elaborate the serial arrangement of religions, but to seek a solution of the question how Christianity, as a religion, is related to general philosophical knowledge. Consequently, it is desirable that the qualities by which *Christianity reveals its religious character* should be brought out with that distinctness which they claim to possess at the level of Christianity. If in doing so we glance at other religions, our business will just be to point out the modifications for the worse which they exhibit when compared with Christianity. The various historical religions are always of a social character, belonging to a multitude of persons. Thence it follows that to assign to religion a merely psychological complexion, in particular to refer it to feeling, is not a solution, but only an abridgement of the problem. In a community the influence of the individual is conditioned by two factors, inasmuch as he is both like and unlike the others, alternately dependent on them and affecting them actively. Consequently a psychological explanation of religion is inadequate, for it deals only with those phenomena of spirit in which all men are alike, and one is the type for all. The above-mentioned dissimilarity of men within the common life of a religion falls under the scope of ethics. Now the multiplicity pertaining to a religion is one of distribution, partly in space and partly in time. An illustration of the latter is presented by the successive stages of life. Thence it follows that every social religion implies a doctrinal tradition. The dispersion in space of the members of the same religion is a direct obstacle to their fellowship, but it is compensated for when the religion takes real shape in the gathering for worship. Feeling, as pleasure or pain, as blessedness or suffering, is the personal gain or the personal presupposition which impels individuals to participate in religious fellowship. Nor in all religions does this aspect stand out so clearly and distinctly from the other functions as it is customary to suppose. In orgiastic faiths, contending emotions of feeling are the very material of worship; in the Roman, religious feeling assumes the form of painful attention to the correctness of ceremonial actions; in the Greek, the same factor appears in the serenity and the seriousness which affect, and are affected by, the worship. Hence it follows that for

G

different reasons the historical religions claim service from all the functions of spirit—knowledge, for the doctrinal tradition, *i.e.* for a particular view of the world; will, for the common worship; feeling, for the alternation of satisfaction and dissatisfaction, moods by which religious life is removed from the ordinary level of existence. No religion is correctly or completely conceived when one element of this succession is regarded as more important or more fundamental than the others. At the same time the question is reserved whether our scientific explanation of the total fact of religion shall give the preference to one or other of the functions of spirit.

In every religion what is sought, with the help of the superhuman spiritual power reverenced by man, is a solution of the contradiction in which man finds himself, as both a part of the world of nature and a spiritual personality claiming to dominate nature. For in the former *rôle* he is a part of nature, dependent upon her, subject to and confined by other things; but as spirit he is moved by the impulse to maintain his independence against them. In this juncture, religion springs up as faith in superhuman spiritual powers, by whose help the power which man possesses of himself is in some way supplemented, and elevated into a unity of its own kind which is a match for the pressure of the natural world. The idea of gods, or Divine powers, everywhere includes belief in their spiritual personality, for the support to be received from above can only be reckoned on in virtue of an affinity between God and men. Even where merely invisible natural powers are regarded as Divine, they are conceived in a way analogous to that in which man distinguishes himself from nature. For the rest, the ease with which definite stupendous natural phenomena, whether beneficent or destructive, are personified, proves that it is in the spiritual personality of the gods that man finds the foothold which he seeks for in every religion. The assertion that the religious view of the world is founded upon the idea of a whole certainty holds true of Christianity: as regards the other religions it must be modified thus far, that in them what is sought is a supplementary addition to human self-feeling or to human independence over against and above the restrictions of the world. For in order to know the world as a totality, and in order himself to become a totality in or over it by the help of God, man needs the idea of the oneness of God, and of the consummation of the world in an end which is for man both knowable and realisable. But this condition is fulfilled in Christianity alone. For in the religion of the Old Testament the presuppositions, indeed, are given, but the world-end aimed at is merely the perfecting of the one chosen people in moral, political, and economical independence; the human perfecting of the individual Israelite, each in his own personal character, is not kept in view, as it is in the Christian conception of life and blessedness. Nevertheless, in heathen and even in polytheistic religions there is always a tendency at work towards belief in the unity of the Divine power, and in the measure in which this is the case the supplement to his own resources which man seeks in religion becomes more clear and more worthy. When, as in Brahminism, the world which has sprung from the original Being is so constituted that it returns to the distinctionless unity of real existence, what takes the place of the maintenance of selfhood is its absorption in the Divine Being. In its own way, this too is a kind of unity, for it is viewed as the consummation of asceticism and quietistic piety.

Christianity, by its completely rounded view of the world, guarantees to believers that they shall be preserved unto eternal life in the Kingdom of God, which is God's revealed end in the world—and that, too, in the full sense that man is thus in the Kingdom of God set over the world as a whole in his own order. Not only the Christian's tone of feeling, but also his estimate of self is determined by this highest and all-inclusive good. For this religion offers no passionate impulse, no vacillation between changing tones of feeling arising from confused ideas, no voluptuous alternation of aesthetic pleasure and pain; on the contrary, such emotions must be viewed in the light of the antitheses of sin and grace, of bondage as to what is good, and liberty to give God thanks and to act aright. The temper produced by these conclusions, therefore, normally issues in the reverence for God proper to the level reached by Christianity. This combination is the rule in other religions also. Those religious affections of feeling which are called forth by the effort to secure blessings obtainable from the gods, and which have a complexion of their own, universally manifest themselves solely in correlative acts of worship. At this point, however, in the sacrifice of acquired property, and in religious and moral self-abnegation, there comes into view a universal characteristic of all religions. In this way the domain of religious action is marked off from secular life as a sacred domain; at the same time, however, the value of the blessings bestowed by the gods is gauged by pleasurable feelings of another class than those which accrue to man naturally or as a result of work. Religious feeling, with or without the accompaniment of a clear estimate of self, will always be found to be the material of worship; but the form which such feeling assumes witnesses at the same time to a decision of the will, which gives reality to the acknowledgment of God and the personal satisfaction this entails. The idea of God is the ideal bond between a definite view of the world and the idea of man as constituted for the attainment of goods or the highest good. Worship is the realisation of the blessing sought by the practical acknowledgment of the power that bestows it. In Christianity, thanksgiving for God's grace, prayer for its continuance, and service of God in his Kingdom, have attached to them eternal life and that blessedness which corresponds to the highest good, the Kingdom of God.

Common worship has a still closer relation to the revelation which forms the organic centre of every connected religious view of the world. This factor, too, appears with various modifications at the various stages of religion. In the religion of sorcery, acts of worship are employed to elicit revelations from mysterious superhuman powers. In Christianity, revelation through God's Son is the *punctum stans* of all knowledge and religious conduct. In the developed natural religions, success in obtaining Divine revelations is bound up with their being regularly acknowledged in worship. No idea of a religion complete after its own order can be formed if the characteristic of revelation which belongs to it is either denied or even merely set aside as indifferent. True, this very method has long been customary. People think themselves justified in abstracting from the characteristic of revelation found in every religion, inasmuch as they regard the myths of natural religions, and the doctrines of the religions of the Bible, as veiled or undeveloped philosophy. But the original purpose of myths is to explain why particular acts of worship, intended to do honour to Divine self-manifestations, are performed at some definite spot and at regularly recurrent intervals. What we may regard as the doctrinal material of the religion of the Old Testament—the free creation of the world by God, and his intention that man, who, as spirit, is the image of God, should bear rule over it—denotes the presuppositions of the belief that the Israelites are called by God in an especial covenant, under which they have to achieve their historical destiny in the world under

the government of their Divine King. The speciality of the spot at
which a god has ordained that he shall be adored, the speciality of the
times at which the gods move through the land and summon their
worshippers to celebrate their festivals, the speciality of the choice of
Israel by the Lord of all nations—in short, *speciality* is the element
which impels men to grasp the different aspects of religion, and to
combine them practically in worship. The significance which revelation thus has for common worship also indicates an indispensable
precondition of our understanding Christianity. The Person of its
Founder is not only the key to the Christian view of the world, and the
standard of Christians' self-judgment and moral effort, but also the
standard which shows how prayer must be composed, for in prayer
both individual and united adoration of God consists. At the same time
the acknowledgment of the revelation of God in Christ yields this pre-
eminent excellence of Christianity, namely, that its view of the world
is a rounded whole, and that the goal it sets to life is this, that in
Christianity man becomes a whole, a spiritual character supreme over
the world. For speciality is ever the condition under which a universal
end is realised through the combination of individual things and
relations.

2. *The Nature of Religious Knowledge*

How, then, is *religious knowledge* related to theoretical or philosophical knowledge? This question, indeed, has already been raised by
the very fact of Greek Philosophy; still, much more tangible and
comprehensive reasons for raising it are to be found in the mutual
relations of Christianity and philosophy. Accordingly, it is best that we
should limit the question to Christianity in so far as it is a religion,
intelligible as such from the characteristics noted above. The possibility
of both kinds of knowledge mingling, or, again, colliding, lies in this,
that they deal with the same object, namely, the world. Now we cannot
rest content with the amiable conclusion that Christian knowledge
comprehends the world as a whole, while philosophy fixes the special
and universal laws of nature and spirit. For with this task every
philosophy likewise combines the ambition to comprehend the
universe under one supreme law. And for Christian knowledge also
one supreme law is the form under which the world is comprehensible

as a whole under God. Even the thought of God, which belongs to religion, is employed in some shape or other by every non-materialistic philosophy. Thus no principle of discrimination between the two kinds of knowledge is, at least provisionally, to be found in the object with which they deal.

Now, in order to elicit the distinction between the two from the realm of the subject, I recall the twofold manner in which the mind (*Geist*) further appropriates the sensations aroused in it. They are determined, according to their value for the Ego, by the feeling of pleasure or pain. Feeling is the basal function of mind, inasmuch as in it the Ego is originally presented to itself. In the feeling of pleasure or pain, the Ego decides whether a sensation, which touches the feeling of self, serves to heighten or depress it. On the other hand, through an idea the sensation is judged in respect of its cause, the nature of the latter, and its connection with other causes: and by means of observation, etc., the knowledge of things thus gained is extended until it becomes scientific. The two functions of spirit mentioned are always in operation simultaneously, and always also in some degree mutually related, even though it be in the inverse ratio of prominence. In particular, it must not be forgotten that all continuous cognition of the things which excite sensation is not only accompanied, but likewise guided, by feeling. For in so far as attention is necessary to attain the end of knowledge, will, as representing the desire for accurate cognition, comes in between; the proximate cause of will, however, is feeling as expressing the consciousness that a thing or an activity is worth desiring, or that something ought to be put away. Value-judgments therefore are determinative in the case of all connected knowledge of the world, even when carried out in the most objective fashion. Attention during scientific observation, and the impartial examination of the matter observed, always denote that such knowledge has a value for him who employs it. This fact makes its presence all the more distinctly felt when knowledge is guided through a richly diversified field by attention of a technical or practical kind.

But even if we have made up our mind that religious knowledge in general, and therefore Christian knowledge too, consists of value-judgments, such a definition is as lacking in precision as it would be to describe philosophical knowledge contrariwise as disinterested. For without interest we do not trouble ourselves about anything. We have therefore to distinguish between *concomitant* and *independent* value-judgments. The former are operative and necessary in all theoretical cognition, as in all technical observation and combination. But all perceptions of moral ends or moral hindrances are *independent* value-judgments, in so far as they excite moral pleasure or pain, or, it may be, set in motion the will to appropriate what is good or repel the opposite. If the other kinds of knowledge are called "disinterested", this only means that they are without these moral effects. But even in them pleasure or pain must be present, according as they succeed or fail. Religious knowledge forms another class of independent value-judgments. That is, it cannot be traced back to the conditions which mark the knowledge belonging to moral will, for there exists religion which goes on without any relation whatever to the moral conduct of life. Besides, in many religions religious pleasure is of a purely natural kind, and is independent of those conditions which lift religious above natural pleasure. For only at the higher stages do we find religion combined with the ethical conduct of life. Religious knowledge moves in independent value-judgments, which relate to man's attitude to the world, and call forth feelings of pleasure or pain, in which man either enjoys the dominion over the world vouchsafed him by God, or feels grievously the lack of God's help to that end. This theory is almost more easily intelligible if it be tested by religions which possess no moral character. Orgiastic worships represent contending natural feelings with extraordinary intensity and with abrupt changes, in virtue of their recognition of the value which the identity of the Godhead with the vegetation as it decays and again revives, has for the man who modifies his attitude towards the world of nature in sympathy with the Godhead which he adores. The peculiar nature of religious value-judgments is less clear in the case of religions of an explicitly ethical character. Nevertheless, in Christianity we can distinguish between the religious functions which relate to our attitude towards God and the world, and the moral functions which point directly to men, and only indirectly to God, whose end in the world we fulfil by moral service in the Kingdom of God. In Christianity, the religious motive of ethical action lies here, that the Kingdom of God, which it is our task to realise, represents also the highest good which God destines for us as our supramundane goal. For here there emerges the value-judgment that our blessedness consists in that elevation above the world in the

Kingdom of God which accords with our true destiny. This is a religious judgment, inasmuch as it indicates the value of this attitude taken up by believers towards the world, just as those judgments are religious in which we set our trust in God, even when he condemns us to suffering.

In its day the Hegelian philosophy represented theoretical knowledge as not merely the most valuable function of spirit, but likewise the function which has to take up the problem of religion and solve it. To this Feuerbach opposed the observation that in religion the chief stress falls upon the wishes and needs of the human heart. But as the latter philosopher also continued to regard professedly pure and disinterested knowledge as the highest achievement of man, religion, and especially the Christian religion—which he held to be the expression of a purely individual and therefore egoistic interest, and a self-delusion in respect of its object, God—was by him declared to be worthless, as compared not merely with the knowledge of philosophic truth, but also with purely moral conduct. But an interest in salvation in the Christian sense, when rightly understood, is incompatible with egoism. Egoism is a revolt against the common tasks of action. Now, people might say that faith in God for our salvation, and a dutiful public spirit towards our fellows, have nothing to do with one another, and that therefore there is no conceivable reason why religion, as a rule, should not be egoistic. But in Christianity precisely faith in God and moral duty within the Kingdom of God *are* related to one another. As a rule, therefore, it is impossible that Christian faith in God should be egoistic. On the other hand, theoretical knowledge in itself, as has been shown, is not disinterested; but moral conduct is still less so. For in the latter domain the vital point is that one realises as one's own interest the interest of others to whom the service is rendered. The moral disposition can nowhere strike root save in such motives. It is true that, contrary to the rule, faith in God may be combined with egoistic arrogance towards others. But the same danger attaches to both of the other kinds of activity which have been compared. It is possible for one occupied with theoretical knowledge to be vain and haughty, and for one devoted to the moral service of others to be tyrannical or sycophantic.

Scientific knowledge is accompanied or guided by a judgment affirming the worth of impartial knowledge gained by observation. In

Christianity, religious knowledge consists in independent value-judgments, inasmuch as it deals with the relation between the blessedness which is assured by God and sought by man, and the whole of the world which God has created and rules in harmony with his final end. Scientific knowledge seeks to discover the laws of nature and spirit through observation, and is based on the presupposition that both the observations and their arrangement are carried out in accordance with the ascertained laws of human cognition. Now the desire for scientific knowledge carries with it no guarantee that, through the medium of observation and the combination of observations according to known laws, it will discover the supreme universal law of the world, from which, as a starting-point, the differentiated orders of nature and spiritual life, each in its kind, might be explained, and understood as forming one whole. On the contrary, the intermingling and collision of religion and philosophy always arises from the fact that the latter claims to produce in its own fashion a unified view of the world. This, however, betrays rather an impulse religious in its nature, which philosophers ought to have distinguished from the cognitive methods they follow. For in all philosophical systems the affirmation of a supreme law of existence, from which they undertake to deduce the world as a whole, is a departure from the strict application of the philosophic method, and betrays itself as being quite as much an object of the intuitive imagination, as God and the world are for religious thought. This is the case at all stages and in all forms of Greek philosophy, especially in those forms in which the ultimate universal grounds of existence, through which the universe is interpreted, are identified with the idea of God. In these cases the combination of heterogeneous kinds of knowledge—the religious and the scientific—is beyond all doubt; and it is to be explained by the fact that philosophers who, through their scientific observation of nature, had destroyed the foundations of the popular faith, sought to obtain satisfaction for their religious instincts by another path. In a certain respect, too, they were able to follow this tendency with especial confidence, so far as they succeeded in making out the unity of the Divine Being to be the ground of the universe. But in another respect they failed to satisfy the essential conditions of the religious view of the world, partly in so far as they surrendered the personality of the Godhead thus identified with the ground of the world, partly because they had to give up the active influence of a personal God upon the world. Nor, under these circumstances, could any worship be deduced from the idea of God. Thus the collision of Greek philosophy with the popular faith was twofold, and in both respects inevitable. For one thing, the actual observation of nature and her laws is incompatible with the religious combination of popular views of nature and the idea of God. Further, the rigidly unified view of the world held by philosophers is incompatible with the religious view of the world which is only loosely developed in polytheism. But the real force of the latter incompatibility is to be found in the fact that, under the guise of philosophic knowledge, what was really only the religious imagination has been operative in designing the general philosophic view of the world, the supreme principle of which is never proved as such, but always merely anticipatively assumed. *Ibid.*, pp. *193–208*

3. The Moral Argument for God's Existence

Since, whenever religion appears, it is subject to the presupposition that man opposes himself, as spirit, to surrounding nature, and to human society acting on him through the media of nature, it is a mistake to employ the idea of God as Author or Creator of the forces of nature in order to compel natural science, aware of its limits, to recognise God's existence. Inferences drawn from the observation of nature lead us to consider the multiplicity and interaction of material forces as the causes of natural things; many therefore suppose that they are justified in concluding further that this multiplicity of forces—which must all be conceived as limited—is derived from one creating and limiting Will. But this special modification of the cosmological argument for God's existence is just as incorrect as its metaphysical and academic form. Were the presupposition of the elements of nature, thus sought, really conceived as God, such a conclusion could not be justified by natural science. Besides, the affirmation of a creative Will, desiderated as the ground of the elements of nature, would not be a religious judgment, and to use the name God to designate the entity thus sought would be premature. For we never exercise religious cognition in merely explaining nature by a First Cause, but always and only in explaining the independence of the human spirit over against nature. The same confusion, therefore, as that of which Scholasticism is guilty when it treats the idea of God as an element in metaphysical science, is to be detected in the combination we are now discussing of natural science with the idea of God.

In religious cognition the idea of God is dependent on the pre-supposition that man opposes himself to the world of nature, and secures his position, in or over it, by faith in God. Consequently no proof of God's existence starts properly save that which accepts as given man's self-distinction from nature, and his endeavours to maintain himself against it or over it. This condition is satisfied in the case of the so-called moral argument, stated by Kant in his *Critique of Judgment*. . . .

Now, when we mark the attitude taken up by the human spirit towards the world of nature, two analogous facts present themselves. In theoretical knowledge, spirit treats nature as something which exists for it; while in the practical sphere of the will, too, it treats nature as something which is directly a means to the realisation of the common ethical end which forms the final end of the world. The cognitive impulse and the will both take this course without regard to the fact that nature is subject to quite other laws than those which spirit obeys, that it is independent of spirit, and that it forms a restraint on spirit, and so far keeps it in a certain way in dependence on itself. Hence we must conclude either that the estimate which spirit, as a power superior to nature, forms of its own worth—in particular, the estimate which it forms of moral fellowship, which transcends nature— is a baseless fancy, or that the view taken by spirit is in accordance with truth and with the supreme law which is valid for nature as well. If that be so, then its ground must lie in a Divine Will, which creates the world with spiritual life as its final end. To accept the idea of God in this way is, as Kant observes, practical faith, and not an act of theoretical cognition. While, therefore, the Christian religion is thereby proved to be in harmony with reason, it is always with the reservation that knowledge of God embodies itself in judgments which differ in kind from those of theoretical science.

The meaning, therefore, of this moral argument for the necessity of the thought of God differs altogether from the aim of the other argu-ments; and for that reason the success it attains surpasses that of the others. The cosmological and teleological arguments are intended to show that the conception of God—necessary to complete the circle of knowledge—is similar in kind to the results of science. A truth which for religious faith is certain is thus proved, it is held, to be at the same time the result of scientific cognition as it advances from observation to observation and crystallises into conclusions, and should be set up as the criterion of theological science. But this method ends in failure, partly because neither argument takes us beyond the limits of the world, partly because their pretended results, even if they were correct, differ from the Christian conception of God in this, that they fail to express his worth for men, and in particular his worth for men as sinners.

Ibid., pp. *218* f., *224* f.

THE UNIQUENESS OF JESUS CHRIST

The nature of Christianity as a universal religion is such that *in the Christian view of the world a definite place is assigned to its historical founder.* In the two ethnic religions which come nearest to Christianity (though in different degrees), and which have preserved some recollection of their historical founders, namely in the Persian religion and in the religion of Israel, Zoroaster and Moses are indeed acknowledged as the founders and lawgivers of the faith; but there is no need of a personal confession either of the one or of the other, because for the religions which they founded the religious community is the nation, and the nation is the community. In the universal religions, on the other hand, it is through express recognition of the founder of the religion that membership in the religious community is described and attained. At the same time, in these religions a certain gradation presents itself in the worth and significance of personal adherence to the founder. In Islam it is enough to name the Prophet alongside of God, because for this religion of law he is merely the lawgiver. Nearer to the religious estimate of Jesus Christ in the Christian religion comes the significance which in Buddhism is attached to Sakyamuni Buddha as an incarnation of Deity. But in this case there is the difference that, whereas what Buddha aimed at was not by any means what his followers believe themselves to have received from him, Jesus, on the other hand, had in view for his own Person essentially that significance which is claimed for it in his religious community. In other words, Buddha had no intention of founding a religion; he did not so much as set forth any conception of God, or any explanation of the world in its relation to

God; he did not explain how man is to reach a definite attitude towards the world or a definite position in the world: he merely indicated the direction along which man is to achieve his own redemption from the misery of actual existence, namely, by the ascetic annihilation of personal life. A philosophy or ethic such as this, which addresses itself to human freedom, may be the basis of a school, but not of religious fellowship; therefore, the significance it secures for its author is that of the founder of a school. That it was afterwards associated with the Indian idea of God, and that the corresponding idea of Divine incarnation was applied to Buddha and to his successors, was a result utterly foreign to the view of the antagonist of Brahmanism. It is true that within the Christian community there are those who hold exactly the same view with regard to the purpose of Jesus, and the fate which has befallen the doctrine of his Person in the Christian Church. According to their reading of the Gospels, Jesus taught a lofty morality, but in the exercise of this vocation never transgressed the limits of a purely human estimate of himself; only through influences that are wholly external have his followers been led to regard him as an incarnation of the Deity. But this view is historically inaccurate. For beyond all doubt Jesus was conscious of a new and hitherto unknown relation to God, and said so to his disciples; and his aim was to bring his disciples into the same attitude toward the world as his own, and to the same estimate of themselves, that under these conditions he might enlist them in the world-wide mission of the Kingdom of God, which he knew to be not only his own business, but theirs. But this involves the assumption that he himself means more for his disciples than the passing occasion of their religion or a lawgiver for their conduct, who would be of no more account when once the law which he proclaimed was thoroughly learned. In the case of Buddhism, on the other hand, the system as a system does not secure for its founder any abiding significance. For if Buddha himself has attained to that personal annihilation to which he showed his followers the way, he can be remembered by them only as a pattern of past days, because each one becomes himself a Buddha, an enlightened one, that is, he too recognises the worthlessness of existence, and acts accordingly, with a view to his own annihilation.

In Christianity the case is otherwise. The aim of the Christian is conceived as the attainment of eternal life. This means the consistent realisation of the personal self-end, of which the test is that the whole world does not compare in worth with the personal life, and that by the acquisition of spiritual lordship over the world, this, the true worth of life, is vindicated. Now this religious vocation of the members of the Christian community is prefigured in the person of its Founder, and rests upon his person as its abiding source of strength for all imitation of him, because he himself made God's supreme purpose of the union of men in the Kingdom of God the aim of his own personal life; and thereby realised in his own experience that independence toward the world which through him has become the experience of the members of his community. This ideal, the true development of the spiritual personality, cannot be rightly or fully conceived apart from contemplation of him who is the prototype of man's vocation. Thus what in the historically complete figure of Christ we recognise to be the real worth of his existence, gains for ourselves, through the uniqueness of the phenomenon and its normative bearing upon our own religious and ethical destiny, the worth of an abiding rule, since we at the same time discover that only through the impulse and direction we receive from him, is it possible for us to enter into his relation to God and to the world.[1] On the other hand, this specific estimate of their founders, even when known, is quite alien to the ethnic religions, because in these there is not posited as ideal aim the independent development of the personal character to the worth of a whole, as against the natural and particular impulses of life. The genius of an ethnic religion is satisfied if there be participation in the fixed tradition and custom of the nation; and such participation, when regarded as the supreme standard of human fellowship, imposes on personal independence impassable limits. Because this ideal of self-realisation has not come within the horizon of any of the ethnic religions, therefore in none of these has the founder received a place which can be compared with the significance of Christ. Even in the case of Zoroaster and of Moses, the ideal interests of their religions are so bound up with the natural consciousness of belonging to a particular nation, that the decision of the Parsees for Zoroaster, and of the Israelites for Moses, was the inevitable result of hostility toward the Hindus in the one case, and toward the Egyptians in the other.

[1] By this is meant that the disciples of Jesus take the rank of sons of God (Matt. xvii. 26), and are received into the same relation to God in which Christ stands to his Father (John xvii. 21–23).

There is yet another reason why the Person of Christ maintains its place in the Christian view of the world. Christ founds his religion with the claim that he brings the perfect revelation of God, so that beyond what he brings no further revelation is conceivable or is to be looked for. Whoever, therefore, has a part in the religion of Christ in the way Christ himself intended, cannot do other than regard Christ as the Bearer of the final revelation of God. At the same time, this point of view is conclusive only in connection with what has already been set forth. For Islam also claims to be the perfect religion, and yet is content with a superficial recognition of its prophet, to whom, under this title, there is actually no place assigned in the Mohammedan view of the world. Thus the claim Christ makes to the perfect revelation of God in himself is only defined as against the rival claim of Mohammed, by the fact that on the ground of his peculiar relation to God, Christ lived a life of mastery over the world, such as makes possible the community in which each Christian is to attain the similar destiny of the life eternal. Because this goal is not the reward of fulfilling a statutory law, Christ does not count, like Mohammed, merely as a lawgiver. On the contrary, since the aim of the Christian is to be attained under the form of personal freedom, therefore the twofold significance we are compelled to ascribe to Christ as being at once the perfect revealer of God and the manifest [*offenbar*] type of spiritual lordship over the world, finds expression in the single predicate of his Godhead.

Ibid., pp. *385–9*

PART III

WILHELM HERRMANN

CHRISTIANITY IN AN AGE OF SCIENCE

1. Protestantism Today

He to-day who is willing to see, can find the way which, even in a world altered by science, leads those who seek God to Christ.

Of course, with all our efforts, we cannot make it clear to all Christians how profoundly our whole existence, down even to that arrangement of our habits of thought which is fixed by mere caprice, has been altered, not so much through the results of science as through the method which, in point of fact, it follows, and which is, in point of fact, unassailable. There will be many Christians for a long time yet on whose consciousness this has not dawned.

But the task for the Church and for theology which grows out of this change is now facing us in fullest distinctness. The Church must endeavour to satisfy the spiritual wants of the thousands who are able to move so freely in the traditional forms of Christianity that they can find in them the means of expression for their own religious conviction. But this does not imply that these Christians, who are not compelled by their course in life to clear up their mental attitude to what is real in the world, are to be made lords over the Church. The leaders of the Church must not avail themselves of these docile masses in order to close the Church to others who are so controlled in their life that they are simply obeying the truth, when they regard the things of this world in a different manner. One may call those happy who do not see themselves forced out of the traditional forms of Christianity by the duty of sincerity. But the Church does not make itself indifferent to them; if she does she will become a sect; that is to say, she will sever herself from the historical movement of humanity. She ought to stand at their service. It is just these men who are in crying need of help if they are rightly to use the precious inheritance that is theirs and not make it an instrument of their ruin.

First of all, they need to be preserved from making the Biblical tradition a law for themselves or others, by the fulfilment of which they may inherit or appropriate salvation. For thus they block the way to God for themselves and hinder others from finding it. . . . It is by the right use of the Biblical tradition that a Christian grows out of its misuse.

The Church must also aid the Christian democracy to see to it that the Bible holds its place. When the perception grows within the Protestant Church that the Bible is given us in order that in the stress of life and stilled in prayer we may listen to its words, if haply we may catch in it the voice of God speaking to our own hearts, then surely must perish the sacrilege that makes a law out of this gift of God's grace. Of course we have in view the fact that in our Church such a deliberate profanation of the holy place gives itself out for "positive Christianity". But in the midst of the darkness, guarded as it is by ecclesiastical authorities and by the State, God sends light into many a heart, so that, in fear of the judge of the conscience and in joy in the Creator and Father, it escapes from all the vulgar arts by which the world and its potentates dress up their Christianity. Among us as well as among Catholics this profound injury to the Church, this reduction of the holy Scriptures to a rule of doctrine, is limited in its practical working by the power of the Spirit that is met with in the holy Scriptures. One who comes under the grasp of the spiritual character of Jesus wins a right appreciation of the doctrines about the Person of Jesus, so that he can find in even them that one thing great and precious to him above all else in the world, the power of this personal spirit over men who are yearning to become conscious of God. . . .

This is the religious way to overcome the delusion that we ought to constitute the means of God's revelation a rule of doctrine, and that the observance of such precepts, a thing which always makes us sink into insincerity, can unite us with God. But Protestant Christians would be much more quickly set free from that most influential of Roman Catholic ideas, if among us the Church had some help to give to the millions who have become conscious of their inward dissatisfaction with many Biblical representations. Through their mental attitude these people feel themselves shut out from a Church that regards and demands as the beginning of Christianity the assent to the teaching and narratives of the Bible. Short-sighted critics may hold that for this reason the Roman Church is better suited than the Protestant to the spiritual needs of moderns. For she declares herself content with the man who, even if he does not share her doctrines at least does not contradict them. In the Protestant Church, on the other hand, the demand is made that the Scriptural doctrines shall be echoed as personal conviction. The lesser seriousness of the Roman requirement will thus make it possible for many to rest in the Church of Rome who could not remain with the Protestant communion. But it is those spiritually asleep who, in this manner, remain inside the Church. We will, therefore, be glad that for such people attachment to the Church is made harder among us than among Catholics. Yet it is a pity, too, that it is not made easier for the sincere. How shall they make a start with talk of "facts which demand faith", when by these facts are meant the miracles reported in the Holy Scriptures, or, indeed, anything that is an event of the past and not something that can be experienced here and now? They must feel repelled by a Church that through multitudes of its ministers spreads among the people the belief that a man does not become a Christian by reverently reflecting on what is undeniably real, but by being ready to obey a general invitation to declare as true things which are doubtfully apprehended, or, in any case, are not grasped as real by himself. Further, however, in the majority of those who are thus injured and left unsuccoured by the Church, there is developed an extraordinary want of comprehension for the Biblical tradition. They count it a meaningless thing, because they are tormented with it in a meaningless way. When, therefore, earnest Christians see how the multitude regards the Bible without reverence or piety, they imagine they must be up in defence of their holy thing and thus they become compliant tools of those very guardians of it who, by their violence, have done it most harm.

2. The Freedom of Faith

There is only one way out of this vicious circle of destruction. . . . Help can be expected only from a reawakening within the minds of those who have lapsed from the Church of an intelligent reverence for a Bible which has been degraded in the Church to a rule of doctrine.

Now this will happen in so far as they observe that the Bible itself, instead of making an inhuman demand on us, offers us an incomparable gift. When it becomes clear to them that the Bible introduces us to a marvellously vivid personal life that compels us to self-examination, that shakes us up, that humbles us, and yet that also fills us with comfort, joy, and courage, then they will look away beyond all that has hitherto been strange and repellent in this tradition to the redeeming vision of God that they see dawning there. They learn, too, to understand at last how good such hindrances have been for them, for thus they have been preserved from the abomination of making the Bible a law of doctrine. And they even learn at last to think with heartfelt pity of the leaders of the Church, who by their high-handed action make the Bible a stumbling-block on which many fall never to rise.

When, however, those who are thus set free by Christ begin the work of self-conquest, they are blessed by continually finding in parts of the Christian tradition that had been previously repellent to them more that is now able to enrich and rejoice their souls. Perhaps, to take an example, they may never succeed in sharing the apostle Paul's conception of the Person of Christ. But it will certainly be given them to rejoice in the fact that such thoughts did rise in a Christian soul. They see there the effect of the *one saving fact* that they themselves, just as much as the apostle Paul, have before their eyes, namely, the personal life of Jesus. This joy in the Christian tradition will spread among our people the more hearts are made to glow with the glorious knowledge that true religion, the blessed life of the spirit, is given to us only when we are willing to obey the simplest demand of the moral law, namely, to know ourselves. We must let ourselves be ready to take to heart in its weightiest characteristics that which is undeniably real, and gladly despise the suggestion that for God's sake we are to adopt the thoughts of other men. The right dependence on the Christian tradition must not, in the way the Church has up till now desired, draw its strength from want of moral insight or purity, but must result from moral earnestness alone. . . .

The new day of Protestant Christianity can dawn only in hearts that have perceived that truly religious faith recognises no other law than the moral law of sincerity and love. The day will break when these people will joyfully make, in quite another sense, the old demand of the legal party, that nothing of the treasure of the Church's tradition shall be lost; and when, with faith free and infinitely various in its individual forms, they take up the unavoidable duty of bringing together into one truly Christian community all who are working for the same good.

3. Personal Christianity

The unity of Protestant theology in a common peaceful task far removed from the noise of ecclesiastical party strife will at last be attained if we devote our attention to that which is usually expressly conceded by the one opponent to the other. Our opponents do not deny our personal Christianity. Well, then, let the endeavour be made on both sides to describe what we understand by personal Christianity. Christians are fully agreed as to its general meaning. It is a communion of the soul with the living God through the mediation of Christ. Herein is really included all that belongs to the characteristic life of Christendom—revelation and faith, conversion and the comfort of forgiveness, the joy of faith and the service of love, lonely communion with God, and life in Christian fellowship. All this is then only truly Christian when it is experienced as communion with the living God through the mediation of Christ. When we believe in a man's personal Christianity we are convinced that he stands in that relation towards God in which all this takes place. The reformers never doubted that Christianity in this sense might exist, and continue to exist, even amid the perverted teaching of the Roman Church. Of couise, they maintained that two of the Roman ideas destroyed the very basis of Christianity. Besides the idea of the meritoriousness of good works, the notion seemed equally obnoxious to them that the Sacraments had a saving efficacy, not the outcome of a religious comprehension of God's promise as expressed in their dispensation. But although they knew the Christianity that was under the guidance of Rome reckoned on its own merits and ascribed to the Sacraments magical effects, for instance, baptismal regeneration, yet they held that even there true Christian life was to be found, the inward strength of which made all these hurtful doctrines mere external additions. ...

This faith in the power of a personal Christianity that is awakened by God is indispensable to us who are Protestants. We must believe that personal Christianity can arise in spite of wrong teaching, and can remain alive amid obsolete ecclesiastical forms. If this be the case, then

Protestant theology is bound to set forth and expound precisely this personal Christianity in which we believe all Christians to be at one.

4. Christian Doctrine not Uniform

Again, the need for treatment of this subject is seen still further when we remember that there must be different teaching among Christians, and this not only on matters where we may feel it necessary to make some distasteful compromise with tradition, but also where the question may concern the expression of our inmost faith. The doctrine which really springs from faith has necessarily an infinite variety of forms. The Christian seeks to express in it the reality amid which his faith lives. But since that reality is infinite, therefore the doctrine in which one Christian seeks to express what his faith sees, cannot be laid down as the limit for other believers. Different men see differently, and therefore, since they ought to be truthful, they must express themselves differently. All attempts at union through uniformity of a compendium of doctrine, large or small, are futile, even when men succeed in building up such a structure as outlasts a millennium. Personal, living Christianity will always follow its own free course in unfolding its thoughts; it is inaccessible to that spirit of legalism which controls the world. We may see this fact illustrated in every sermon that comes truly from the preacher's heart. That heart, deeply moved by the Spirit of God, thinks very little of any doctrinal theory or of any theological system ruled by such, but reveres the free testimony of the faith of other men. In the outpourings of such a heart, therefore, the old faith, on which the characteristically new is climbing, will certainly be expressed in some measure; but the man, being really taught of God, will bring forth out of his treasure, along with the old, some new things also, which are by no means to be understood as the mere logical consequences of the old.

In the origination of particular doctrines, there have been many contributory thoughts all springing from the Spirit of God. But the idea of dogma as a uniform doctrinal theory is contrary to the working of the Holy Spirit. A uniform doctrinal theory seeks to dominate the thinking of the Christian community, and it demands that its own logical implications shall be developed in the thoughts of the Christian. But the Holy Spirit creates men of faith.

The actual composition of the New Testament clearly shows this. If Christians seek unity by means of unalterable doctrine, then they must give up the authority of the New Testament. For in the New Testament there is no unalterable doctrine which embraces the whole scheme of Christian thought. If in spite of this the effort be made, with the New Testament as guide, to construct a system which shall guarantee the unity of the Church, then the wonderful variety of the forms of thought contained in those Scriptures will be found to be an imperfection. Such a feeling is unavoidable if we attempt at once to teach according to Scripture, and, at the same time, to have unalterable doctrine as a condition of the unity of fellowship. He who wishes to teach according to Scripture needs rather to make up his mind that the ideal of doctrines which shall be unalterable, and equally binding upon all, is a false one. Were it a true ideal, then we should have to get beyond the Christianity of the New Testament. But we must rather intrench ourselves within it. It is no imperfection, it is rather most fitting that the Epistles of the New Testament are letters written in view of special circumstances, and not contributions to a doctrinal system which shall be valid to all eternity. . . .

5. The True Principle of Christian Unity

We hold a man to be really a Christian when we believe we have ample evidence that God has revealed himself to him in Jesus Christ, and that now the man's inner life is taking on a new character through his communion with the God who is thus manifest. But if this is certain, then it is the first business of theology to set forth and expound the communion of the Christian with God which is mediated through Jesus Christ.

For, in the first place, in this way alone can the Christian be guided by the New Testament as the principle of Protestantism demands, while, on the other hand, the notion that it is possible for the Christian to know and hold all the various doctrines uttered in the New Testament is, to put it plainly, a monstrous fiction. No Christian does so, and none can. To state all these doctrines correctly is the business of historical inquiry; it is an arduous task, and one that is never accomplished with certainty. Such an inquiry is not within the power of every Christian. The manifold nature of the doctrines uttered in the Scriptures corresponds indeed to the real nature of the life of faith, but it forbids a Christian to appropriate to himself equally all the processes of thought recorded by those writers. The authority of the New Testament, which gives the needed and safe guidance to every Christian, has for its sphere something quite different from fixity of doctrine, namely, the communion of the Christian with God which is mediated through Jesus Christ. Whenever the authority of the New Testament is extended so as to belong to its doctrines, that authority is diminished. Into the place of the New Testament there inevitably step those theological products which offer a unity of doctrine not found within its pages. If, however, we have learned to fix our eyes on that which God's revelation produces in the inner life of a Christian, then, in our reading of Scripture, we shall constantly meet with an authority by which we shall be safely led and wonderfully uplifted.

Second, in the vision of the communion of the Christian with God, we see wherein Christians are truly at one. In the inner life of faith all is ruled by the one God and the one Christ. Of course, in the exposition of such a life the development of particular doctrines must be set forth; but unities of doctrine beyond these limits are not legitimate, because not vital to faith. They are worthless dreams which arouse useless strife, and hinder the unity of the Christian Church. To fix doctrines that are thus severed from the stem of real life, and to frame them into a system, is the last thing the Christian Church should undertake, and the more important the matter worked up in this way is, the more harmful it is. But if, on the other hand, we keep our attention fixed on what God is producing in the Christian's inner life, then the manifoldness of the thoughts which spring from faith will not confuse us, but give us cause for joy. For we can then understand that the manifoldness is both necessary and valuable. Hence we must cease attempting to bind together into one system thoughts of faith coming from various sources, and to make the unity of the Church depend on any product of the kind. No confession ever arose thus which believers could unanimously and heartily accept. The Church's confession of faith ought to be the confession of real faith. But this is only possible where faith itself, or the personal life of the Christian, the life redeemed by God, becomes clearly conscious of itself. Whatever faith conscious of itself says concerning itself, its origin and the forms of its own life, that alone is the real confession of faith. In this confession Christians understand each other if the faith which God has wrought is alive within them at all. On these grounds, for a Church which desires to be really a fellowship of believers, there can be no theological task more important than that of setting forth that inner life of faith, or that communion with God in which we really find ourselves at one.

6. The Objectivity of Christian Knowledge

Of course, many persons fear that if we set the problem in this way, we are going to resolve Christianity entirely into subjective experiences. Their conviction is certainly right that the inner life of the Christian faith is extinguished if we lose the Christian knowledge in which we lay hold of a certain objective reality, which is our support. It remains to be seen whether, as we proceed, our exposition will disarm this suspicion; but the error of subjectivity by no means necessarily follows from the problem as now stated. This certainly does follow: that the knowledge of the objective Christian realities is the only nourishment on which faith is fed. It is not possible to prove to an unbeliever the truth of these things. That knowledge is inseparable from faith; and no one can gain an insight into its truth who is not sensible to the peculiar problems of the personal life that asserts itself in the sphere of moral thought. But just because this Christian knowledge is grasped in its truth only by those who occupy already the standpoint of faith, it is all the more needful to describe quite clearly the inner life of faith, wherein that Christian knowledge has its place. If we wish to settle our differences concerning doctrine, then, above all things, we must know what we mean by the inner life of faith, or, in other words, how we represent the communion of the Christian with God. Every theological discussion which does not sound these depths is in danger of that very calamity of subjectivity which others prophesy for us. The true objectivity of Christian knowledge, its truth for believers, must be lost unless it is protected by clear views concerning the life of faith. . . .

The Communion of the Christian with God
(trans. by J. S. Stanyon, revised by R. W. Stewart), pp. 1–17

COMMUNION WITH GOD THROUGH JESUS CHRIST

1. Revelation as Communicated Knowledge

We may speak of having communion with God only when we are certain that God speaks clearly to us, and also hears and considers our speech in his operations.

In order to commune with us, God makes himself known to us. The God of whose communion with men the Sacred Scripture tells, does not, for his own holiness' sake, suffer men to reach him through any efforts of their own. He will vouchsafe this in one way alone, and that way he opens to us himself. Now, further, if it is impossible for a man to rise unaided above all fightings and doubts into the realm of real communion with God, it is equally certain that no mere information of any kind concerning God could thus raise a man, even although that information should claim to be a divine revelation. We might indeed form a conception of God on the ground of such information. We might consent to acknowledge the reality of that revelation, and we might therefore believe our conception of God to be correct. But in that case we should still have to win for ourselves the impression that the God thus revealed did actually commune with us. If we had received only information concerning God, it would still be left to us to obtain the certainty of a real communion of God with ourselves. And no such endeavour of ours could ever conquer doubt, for it is just amid such endeavours that doubt does always rise. *Information concerning God*, therefore, although it may claim to be of divine revelation, can only bring that troubled piety which lives by no delivering act of God, but by men's own exertions. God has left us in no such miserable condition, and Protestants, at least, may know this, if they will only refuse to be led aside from the one thing needful by common cries like the following: "You must believe that God made the world; that men sprang from a single pair; that God's Son became a man; that God's demand for the punishment of the guilty has been satisfied by the death of his Son; and finally that all this happened for your sake." He who determines so to believe, can only cause distress to his soul. For in such doctrines, however true they may be in themselves, we are not brought face to face with that reality which gives faith its certainty; they simply

tell us something, and we are then expected by our own efforts to hold
that information to be true.

2. Revelation as Inward Experience

But we leave all these fruitless endeavours at religious self-help
behind, when we entirely reject the idea that we are to believe doctrines.
Untroubled by these suggestions we must put ourselves the one
question: "Whereby shall we know that a living God is communing
with us?" Then, when we come to see and understand the reality which
makes us certain of this fact, we see also that the painful effort which
had been demanded of us is taken away by God's own act. For when
the Christian has once experienced the fact that God is striving to make
himself known to him, and when he sees how God so strives, then he
begins to see also what is true in those aforesaid doctrines.

God makes himself known to us, so that we may recognise him,
through *a fact, on the strength of which we are able to believe on him.* No
doctrine of any kind can do more than tell us how we ought to
represent God to ourselves. No doctrine can bring it about that there
shall arise in our hearts the full certainty that God actually exists for us;
only a fact can inspire such confidence within us. Now we Christians
hold that we know only one fact in the whole world which can overcome every doubt of the reality of God, namely, the appearance of
Jesus in history, the story of which has been preserved for us in the
New Testament. Our certainty of God may be kindled by many other
experiences, but has ultimately its firmest basis in the fact that within the
realm of history to which we ourselves belong, we encounter the man
Jesus as an undoubted reality.

Of course, we may have heard about Jesus for a long time without
his becoming manifest to us in his power. We can hardly put it that it
is only in the vision of the Person of Jesus that our eyes are first opened
to the invisible. Probably for all of us that revelation comes from those
in our immediate circle, and we ought in our turn to do a like service to
others. But such men, in whose earnestness and brotherly love we can
trace a hidden life with God, are fragments of God's revelation. The
whole revelation that God has ordained for us in our historical situation
is ours only when we can see that the Person of Jesus surpasses all else
that is great and noble in humanity, and that behind those whose

influence upon us is strongest, he is visible as their life-giver and their Lord. The revelation of God that we get from those of our most immediate circle is not pushed aside or emptied of its value, but only deepened and perfected as we become acquainted with Jesus himself.

The true Christian confession is that Jesus is the Christ. Rightly understood, however, it means nothing else than this: that through the man Jesus we are first lifted into a true fellowship with God. If it be asked what we are to understand by that, the reply is that for those who truly seek God it should be wonderfully simple. But it is often made difficult by those thieves amid Christendom (John x. i), who pretend to come into fellowship with God by some other way than through the man Jesus. The by-path most frequented is that of doctrines concerning Jesus which give him the highest praise, and so form the most convenient means of avoiding his Person. By this means the only way of salvation is closed to persons without number. The divinely simple fact that the man Jesus is the Christ is made distasteful to them by the idea instilled into them that they may come into possession of much higher things, namely, a number of wonderful doctrines, the *fides quae creditur*, by simply believing them. The result is that even among us Protestants it has become very difficult for the majority to regard the finding of God as the highest good, or even to look upon it as a wonderful gift from him at all. Most men think it of small importance that Jesus alone makes us certain of a living God, for they imagine that of all the doctrines in which they "believe" the doctrines of the existence of God is the most elementary.

3. The Person of Jesus

From this there has arisen a bad practice now widely spread among us. When the question is asked: "On what depends our certainty of a Living God who works in us?" it is quite a common practice to look away from ourselves and our own particular position, and to think of as many men as possible, who stand at the greatest possible distance from us, such as the savages of New Holland or the ancient Egyptians. None of these, it is urged, have been utterly without the capacity for recognising God, as indeed the apostle Paul testifies. We are also further reminded that Israel had the knowledge of God and enjoyed communion with him before Christ came, and therefore it is finally concluded that what was possible to the Jews must also be possible to us. Such arguments are frequently set up in contradiction of our proposition that for us Jesus is the revelation of God. And then that proposition of ours looks like an exaggeration. It seems as though, in order to reduce it to its right proportions, we ought rather to say that we may have the revelation of the being of God quite apart from Jesus, but that Jesus makes some addition to that revelation, as, for example, the knowledge that God has a Son and constitutes one Being with him.

Now to all this we may reply that we by no means wish to assert, even for a moment, that the savages of New Holland have no knowledge of God, no pulsations of true religion, and therefore no communion with God. But we do not know through what medium such knowledge and such communion reach them. We cannot enter fully into the religious life even of a pious Israelite, for the facts which worked upon them as revelations of God have no longer this force for us. Israel stood in communion with God as *his people*; hence national feeling was an indispensable element in Jewish piety; and just because the Israelite knew what it meant to belong to Israel instead of to any other nation, he was able to grasp as revelations of God those features in the course of Hebrew history which he did so apprehend. Since we cannot feel as Jews, the revelation which was given to Israel can no longer satisfy our need. Our position is different; we stand in such historical relationships that Jesus Christ alone can be grasped by us as the fact in which God so reveals himself to us that everything that hides him from us vanishes away. The knowledge of God and the religion which have been and which are possible to men placed in other historical conditions are impossible to us. Indeed, there exists in our case a hindrance to the religious life of which men were quite ignorant in olden times, namely, that deepening of the moral consciousness which has come about, and the consequent moral need. We feel ourselves to be separated from God, and consequently crippled in our faith by things which troubled the ancients very little. We cannot go back to our first simple indifference to moral demands after our conscience has once been sensible of them. Above all, the knowledge that we are bound to unconditional obedience can never die away into sloth and inactivity after it has once dawned upon us. So that when we are faced by something that wants to force itself on us as a Power over our entire life, the doubt arises in our minds whether in it we really find something we can be conscientiously willing to obey unconditionally. He who is morally free will mock at a religion that is above morality just as he pities one that is beneath it. Therefore, the only God that can reveal himself to us is one who shows himself to us in our moral struggle as the Power to which our souls are really subject. This is what is vouchsafed to us in the revelation of God in Jesus Christ. He gives a fulness to our personal life which burst all other moulds of religion and allows us to find rest only in that communion with God into which he brings us.

If we wish to come to God, we must not, above all things, turn our back upon the actual relationships in which we stand. The concrete reality amid which we actually live must be the nourishment of our inner life. When we take this reality to heart, then God enters our life. For the earth is the Lord's. Dreams which soar away from reality lead not to God but to nothing. They are a form of original sin, a form of untruth in which we spin a web of emptiness about ourselves, and so cut ourselves off from true life.

That is the right in the efforts that have cost honest thinkers so much toil, as they have tried to discover for human reason the activity of the Creator in the reality of nature. Those attempts belong, however, to a period of Christian life that has now been outlived. We do not apprehend ourselves as what we really are when we conceive ourselves as part of nature, for we have become conscious that our realm of life is human society and its history. Nature alone cannot show us all the reality in which we stand. She belongs to that reality, being herself a means to the existence of society; but it is in this society itself, this historical life, of which nature is thus a subordinate part and means, that we first reach the true reality, of which we must become conscious if our inner life is to have any content at all. For this reason we can no longer hope to find God by seeking him in nature. God is hidden from us in nature because we do not find our whole selves there, we do not find there the full riches of that reality, which crowds in upon our consciousness. It is only out of life in history that God can come to meet us. In proportion as what is essential in our historical environment becomes an element of our consciousness we are led into the presence of those facts which can reveal God to us. If our souls do not awake to a clear consciousness of these facts, if we simply endure our relationship to other men, instead of living it, then the personality within us to which God desires to reveal himself remains dormant, and we do not see the facts through which alone God can reveal himself to us.

In that historical environment which ought to give our personal life its fulness, there is no fact more important for each individual than Jesus Christ. To overlook him is to deceive ourselves as to the best treasure which our own life possesses. For he is precisely that fact which can make us certain, as no other fact can, that God communes with us. This assertion will no doubt give to many the impression of a manifest exaggeration. All who are accustomed to follow the orthodox method of teaching will esteem it such, but so, too, will those who think along rationalistic lines. The former think they find the support of their religious life in doctrines concerning God and Christ which are vouched for by others; the latter wish to found their inward peace neither upon authorities nor upon past events in history, but upon that eternal truth which they grasp in their own thinking here and now. Both classes must find a stumbling-block in our proposition that the person of Jesus is the fact by which God communes with us. Both are inclined to imagine that the communion with God with us is an inward experience into which external facts do not intrude. The objections they raise against our proposition are, *first*, that the person of Jesus is a fact vouched for by authorities, and, *secondly*, that it is a thing of the past. They hold that the first objection forbids us to say that, strictly speaking, *Jesus himself* is an element of the reality in which we stand; they hold that such can be said only of the *tradition concerning Jesus*. They contend that the second objection above forbids us to say that God communes with us by this fact, *i.e.*, the person of Jesus, because this fact is a thing of the past, whereas God's communion with us must be a thing of the present.

4. Faith and Historical Evidence

The former contention has the greater weight. Men must indeed be powerfully moved by the supposition that Jesus himself cannot be held to be an undeniable element in our actual environment, and that it is only the story of Jesus, as vouched for by others, that can be called such an element. Many within the Christian fellowship find this supposition to be a very slave-chain, and for many outside that fellowship it is a drag holding them back from entering. But are the chains as adamantine as they seem? If not, then we, too, can overcome a serious hindrance which the faith of the Reformers reached beyond, but from which they could not get free.

It is true that we should have no certain knowledge of Jesus if the New Testament did not tell us about him. Narratives by others contribute in all cases not a little to the picture we form for ourselves of historical reality. If tradition of some sort did not show us what others have experienced of human life we should lack the most valuable of the interchanges of spiritual possessions. But given this exchange, then the narrative which comes to us, either by word of mouth or in writing, is not the only fact which we incorporate into our picture of historical reality; the content of those narratives may also become a fact for us. This happens only when we can ourselves establish its reality, and we may do this in various ways.

The most elementary form of doing so consists in extending the confidence we place in the trustworthiness of the narrator to that which he narrates. This constantly happens in our daily life, whenever we base our plans of action upon information given by others. We are guided by the content of their report just as by a reality we have grasped for ourselves. But it does not occur to us to offer ourselves as witnesses that things are really as they are said to be. Hence we can remain in this attitude only so long as we are concerned with matters of minor importance. But as soon as the contents of the information affect seriously the most important interests of life, our trust in the mental power and moral goodness of the narrator no longer suffices to assure us that what he reports is a fact beyond all doubt. If even in such a case we are compelled to take action in reliance on the report, our action takes the character of a venture. We are often obliged to act thus when the pressure of necessity does not permit of inaction; under such compulsion we may find ourselves obliged to treat the contents of the narrative as fact. But it is obvious that no such compulsion exists when the information received in any way concerns our religious faith. If we do put confidence in the trustworthiness of a narrator, and are thus led to receive his narration as a fact among the subjects of our religious thought, then, whether the confidence be really felt or be only arbitrarily assumed, it is always very certain that the matter reported is nothing that affects the vital interests of religion. This may be clearly seen in Roman Catholicism. The historical appearance of Jesus is there really accepted on the authority of the narrators, and so we find that

that appearance has nothing to do with the highest concern of religious life, namely, how a man is to find God. It serves as a stimulus to the imagination, as an example and as a symbol, but it is not to the Roman Catholic the great fact in which he sees God entering into his own life and revealing Himself to him. Whenever we find the proclamation of the appearance of Jesus thus based entirely on the authority of the narrators, it will also be observed that the Person of Jesus is put on one side so soon as the deepest religious interest comes forward for consideration. A believer cannot base his very existence entirely on what may be given him by other men.

Our mental activity in the matter of receiving reports is certainly greater when we do not form our conception of the actual event from the narrative alone, but seek to obtain it by a combination of the narrative with something else which we know to be real. This procedure is frequently exemplified in daily life, and it has been developed into an art in historical criticism. The contents of the narrative are viewed in the light of the evident character of the narrator as seen through his writings, the position he occupied and its impress on him, and the culture of his age which influenced his way of looking at things. From a consideration of these circumstances we decide how far the contents of the story may be incorporated into our picture of what actually happened. But the decision thus reached of necessity lays claim to nothing more than probability. We are always prepared to modify our results upon more exact examination of the narrative or upon the discovery of new information. It is obvious, then, that such decisions do not give us facts on which our religious faith could be based. Hence it is quite explicable why historical criticism of the sacred records is so much disliked in many quarters. If men will imagine that the reliability of the sacred records is the proper ground of religious faith, then they must necessarily be rendered in the highest degree uneasy by faithful attempts to estimate the historical probability of what is narrated in these records. We have no such anxiety; on the contrary, we declare that the historical appearance of Jesus, in so far as it is drawn into the sphere of this attempt to establish the probable truth, cannot be a basis of faith. It is only a part of that world with which faith is to wrestle.

At this point, of course, the question arises whether we can maintain our position that the historical Christ has become for us the absolutely

I

convincing ground of our faith in God. For how is it at all possible to lift out of the mist of probability the content of a tradition that is subject to historical criticism?

It may be said that we learn with certainty that at least Jesus lived, from the fact of the existence of his church and its historical significance, and that just as little can we question the correctness of certain features in that portrait of Jesus which his followers have preserved in the records of the New Testament. From the standpoint of the mere historian this is certainly the case. A historian may doubt much that the New Testament tells us concerning the glory of Jesus. Because it is possible to attribute it in some measure to the transfiguring enthusiasm of his disciples, it is open to the suspicion of exaggeration. But, on the other hand, the correctness of his portrait in its other features must be admitted by every one who is not prepared to adopt the absurd supposition that in the case of a man who has exerted the greatest influence on history all traces of his earthly life have disappeared. On the strength of those elements in Jesus which, beyond all doubt, are with us to-day, every reasonable man will hold the more general features of the common story of his life to be correct. Now, one might in theory hold the opinion that we have only succeeded in establishing the probability of those facts concerning Jesus; none the less in practice, even if our interests in Jesus be only historical, we do all include his picture with its well-known features as a part of the historical reality amid which we live, and here we are evidently in no way dependent upon the authority of the chroniclers who give us those features of the life of Jesus. On the contrary, the decision which we reach that these things are facts, proceeds from our own independent activity, and is based upon that which we regard as real at present exactly as the decisions of historical criticism are. It is thus perfectly clear that we are quite in a position to detach the content of a narrative both from the narrative itself and from its author, and to regard it as an element of the reality to which we have to adjust our lives.

5. Jesus and the Believer

Yet this helps us little. The historian may succeed thus in removing doubts as to the historical reality of some person long since dead; but if he seeks to base his faith in God upon this, his argument collapses immediately. Once again a doubt lifts its head, one which perhaps can have no meaning for the mere historian. There comes back the feeling that it is a fatal drawback that no historical judgment, however certain it may appear, ever attains anything more than probability. But what sort of a religion would that be which accepted a basis for its convictions with the consciousness that it was only probably safe? For this reason it is impossible to attach religious conviction to a mere historical decision. Here Lessing is right. If, notwithstanding all this, the person of Jesus is so certainly a fact to us Christians that we do see in him the basis of our faith, and the present revelation of God to us, this conviction is not produced by a historical judgment. The calmness with which Christendom holds by the historical reality of Jesus has certainly not been won by the forcible suppression of historical doubt. Any such effort would be made contrary to the dictates of conscience, and it could give no man peace. It is something quite different which removes all doubt from the picture of Jesus; if we have that picture at all, we have it as the result, not of our own efforts, but of the power of Jesus himself.

In the Christian fellowship we are made acquainted, not merely with the external course of Jesus' lot in life and of his work in history, but we are also led into his presence and receive a picture of his inner life. For this we are certainly dependent, in the first instance, upon other men. For the picture of Jesus' inner life could be preserved only by those who had experienced the emancipating influence of that fact upon themselves. The personality of Jesus remained hidden from all others; it could only reveal itself to such as were lifted by it. Such men were able to understand and to retain the utterances of Jesus which were expressions of his peculiar power. Hence the picture of his inner life could be preserved in his church or "fellowship" alone. But, further, this picture so preserved can be understood only when we meet with men on whom it has wrought its effect. We need communion with Christians in order that, from the picture of Jesus which his church has preserved, there may shine forth that inner life which is the heart of it. It is only when we see its effects that our eyes are opened to its reality so that we thereby experience the same effect. Thus we would never apprehend the most important element in the historical appearance of Jesus did not his people make us feel it. The testimony of the New Testament concerning Jesus arose within his church, and its exposition is the work of the Church, through the life which that Church develops and gains for itself out of this treasure which it possesses. Something similar is the case with every personality; one must stand within the sphere of life which it created or influenced in order to be able to understand its innermost reality. So if we would understand what is most important in history, we must look not only to the records but also to the men whose actual present life expounds those records to us.

What we are thus seeking is certainly the hardest part to grasp in the whole sum of the historical reality of Jesus; nevertheless it is just this which sets us free from the mere record, because it presses in upon us as a power that is present through its work upon us. He who has found the inner life of Jesus through the mediation of others, in so far as he has really found it, has become free even of that mediation. He is so set free by the significance which the inner life of the man Jesus has for him who has beheld it. If we have experienced his power over us, we need no longer look for the testimony of others to enable us to hold fast to his life as a real thing. We start, indeed, from the records, but we do not grasp the fact they bring us until the enrichment of our own inner life makes us aware that we have touched the Living One. This holds true of every historical personality; the inner content of any such personality is laid open only to those who become personally alive to it, and feel themselves aroused by contact with it and see their horizon widened. The picture of a personality becomes visible to us in this way, and cannot be handed over to us by any communication from others; it must arise within ourselves as the free revelation of the living to the living. It is thus, therefore, that the inner life of Jesus becomes part of our own sphere of reality, and the man who has experienced that will certainly no longer say that, strictly speaking, he can know only the story of Jesus as a real thing. Jesus himself becomes a real power to us when he reveals his inner life to us; a power which we recognise as the best thing our life contains.

Any conscientious reader of the Gospels will be constantly questioning whether the events actually happened as they stand in the narrative. Of course, we can forcibly suppress this doubt, and many a Christian will think it an inevitable necessity to do so. But such suppression will not help him. Help lies for each of us, not in what we make of the story, but in what the contents of the story make of us. And the one thing which the Gospels will give us as an overpowering reality which allows no doubt is just the most tender part of all: it is the inner life of Jesus itself. Only he who yearns after an honest fulness for his own inner life can perceive the strength and fulness of that soul of Jesus, and whenever we come to see the Person of Jesus, then, under the impress of that inner life that breaks through all the veils of the story, we ask no more questions as to the trustworthiness of the Evangelists. The question whether the portrait of Jesus belongs to history or fiction is silenced in every one who learns to see it at all, for by its help he first learns to see what is the true reality of personal life. We must allow the abstract possibility of the view that the historical portrait of Jesus was constructed in good part by men who were able, like ourselves, to fashion visible symbols of religious and moral ideas, and if we look at it thus we shall feel we are in a superior position, for what we can thus explain does not enrich us, but shows us what we already possess. But we cannot think thus of the total picture of Jesus' inner life, for it compels us to simple reverence.

The man who has had this experience can with heartfelt confidence allow the historical criticism of the New Testament writings to have full play. If such investigation discovers contradictions and imperfections in the story, it also discloses by that very fact the power of the personality of Jesus, for that personality never lets the contradictions and imperfections of the story disfigure the clear features of that which it gave to men, namely, Jesus' own inner life. It is a fatal error to attempt to establish the basis of faith by means of historical investigation. The basis of faith must be something fixed; the results of historical study are continually changing. The basis of our faith must be grasped in the same independent fashion by learned and unlearned, by each for himself. Howsoever the story may come to us, whether as sifted and estimated by historical criticism or not, the same results ought to follow, and may follow, in both cases, namely, that we learn to see in it the inner life of Jesus. Whether faith then arises in us or not depends on whether this personal spirit wins power over us, or we hold ourselves back from him. Thus in a moral experience there becomes clear to us what it is that can be the basis of our faith. So far as establishing our faith is concerned, historical work on the New Testament can bring us no nearer, and neither by this nor by any other means can we compel any other man to recognise even the bare reality of that which has an effect upon ourselves so powerful as to give us courage to believe on God.

But, nevertheless, historical work on the New Testament is not without value for faith. In the first place, it shows us how small a foundation those writings afford for a historical account undertaking to set forth as the result of scientific processes what the Person of Jesus shall signify for the Christian. In shattering such hopes it destroys certain false props of faith, and that is a great gain. The Christian who imagines that the reliability of the records as historical documents gives certainty to his faith, is duly startled from his false repose by the work of the historian, which ought to make it clear to such a man that the possession of Christianity cannot be obtained so cheaply as he thinks. Secondly, historical work is constantly constructing afresh, with every possible new modification, whatsoever results can be obtained from the records. By this means the Christian believer is constantly called upon to compare afresh that portrait of Jesus which he carries within him as absolute truth, with the relative truth obtained by historical research. And this helps us not to forget that the most important fact in our life cannot be given to us once for all, but must be continually laid hold of afresh with all our soul. And it helps us also to increasing knowledge of the inexhaustible treasures of the inner life of Christ, and to growing acquaintance with the ways of his sovereignty over the real world. Of course, we lose this advantage entirely if historical research is made to serve the ends of apologetics instead of remaining true to its own laws. It must make us thankful to feel that we have got beyond the temptation to misuse science in this way. For when we speak of the historical Christ we mean that personal life of Jesus which speaks to us from the New Testament, as the disciples' testimony to their faith, but which, when we perceive it, always comes home to us as a miraculous revelation. That historical research cannot give us this we *know*. But neither will it ever take this from us by any of its discoveries. This we *believe*, the more we experience the influence that this picture of the glory of Jesus has upon us.   *Ibid.*, pp. *57–78*

PART IV

JULIUS KAFTAN

DIVINE REVELATION AND HUMAN REASON

The history of the human race becomes intelligible as a whole only if there is such a revelation in it as that to which Scripture witnesses, and to which the Christian Church confesses adherence: therefore it is reasonable to believe in that revelation. Again, men take the only possible way to arrive at an answer to the question of the origin and final purpose of all things when they understand and interpret the world by starting with the highest result that has been disclosed to them in their history, by which their history gains unity and meaning: therefore it is reasonable to recognise in this revelation and its content that principle for interpreting the world which answers to reason. That is the intention of [the proof of Christianity's truth by the reasonableness and absoluteness of the faith reposed in the Christian Revelation].

And now we maintain that in this proof the fundamental problem of theological doctrine, *the old question of the relation of Reason and Revelation*, also finds its solution. A real reconciliation of the principles attained by it, a reconciliation with regard to which we previously found that on the old ground it was neither attained nor attainable at all: on the old ground—that, viz., of objective apprehension or of *knowledge* in regard to these questions. The *way* to the solution is indicated, it is true, even there. And it is no other than that which we are traversing: it must be shown that it is reasonable to believe in revelation. But the true conception could not be carried out under the presuppositions which determined theological tradition. Or more precisely, the mode in which it was carried out and had in that connection to be carried out, prevented any reconciliation of the principles from being arrived at, entailing rather an infringement of the one by the other. On the ground of knowledge, the reasonableness of faith in revelation can be maintained only in such wise that Reason has its defects and imperfections made clear to it, and it is required to accept Revealed knowledge on authority and without a sincere appropriation of it—a course with which Reason never will be contented and never can. Furthermore, the transference of the question to this sphere of objective knowledge already occasions in itself a subordination of our Faith in Revelation to the judgment of Reason, such as runs counter to the interests of Faith. Therefore no reconciliation of the principles can be arrived at so long as the discussion of the question is carried on on this ground.

The matter assumes, on the other hand, quite a different form when we found on the perception that the highest knowledge can be established only by means of a practical idea, that of the chief good. For now it can be shown that Reason and Revelation meet in the *same conception of the chief good*, that chief good which the former requires as the true principle of a rational interpretation of the world, without, however, being able to attain it by its own resources, while Revelation proclaims it as an eternal fact. And then there is implied in that a *reconciliation of the principles* by which neither the one nor the other is compromised, in which they are completed precisely in and through each other. Reason finds in the existence of Revelation a confirmation of itself as Reason; if there were not Revelation, the highest knowledge would remain incomplete, a Postulate or a hypothesis; on that very amount the proper attestation of the highest knowledge is found not in Reason, but in Revelation. Reason could not be trusted with regard to this highest knowledge if there were not Revelation to attest it. And Revelation would not be really Revelation, the proclamation of fruitful and world-embracing truth, unless it were met by the demand of Reason. Here the position is similar to that of *religious certainty*. In respect to the latter also the subjective and the objective factors must meet and mutually penetrate each other. The subjective need in itself engenders no certainty, and just as little does the latter spring from the acceptance on authority of an objectively existing Revelation. Only where the subjective need lays hold of Revelation as objectively given and self-announcing is there such certainty attained. What makes Revelation as such intelligible is the subjective need; that on which certainty as such rests and to which it appeals is the existence of objective Revelation. In the same way Reason and Revelation mutually condition and require each other. We may repeat what has been said almost in the same words: what attests Revelation as such is the need shown by Reason; that on which Reason as such rests and to which it appeals is the existence of Revelation.

But in regard to one point this proof still needs completion. What has been taken into consideration in it in the first instance is only the kingdom of God as the content of Revelation and of the Christian faith. That, indeed, is the fundamental idea of the Christian religion and the main content, properly speaking, of Divine Revelation. Christianity is, however, on the other hand, the religion of the *Atonement*; the Revelation of God in Christ contains as a further and essential head the proclamation of the love of God which justifies sinners and reconciles them to himself. The proof therefore seems to be incompleteu nless it also refers at the same time to this matter.

However, this completion naturally follows from what was previously said regarding the close and essential connection between the kingdom of God and the Atonement.[1] Here it only remains for us, founding on the exposition already given, to take up this further element in connection with the rational proof. Now that is done simply by looking to the consideration that the kingdom of God would not be for men at all as they exist empirically, if the message of Justification and Reconciliation were not combined with the preaching of it. Men cannot think of accepting the great gift of God in Christ if guilt interposes to separate between them and a holy God, unless God blots out the guilt and purifies the conscience. Only by reconciling men to God was Christ able to set up the kingdom of God among mankind. Not by accident or by arbitrariness on God's part, but intrinsically and necessarily, are the two realities combined with each other—as was

---

[1] *Das Wesen der christlichen Religion*, pp. *312 ff.* The notion of the Atonement and the kindred notions of Justification and the Forgiveness of sins always give expression merely to the fact that a hindrance has been removed or that the normal relation is established. But they do not state what it is that is now unhindered, or in what the normal relation consists. What decides on these points is the idea of the chief good, the idea which governs the religion in question. On it therefore depends among other things our understanding of the Atonement, etc. Now, the chief good as apprehended by Christianity is itself determined by ethical considerations. For that reason the Atonement cannot be conceived as proceeding from the side of man; it must rather proceed from the side of God; and the good works of men cannot be regarded as a condition of the Atonement, as they are rather expected only as its fruit. On the other hand, without the Atonement the chief good would not be attainable by man at all owing to his sin and guilt. These two realities, the chief good and the Atonement, are in every respect most intimately connected.

shown on the former occasion alluded to. If, therefore, it is reasonable to believe in a revelation which has the kingdom of God as its content, the same holds good with regard to faith in the Atonement. Owing to the essential interdependence of the two elements in Divine revelation, in view of the actual state of things among men, the proof naturally extends to this further element of revelation and of Christianity.

And in connection with this matter it remains to be considered what is the meaning of the proof here again, and what the meaning can only be. It is not, then, meant as a proof of the objective necessity of the Atonement. As to this aspect of the matter, it is always an *unfathomable free* decree of the love of God that he was willing toreconcile sinners to himself in Christ, without and contrary to their desert. It is only shown that the Atonement is necessary *if* a realisation of the kingdom of God is to be attained. Here as always the historical fact of revelation, a revelation which has this and no other content, forms the presupposition of the proof. Reason cannot arrive by its own resources at the fact of the eternal kingdom of God as the purpose of the world and of history, or at most it reaches it as a conjecture (which, however, does not suffice). Just as little can it make out anything by its own means as to the fact of the Atonement, of the Divine decree bearing upon it. Both required to be announced by Divine Revelation. And the first, moreover, would not suffice in any way by itself alone to make a safe conclusion possible as to the second. For *the conscience* would judge that guilt excludes us from participation in the kingdom of God. The Atonement must therefore by itself and *expressly* be a matter of Divine Revelation. The essential interdependence of the two doctrines always reaches only so far that we must conclude:—as it is only by the Revelation of the Kingdom of God that a rational interpretation of the world is rendered possible for us, so it is only through the Atonement effected by Christ that we are enabled to complete that interpretation.

Hence: the proof of Christianity is the proof of the reasonableness of the faith which is reposed in revelation, which has this and no other content. By faith in Christ we do not put ourselves in opposition to reason, but by that faith we attain first of all the unity of our personal life and also the consummation of our reason.

There remains the question whether the knowledge thus attained is in harmony with the rest of the knowledge which we men possess or can attain as the case may be, or whether a contradiction between the two kinds is to be feared. Hitherto this matter has remained unnoticed: we have simply sought on the path acknowledged to be right the *direct* proof of the supreme principle of all Christian knowledge, without looking about for such *possible conflicts*. But we must not pass by that question altogether. It is an imperative requirement of reason that no contradiction shall prevail in our knowledge. By way of completing the direct proof we shall therefore have to show that any such drawback is precluded. As part of our task in doing so we shall have to bring forward simple inferences from the first three chapters. And in part some isolated points which must not remain undiscussed will have to be treated in connection with these.

And here now as respects the general question in the first instance, the truth holds good that a contradiction between Christian knowledge and man's common experimental knowledge of things generally is in no wise to be feared. That follows from the fact which has formerly been proved at sufficient length that the two bodies of knowledge are of quite different kinds. In the two cases the same set of facts is conceived and looked at from *totally different points of view*. Christian faith always acknowledges the world as a whole, and everything in particular in it as well, to be the work of God and to be a means for God's eternal purpose. As the object of Christian knowledge everything is placed in these last and highest relations. But of these relations common experience knows nothing, absolutely nothing whatever. Its aim is directed at the finite connections of things and only at these. How then should a contradiction be possible between the two kinds, whether on the whole or in detail? Things that are to contradict each other must lie somehow on the same ground. Just as little as a mathematical proposition and a moral judgment can contradict each other, can a contradiction intervene between Christian faith and our empirical knowledge of the world.

But if it is said that man is a *unity*, and so his knowledge too must be a *unity*, and therefore that, however true it may be that faith draws from one source and empirical science from another, there still remains the problem of reconciling the two, and so, *e.g.* where we have to do with the same body of facts, of gathering up the two forms of knowledge in *one* proposition; if it is affirmed that this is the real problem, and that only the solution of it guarantees the non-existence of a contradiction, the answer to all this also follows naturally from our previous discussions. Certainly man is a *unity*. Of course there remains the problem of reducing the two forms of knowledge relating to the same body of facts to harmony with each other. But that can and ought to be done only from the point of view which determines the comprehension of our knowledge as a whole in a *unity*, from the point of view, viz., of the *practical position of man in the world*. From that point of view the combination is obtained in quite a simple and easy manner. The fact that the Christian acknowledges a finite body of facts to be the work of God and the means for God's purpose, immediately involves the other fact that he discerns therein something that has to serve as material for moral action; but in order to be able to do so he must attend to the *finite* connections, and therefore even *as a Christian* he assumes in no wise an attitude of indifference towards such knowledge; even as a Christian he cannot possibly dispense with it. The completion by him of each of the two kinds of knowledge is not precluded; they are rather the two factors, demanding and conditioning each other, of that position in the world and relatively to it which the Christian adopts and retains as a unity. If, on the other hand, the requirement alluded to is understood in the sense that the two judgments must be brought together in a *third*, that is simply an error which springs from a false appreciation of those judgments and their relation to one another. What experience teaches us is, and remains always, *relative knowledge*, determined by the finite purposes of the knowing mind; faith, on the contrary, knows of an absolute purpose and has to do with *absolute knowledge*. The unity lies in the proper arrangement of these purposes together; but the judgments of knowledge as such cannot be bent together and put into one. The finding of that unity may, it is true, in particular cases involve a practical problem which no one can solve without prayer and without the assistance of the Divine Spirit. But that is a matter by itself. In principle when we follow this path the reconciliation of the two spheres of knowledge is simple and easy.

The same thing recurs next on a large scale. I mean, while there is no contradiction between experience and faith in any particular instance, it is equally true that there is none between the Christian theory of the world and modern science. Often, of course, it is conceived that there is. Modern science, which resolves nature into processes of movement that are governed by laws, is supposed to be incompatible with

Christian faith, which everywhere, even in nature, discerns God's power, God's dispensation and Providence. And it is intelligible how it has been possible for such an opinion to originate and take root among large classes of people. The traditional habits of thought (even in theology) induce people to compare the two *immediately*. Then under that presupposition the overpowering impression which the results of modern Physical Science produce readily leads to such a judgment. But although thus psychologically intelligible, the judgment itself is nevertheless false. We must never aim at comparing and conjoining the two immediately. For if that is done, both faith and science are vitiated. And quite naturally, too. Each of these modes of looking at the world aims at being *complete* in its kind, and suffers no intervention of foreign points of view, without which, however, one cannot get along with such attempts at reconciliation.

These attempts themselves may be divided into two groups; in the one set the emphasis is laid on the results of Physical Science, in the other on the knowledge of Faith. The principle of the former is that in the eternal laws pervading nature the *immutable* expression of the Divine will is to be recognised; they culminate in opposition to miracles. Now that such a view, if it is not tacitly corrected from time to time, cannot be reconciled in practice with the Christian faith does not require to be shown. The God whose will has to be realised to oneself by the intermediate conception of *immutable* laws of nature is not, it must be allowed, the living God of Christian faith. But science too suffers harm on such a view. Its conclusions have in this way a stamp of *absolute validity* impressed upon them which does not answer to the truth: but where the *truth* suffers, *genuine* science also suffers, no matter whether too much or too little is made over to it. On the other hand, the other attempts at reconciliation, which lay the emphasis on faith and the knowledge peculiar to it, also, it is true, hold the action of God to be realised as a rule by laws as intermediaries, but make the reservation that exceptions are always possible and in particular cases become actual. Now it is obvious that for the scientific view that is an *absurd* supposition: he who speaks of "laws" in the sense of science must hold them to be valid without exception, because otherwise his language loses it meaning. Here what has to be brought prominently out is the other fact that by this means faith too is vitiated; on its part it will indeed have *nothing whatever* to do with these laws, but seeks to recognise in everything the *immediate* dispensation and arrangement of the Divine will. Such attempts at reconciliation, as they appear in sundry varieties, rest one and all on the error already mentioned, viz. on the assumption that the two modes of view are homogeneous enough to allow of such a reconciliation and conjunction. In truth that is not the case. In truth by this means Faith as well as Science is *vitiated*.

Here again the true way to reach unity is no other than that which was treated above: unity must be sought in the practical position occupied by man in the world. Both science and Christian faith spring from the need felt by the personal mind to dominate the world and to assert itself together with its purposes in the world; only in the one case we have to do with the purposes of the mental life which runs its course in the world, in the other case with the absolute purpose as it extends beyond the world, the apprehension and attainment of which first of all lead man to the consummation of his personal life. Here again the point in which both coincide is the moral problem. For the work of science is an important means for the solution of that problem, and only in and through his application to the same problem can the Christian attain his absolute purpose. Instead of contradicting each other, therefore, *modern Science and Christian Faith* together form elements of Protestant Christian culture which answer to each other and mutually demand each other. I say, Protestant culture, because in Catholicism another combination of Science and Faith is employed, a combination with which we have nothing further here to do.

But the assertion that contradiction is precluded in this combination which is here advocated may be proved especially by the circumstance that in such connection the two modes of view are at length carried out fully and without abridgment. All thought of pressing on Physical Science the duty of attending to supernatural factors is completely precluded—the fact being apparent that even *the most thoroughly convinced Christian*, as a worker with others at the problems of such science, leaves these factors alone. It is implied by the very nature of the case that that must happen, and that anything else is impossible. The sole reservation always made, a reservation demanded by the nature of the case, apart altogether too from Christian faith, is that the results of that investigation bear a relative character and can never lay it aside. Therefore they leave room for the other view that the Christian knows himself to be encompassed and attended on his path by the wonderful dispensations of his God. This view also is completely carried out, and that too with the consciousness that it is the last and highest truth: here the consideration of law (in the sense of science) is always entirely excluded.

But if the question of "miracle" in the pointed sense of the word is raised, we have to say that a "miracle" as "an exception to the laws of nature", is nothing but a falsely formed notion, one which springs from that *erroneous* combination of the two modes of view which we have just characterised and rejected. The "laws of nature" are nothing real; how then can I affirm that there are exceptions to them? What there is in reality answering to the scientific conception of laws of nature is the fact that the regularity of the course of nature permits the human mind to grasp that course by means of such formulae. At the same time it is true that every concrete occurrence is something by itself after all, nothing being accounted for without a residue by any formula, and that we must always be prepared for unforeseen exceptions. Again, an endless amount of things happen which it has not hitherto been possible to subject to such an interpretation by a law. If it were otherwise, science itself would really have nothing more to do. But neither the one thing nor the other is the miracle that is meant. Rightly defined, a miracle must be declared to be *an extraordinary and unusual* occurrence in nature, the historical relations of which, its *religious and moral import* as derived from these, awaken in a special manner faith in God's living government of the world (which faith embraces everything, even what is least, and no matter whether it is construed in accordance with natural law or not). To emphasise in such a case the special intervention of God is only permissible in the sense of that faith which does not doubt that everything comes from God *after the same manner*. Now, that there are such miracles who will deny? Who will be surprised at our finding them especially in the history of Revelation, in the life of Jesus Christ? But we must go a step farther still. Among the miracles in this narrower sense are such as run counter to the explanation got from "laws of nature", *i.e.* represent a deviation from the course which is otherwise explicable in that way. Can we decree now that anything of that kind is impossible? That those should do so who are led by modern Physical Science and imperceptibly become adherents of a sort of new Natural Religion is perfectly intelligible. That Christian theologians, who as such consciously

acknowledge their acceptance of the Christian faith, should assent to
that view, and should hold that judgment to be one of the sources of
their power, I do not understand. Or else I can only explain it to
myself psychologically as due to the impression which the results of
modern Physical Science, aided by traditional but erroneous habits of
thought, have produced. In any case such a judgment is not well-
founded. Or should the assumption that miracles in this narrower sense
are possible pave the way for the love of marvels, for superstition and
similar aberrations? If so, that assumption would of course be serious.
For one constituent part of Christianity quite as much as faith in God's
living power in the world is the other element that everywhere we
resolutely count on finite causes, for the reason that the moral work
demanded of us so requires. But in fact is there a more effective, or
indeed *another absolutely effective*, safeguard against all such aberrations
than simple inflexible *Christian faith in God*? I should think not. But
on the other hand that very faith in God does not suffer itself to lose
hold of the truth that the earth is the Lord's, that everything comes
from Him, that here and in all quarters He works miracles which daily
encompass us, and that according to His good pleasure He also uses
extraordinary means to enable faith to trace His presence and omni-
potence. The conclusion therefore must be that here there is no
contradiction in our knowledge and in our position in the world.

But now in one other point it is supposed that after all an irreconcilable opposition between Christian faith and modern science comes to
light. God's purpose in and with *men* is posited by Christian faith as the
purpose of the worlds. But the theatre for men and their history is *the
earth*. Modern science, however, has taught us to recognise this earth
on which we live as a vanishing point in the universe. Is it consistent
then with such knowledge to declare a kingdom of God which has to
be realised among the inhabitants of the earth to be the purpose of the
worlds, a faith determined by that conviction to be the highest knowledge answering to reason? Is there not here a contradiction of the kind
mentioned lying open to view? I do not think that can be affirmed on
good grounds. However, some remarks are necessary on the subject.

In the first place, as appears from all that has already been said, it is an
established fact that we can arrive at a highest grade of knowledge, a
view of the world as a whole, only from our *human* standpoint, or can,
say, give a sketch of such knowledge. He who does not renounce the

highest knowledge in every form—and he who does so judges un-reasonably—must conform himself to this inevitable position of matters. It would be unchanged although one declined to take his stand on human history and wished rather to attempt to start with the *knowledge of the universe.* The sole consequence would rather be that such an one would abstract from the peculiarity of human life as mental, from its concrete definiteness, and would take *human existence as it forms a part of finite existence,* and is therefore for an abstract view equal to everything that exists, as his point of departure. But that cannot be justified by any rational rule. No one can even think of it who does not commit the error in principle of wanting to attain the highest knowledge by means of an extension of common knowledge. Apart from that it is impossible that we can be on the right way to the highest knowledge when we purposely forget the more exact and more definite knowledge we have, in order to set out with the most general Category that can be conceived, one which is as abstract as it is meagre, that of Existence. In short, if there is to be a highest type of knowledge, and that is indispensable when we have regard to history, it can be gained only from a standpoint which is chosen in the history of the human race; and the extension of the universe, which is for us un-limited, and of which modern Astronomy gives us a glimpse, cannot be resorted to as the ground on which it is determined.

Further, this challenge addressed to the Christian theory of the world is based on an appreciation of things according to a *merely quantitative standard* which is palpably false. The fact that the earth, as it is said, is a vanishing point in the universe does not in itself by any means prevent its being true that on it that history is running its course in which the purpose of the worlds is to find its realisation. Or is not man too a vanishing point when regarded in comparison with the whole earth? And is the belief thereby refuted that in virtue of his mental endow-ments he is qualified to have *dominion* over the earth? But how then can it be inferred from the place which the earth was said to hold in the sum of things that it cannot in a corresponding manner possess an importance in that sum with which all else there is cannot compare? Such an assertion reckons on the impression which is *instinctively* formed on a comparison of the earth and the universe. On the ground of *rational* reflection it cannot be made good.

Finally, it follows from the nature of the highest knowledge as a

K

practical faith that we can, and indeed must, decline to regard man's scientific knowledge of the universe as an integral part of the highest knowledge. It is true that the relative infinity of the sum of things will always appear to Christian faith a proof of the infinite might and majesty of the Creator, and as such a proof will be precious to it. But we cannot make the universe intelligible as a means for the kingdom of God. This undertaking cannot be *theoretically* carried out even as respects the earth's general relations to the other worlds: in every instance it is imposed on us only as a *practical undertaking*—one, however, which from the nature of the case comes to nothing when we are confronted by the universe. In general the theoretical problem can be treated only in so far as the Christian faith is admitted, and there results from it that attempt at a Philosophy of Nature which we previously alluded to. But that attempt will refer to the universe as well as to the development of the earth, although only in the exceedingly general way which the meagreness of our knowledge of the universe implies. For the rest, the line to be followed here is determined by two considerations. On the one hand, we can and must neither deny nor affirm that our God, the Lord and Creator of the universe, pursues purposes in and with it even apart from the earth and its inhabitants. On the other hand, we must maintain in the most positive manner that these possible purposes coalesce with the purpose of the world as recognised by us, and therefore, if they do exist, presuppose a mental and historical life in the heavenly bodies which in its essence and core coincides with ours: that follows from the Christian conviction that it is participation *in the Divine life* itself to which Christ leads men, and that consequently there can be no supreme Divine purpose which surpasses that which is posited in and with that object.

But our knowledge has reference not merely to the world of sense, and beyond that to the universe as extending in Time and Space and for us infinite; it has reference equally to the mental life of men as it develops and takes form in history. There remains, therefore, the possibility that a contradiction may arise between Christian faith and this part of our knowledge. And in the abstract this *possibility* cannot be denied.

In general, it is true, such a contradiction may be held to be precluded, to be impossible. It is precisely from the facts of history that we have derived the proof of the reasonableness of the faith reposed in the Christian revelation. And already, too, we have mentioned the fact that Freedom, that human guilt springing from it, introduces an irrational element into history: that element cannot be turned against the Christian faith, which teaches us to understand human guilt without, however, declaring it to be necessary, an assertion which would contradict its essential nature. But if much remains unintelligible in detail, even of what we see daily before our eyes, we can content ourselves with the thought that our knowledge is fragmentary, with waiving the claim to possess perfect knowledge, and with living in that *Faith* which impels us to do our endeavour to secure improvement, and for the rest teaches us to *vanquish* what is unintelligible: the right to such self-restraint is involved from the first in the standpoint here adopted. However, if a contradiction accordingly does not require, generally speaking, to be feared, it is not meant that such an issue cannot come to light in connection with a single definite point, viz. *faith in revelation*. And that is the possibility regarding which I said it cannot *as such* be denied and must not be denied. The following is a more particular account of the matter.

Christian faith rests on the revelation of God in the history which reaches its completion in Christ. It includes, therefore, an affirmation as to historical matters, in particular as to the personal historical life of Jesus Christ. And it does so too in such wise that this affirmation as to what is historically *actual* is essential and indispensable to it, so that the faith itself stands or falls with the truth of that affirmation. From that there can be no deduction. The distinction drawn between a historical and an ideal Christ, by means of which an attempt has been made to prove that it is impossible in principle for a contradiction to arise here, must in all its forms be definitively and for ever rejected, because if really carried out it involves as its precise issue the destruction of our faith in the Christian revelation. All depends on the fact that in that faith we have to do not merely with an idea, with a thought, but with a *historical reality*: the historical person of Jesus Christ, his relation to God, has been essentially different from what is seen in the case of all other men; he is the Son who knows the Father, through the knowledge of whom all men are meant to come and can come to the knowledge of God. This fact is *the foundation of Christian faith and Christian hope*. The Christian feels what is a necessary consequence when he feels the denial of this fact to be a denial of the Christian faith.

It is what the religious certainty of the Christian is based upon.

But if we have to do with a historical fact, we have to do with something that is not merely given to faith, but can equally well be matter for *objective* historical study. Here, therefore, there remains a point where it is possible to refute the Christian faith. For if it can be demonstrated by means of historical investigation beyond the possibility of doubt that the Person of Jesus Christ is not of that nature which is assumed in the Christian faith, the faith must be held in that case to be refuted, to be *untrue*. This logical inference cannot be avoided. What is thereby affirmed is only the reverse side of what has just been said: if the fact of the historical revelation of God really has a fundamental significance for Christian faith, the proof that that revelation is not truth, but an illusion, is a destruction of the faith itself. The one thing is inseparably connected with the other.

Now it will be asked, of course, whether it can be conceived to be the case that by such historical argumentation a Christian should allow himself to be led away from the faith which approves itself in all the experiences of his life, the faith with which his whole life is entwined. In reply it has to be said that that case certainly will not occur, since from the nature of the subject the argumentation in question can never take the form of that which involves compulsion; and the inward certainty of faith itself appears as decisive evidence against its correctness. But assuming for a moment that the abstract possibility referred to were realised, that such counter-evidence were furnished—would the great *general* truths of Christianity thereupon cease to be true? would the highest ideals of humanity that history knows thereupon lose their splendour? Our thought instinctively rises up against that assumption, and it is probably from *that* circumstance principally that it has to be explained how the attempt to separate the question of the truth of Christianity from the historical question referring to the Person of its Founder always springs up anew. Nevertheless, that procedure is false. The two questions are inseparably bound up together, as the following consideration shows.

The first and immediate consequence of such a historical refutation of Christianity would be that religious *certainty* would have to cease, and where a person was convinced of the truth of the refutation would cease, too, without fail. The *content* of the faith would not yet lose its significance in consequence, but would in the first instance be affirmed as a Postulate, as a hypothetical truth of reason. But the matter could not permanently rest there. The conscience in its anguish can never find rest in a conjecture. Without faith in the revelation of that love of God in Christ which forgives sins that conscience would have to despair. But since the impulse to seek life is indestructible as such, despair can never be the last word for the community or even for the majority. A way of escape must therefore be sought otherwise. But such a way can only be found when the moral requirement is somehow weakened, when personal responsibility is put in question. On this basis, therefore, the chief and fundamental truth of Christianity itself becomes matter of doubt and practical denial. On the other hand, we have the imperative consideration that if the truth of Christianity is presupposed, there would have to be a corresponding revelation of God in the world If, therefore, it were demonstrated that there was no such revelation, that would be identical with a real demolition of the truth of reason, that being the only form which Christian truth could still claim to possess. It is of no use, therefore, to shade away the facts of the case. The refutation of the faith reposed in the Christian revelation would necessarily take the form of a refutation of Christianity itself; it would be identical with an overthrow of the highest historical ideals of humanity. Not, of course, as if every individual who doubts revelation therefore denies the latter also. In every particular case such consequences may encounter incalculable delay owing to inherited dispositions and an acquired bent of feeling. But nevertheless, if we look at the broad and general aspect of the matter, they are fully realised. If we cease to believe in Christ, our whole civilisation must in process of time sink back from the stage attained by Christianity to that of heathenism—there can be no other result than that. The signs of the times, too, certainly do not contradict the statement.

But if there seems to be implied in this a possible exposure of the Christian faith to danger, there is on the other hand strong support hereby supplied to faith. He who cannot allow himself to despair of the highest ideals of humanity and of the reason in history will have to decide for faith in *the revelation of God in Christ*. And as respects historical research itself it is really not the case at all that the denial of faith would be favoured by it. Only a theory of the world which has ceased to be Christian, not historical research itself, leads to such results. True, that research cannot in itself constrain one to have faith in the revelation of God in Christ. In order that one may arrive at that conclusion faith is required, that view of reason which surveys the world as a whole. The historical facts, however, do not tell against but for him who in faith combines them in the judgment that a revelation of God has to be recognised in Christ. And since that faith has reason at the same time on its side, there is no real danger to be feared from this possible refutation of Christianity. The reflections just offered on subject have not the significance of bringing to consciousness the fact that faith in the perfected revelation of God in the personal historical life of Jesus Christ is the inalienable foundation of the Christian faith, and thereby also of the highest truth of reason.

Consequently we affirm that the apprehension lest a contradiction may arise between the rest of man's knowledge and the knowledge which faith attains is unfounded. Christianity approves itself in this indirect way also as the truth which answers to reason.

The Truth of the Christian Religion
(trans. by G. Ferries), ii, pp. *385–408*

PART V

ADOLF VON HARNACK

CATHOLICISM

The Gospel did not come into the world as a statutory religion, and therefore none of the forms in which it assumed intellectual and social expression—not even the earliest—can be regarded as possessing a classical and permanent character. The historian must always keep this guiding idea before him when he undertakes to trace the course of the Christian religion through the centuries from the apostolic age downwards. As Christianity rises above all antitheses of the Here and the Beyond, life and death, work and the shunning of the world, reason and ecstasy, Hebraism and Hellenism, it can also exist under the most diverse conditions; just as it was originally amid the wreck of the Jewish religion that it developed its power. Not only can it so exist—it must do so, if it is to be the religion of the living and is itself to live. As a Gospel it has only *one* aim—the finding of the living God, the finding of him by every individual as *his* God, and as the source of strength and joy and peace. How this aim is progressively realised through the centuries—whether with the co-efficients of Hebraism or Hellenism, of the shunning of the world or of civilisation, of Gnosticism or of Agnosticism, of ecclesiastical institution or of perfectly free union, or by whatever other kinds of bark the core may be protected, the sap allowed to rise—is a matter that is of secondary moment, that is exposed to change, that belongs to the centuries, that comes with them and with them perishes.

Now the greatest transformation which the new religion ever experienced—almost greater even than that which gave rise to the Gentile Church and thrust the Palestinian communities into the background—falls in the second century of our era, and therefore in the period which we shall consider in the present lecture.

If we place ourselves at about the year *200*, about a hundred or a hundred and twenty years after the apostolic age—not more than three or four generations had gone by since that age came to an end—what kind of spectacle does the Christian religion offer?

We see a great ecclesiastical and political community, and side by side with it numerous "sects" calling themselves Christian, but denied the name and bitterly opposed. That great ecclesiastical and political community presents itself as a league of individual communities spanning the Empire from end to end. Although independent they are all constituted essentially alike, and interconnected by one and the same law of doctrine, and by fixed rules for the purposes of intercommunion. The law of doctrine seems at first sight to be of small scope, but all its tenets are of the widest significance; and together they embrace a profusion of metaphysical, cosmological, and historical problems, give them definite answers, and supply particulars of mankind's development from the creation up to its future form of existence. Jesus' injunctions for the conduct of life are not included in this law of doctrine; as the "rule of discipline" they were sharply distinguished from the "rule of faith". Each church, however, also presents itself as an institution for public worship, where God is honoured in conformity with a solemn ritual. The distinction between priests and laymen is already a well-marked characteristic of this institution; certain acts of divine worship can be performed only by the priest; his mediation is an absolute necessity. It is only by mediation that a man can approach God at all, by the mediation of right doctrine, right ordinance, and a sacred book. The living faith seems to be transformed into a creed to be believed; devotion to Christ, into Christology; the ardent hope for the coming of "the kingdom", into a doctrine of immortality and deification; prophecy, into technical exegesis and theological learning; the ministers of the Spirit, into clerics; the brothers, into laymen in a state of tutelage; miracles and miraculous cures disappear altogether, or else are priestly devices; fervent prayers become solemn hymns and litanies; the "Spirit" becomes law and compulsion. At the same time individual Christians are in full touch with the life of the world, and the burning question is, "In how much of this life may I take part without losing my position as a Christian?" This enormous transformation took place within a hundred and twenty years. The first thing which we have to determine is, How did that happen? next, Did the Gospel succeed in holding its own amid this change, and how did it do so?

Before, however, we try to answer these two questions, we must call to mind a piece of advice which no historian ought ever to neglect. Anyone who wants to determine the real value and significance of any great phenomenon or mighty product of history must first and foremost inquire into the work which it accomplished, or, as the case may be, into the problem which it solved. As every individual has a right to be judged, not by this or that virtue or defect, not by his talents or by his frailties, but by what he has done, so the great edifices of history, the States and the Churches, must be estimated first and foremost, we may perhaps say, exclusively, by what they have achieved. It is *the work done* that forms the decisive test. With any other test we are involved in judgments of the vaguest kind, now optimistic, now pessimistic, and mere historical twaddle. So here, too, in considering the church as developed into Catholicism, we must first of all ask, In what did its work consist? What problem did it solve? What did it achieve? I will answer the last question first. It achieved two things: it waged war with nature-worship, polytheism, and political religion, and beat them back with great energy; and it exploded the dualistic philosophy of religion. Had the Church at the beginning of the third century been asked in tones of reproach, "How could you recede so far from where you began? to what have you come?" it might have answered: "Yes, it is to this that I have come; I have been obliged to discard much and admit much; I have had to fight—my body is full of scars, and my clothes are covered with dust; but I have won my battles and built my house; I have beaten back polytheism; I have disabled and almost annihilated that monstrous abortion, political religion; I have resisted the enticements of a subtle religious philosophy, and victoriously encountered it with God the almighty Creator of all things; lastly, I have reared a great building, a fortress with towers and bulwarks, where I guard my treasure and protect the weak." This is the answer which the Church might have given, and truthfully given. But, some one may object, it was no great achievement to wage war with nature-worship and polytheism, and to beat them back; they had already rotted and decayed, and had little strength left. The objection does not hold. Many of the forms in which that species of religion had taken shape were, no doubt, antiquated and approaching extinction, but the religion itself, *the religion of nature*, was a mighty foe. It even still avails to beguile our souls and touch our heart-strings with effect, when an inspired prophet voices its message; how much more so then! The hymn to the Sun, giving life to all that lives, produced a profound and lifelong religious impression even upon a Goethe, and made him into a Sun-worshipper. But how overpowering it was in the days before science had banished the gods from nature. Christianity exploded the religion of nature—exploded it not for this or that individual; that was already done—but exploded it in the sense that there was now a large and compact community refuting nature-worship and poly-theism by its impressive doctrines, and affording the deeper religious temper stay and support. And then political religion! Behind the imperial cult there was the whole power of the state, and to come to terms with it looked so safe and easy—yet the Church did not yield a single inch; it abolished the imperial system of state-idols. It was to place an irremovable landmark between religion and politics, between God and Caesar, that the martyrs shed their blood. Lastly, in an age that was deeply moved by questions of religious philosophy, the Church maintained a firm front against all the speculative ideas of dualism; and, although these ideas often seemed to approximate closely to its own position, it passionately met them with the mono-theistic view. The struggle here, however, was rendered all the harder by the fact that many Christians—and just the very prominent and gifted ones too—made common cause with the enemy, and themselves embraced the dualistic theory. The Church stood firm. If we recollect that, in spite of these counter-movements against the Graeco-Roman spirit, it also managed to attach this very spirit to itself—otherwise than Judaism, of whose dealings with the Greek world the saying holds, "You had power to draw but not to keep me"; if we recollect, further, that it was in the second century that the foundations of the whole of the ecclesiastical system prevailing up to the present day were laid, we can only be astonished at the greatness of the work which was then achieved.

We now return to the two questions which we raised: How was this great transformation accomplished? and did the Gospel hold its own amid this change, or, if so, how?

There were, if I am not mistaken, three leading forces engaged in bringing about this great revolution, and effecting the organisation of new forms. The first of these forces tallies with a universal law in the history of religion, for in every religious development we find it at work. When the second and third generations after the founding of a new religion have passed away; when hundreds, nay thousands, have become its adherents no longer through conversion but by the influences of tradition and of birth—despite Tertullian's saying: *fiunt, non nascuntur Christiani*; when those who have laid hold upon the faith as great spoil are joined by crowds of others who wrap it round them like an outer garment, a revolution always occurs. The religion of strong feeling and of the heart passes into the religion of custom and therefore of form and of law. A new religion may be instituted with the greatest vigour, the utmost enthusiasm, and a tremendous amount of inner emotion; it may at the same time lay ever so much stress on spiritual freedom—where was all this ever more powerfully expressed than in Paul's teaching?—and yet, even though believers be forced to be celibates and only adults be received, the process of solidifying and codifying the religion is bound to follow. Its forms then at once stiffen; in the very process of stiffening they receive for the first time a real significance, and new forms are added. Not only do they acquire the value of laws and regulations, but they come to be insensibly regarded as though they contained within them the very substance of religion; nay, as though they were themselves that substance. This is the way in which people who do not feel religion to be a reality are compelled to regard it, for otherwise they would have nothing at all; and this is the way in which those who continue really to live in it are compelled to handle it, or else they would be unable to exercise any influence upon others. The former are not by any means necessarily hypocrites. Real religion, of course, is a closed book to them; its most important element has evaporated. But there are various points of view from which a man may still be able to appreciate religion without living in it. He may appreciate it as discharging the functions of morality, or of police; above all he may appreciate it on aesthetic grounds. When the Romanticists re-introduced Catholicism into Germany and France at the beginning of the nineteenth century, Chateaubriand, more especially, was never tired of singing its praises and fancied that he had all the feelings of a Catholic. But an acute critic remarked that Monsieur Chateaubriand was mistaken in his feelings; he thought that he was a true Catholic, while as a matter of fact he was only standing before the ancient ruin of the Church and exclaiming: "How beautiful!" That is one of the ways in which a man can appreciate a religion without being an inward adherent of it; but there are many others, and, amongst them, some in which a nearer approach is made to its true substance. All of them, however, have this much in common, that any actual experience of religion is no longer felt, or felt only in an uncertain and intermittent way. Conversely, a high regard is paid to the outward shows and influences connected with it, and they are carefully maintained. Whatever finds expression in doctrines, regulations, ordinances and forms of public worship comes to be treated as the thing itself. This, then, is the first force at work in the transformation: *the original enthusiasm*, in the large sense of the word, *evaporates*, and the religion of law and form at once arises.

But not only did an original element evaporate in the course of the second century; another was introduced. Even had this youthful religion not severed the tie which bound it to Judaism, it would have been inevitably affected by the spirit and the civilisation of that Graeco-Roman world on whose soil it was permanently settled. But to what a much greater extent was it exposed to the influence of this spirit after being sharply severed from the Jewish religion and the Jewish nation. It hovered bodiless over the earth like a being of the air; bodiless and seeking a body. The spirit, no doubt, makes to itself its own body, but it does so by assimilating what is around it. The influx of Hellenism, of the Greek spirit, and the union of the Gospel with it, form the greatest fact in the history of the Church in the second century, and when the fact was once established as a foundation it continued through the following centuries. In the influence of Hellenism on the Christian religion three stages may be distinguished, and a preliminary stage as well. We have already mentioned the preliminary stage in a previous lecture. It is to be found in the circumstances in which the Gospel arose, and it formed a very condition of its appearance. Not until Alexander the Great had created an entirely new position of affairs, and the barriers separating the nations of the East from one another and from Hellenism had been destroyed, could Judaism free itself from its limitations and start upon its development into a religion for the world. The time was ripe when a man in the East could also breathe the air of Greece and see his spiritual horizon stretch beyond the limits of his own nation. Yet we cannot say that the earliest Christian writings, let alone the Gospel, show, to any considerable extent, the presence of a Greek element. If we are to look for it anywhere—apart from certain well-marked traces of it in Paul, Luke, and John—it must be in the *possibility* of the new religion appearing at all. We cannot enter further upon this question here. The first stage of any real influx of definitely Greek thought and Greek life is to be fixed at about the year *130*. It was then that the religious philosophy of Greece began to effect an entrance, and it went straight to the centre of the new religion. It sought to get into inner touch with Christianity, and, conversely, Christianity itself held out a hand to this ally. We are speaking oj Greek *philosophy*; as yet, there is no trace of mythology, Greek worship, and so on; all that was taken up into the Church, cautiously and under proper guarantees, was the great capital which philosophy had amassed since the days of Socrates. A century or so later, about the year *220* or *230*, the second stage begins: Greek mysteries, and Greek civilisation in the whole range of its development, exercise their influence on the Church, but not mythology and polytheism; these were still to come. Another century, however, had in its turn to elapse before Hellenism as a whole and in every phase of its development was established in the Church. Guarantees, of course, are not lacking here either, but for the most part they consist only in a change of label; the thing itself is taken over without alteration, and in the worship of the saints we see a regular Christian religion of a lower order arising. We are here concerned, however, not with the second and third stage, but only with that influx of the Greek spirit which was marked by the absorption of Greek philosophy and, particularly, of Platonism. Who can deny that elements here came together which stood in elective affinity? So much depth and delicacy of feeling, so much earnestness and dignity, and—above all—so strong a *monotheistic* piety were displayed in the religious ethics of the Greeks, acquired as it had been by hard toil on a basis of inner experience and metaphysical speculation, that the Christian religion could not pass this treasure by with indifference. There was much in it, indeed, which was defective and repellent; there was no personality visibly embodying its ethics as a living power; it still kept up a strange connexion with "demon-worship" and polytheism; but both as a whole and in its individual parts it was felt to contain a kindred element, and it was absorbed.

But besides the Greek ethics there was also a cosmological conception which the Church took over at this time, and which was destined in a

few decades to attain a commanding position in its doctrinal system—
the Logos. Starting from an examination of the world and the life
within, Greek thought had arrived at the conception of an *active
central idea*—by what stages we need not here mention. This central
idea represented the unity of the supreme principle of the world, of
thought, and of ethics; but it also represented, at the same time, the
divinity itself as a creative and active as distinguished from a quiescent
power. The most important step that was ever taken in the domain of
Christian doctrine was when the Christian apologists at the beginning
of the second century drew the equation: the Logos = Jesus Christ.
Ancient teachers before them had also called Christ "the Logos" among
the many predicates which they ascribed to him; nay, one of them,
John, had already formulated the proposition: "The Logos is Jesus
Christ." But with John this proposition had not become the basis of
every speculative idea about Christ; with him, too, "the Logos" was
only a predicate. But now teachers came forward who previous to
their conversion had been adherents of the platonico-stoical philosophy, and with whom the conception "Logos" formed an inalienable
part of a general philosophy of the world. They proclaimed that Jesus
Christ was the Logos incarnate, which had hitherto been revealed only
in the great effects which it exercised. In the place of the entirely
unintelligible conception "Messiah", an intelligible one was acquired
at a stroke; Christology, tottering under the exuberance of its own
affirmations, received a stable basis; Christ's significance for the world
was established; his mysterious relation to God was explained; the
cosmos, reason, and ethics, were comprehended as one. It was, indeed,
a marvellous formula; and was not the way prepared for it, nay
hastened, by the speculative ideas about the Messiah propounded by
Paul and other ancient teachers? The knowledge that the divine in
Christ must be conceived as the Logos opened up a number of problems, and at the same time set them definite limits and gave them
definite directives. Christ's unique character as opposed to all rivals
appeared to be established in the simplest fashion, and yet the conception provided thought with so much liberty and free play that
Christ could be regarded, as the need might arise, on the one side as
operative deity itself, and on the other as still the first born among
many brethren and as the first created of God.

What a proof it is of the impression which Christ's teaching created that Greek philosophers managed to identify him with the Logos! For the assertion that the incarnation of the Logos had taken place in an historical personage there had been no preparation. No philosophising Jew had ever thought of identifying the Messiah with the Logos; no Philo, for instance, ever entertained the idea of such an equation! *It gave a metaphysical significance to an historical fact; it drew into the domain of cosmology and religious philosophy a person who had appeared in time and space;* but by so distinguishing one person it raised all history to the plane of the cosmical movement.

The identification of the Logos with Christ was the determining factor in the fusion of Greek philosophy with the apostolic inheritance and led the more thoughtful Greeks to adopt the latter. Most of us regard this identification as inadmissible, because the way in which we conceive the world and ethics does not point to the existence of any logos at all. But a man must be blind not to see that for that age the appropriate formula for uniting the Christian religion with Greek thought was the Logos. Nor is it difficult even to-day to attach a valid meaning to the conception. An unmixed blessing it has not been. To a much larger extent than the earlier speculative ideas about Christ it absorbed men's interest; it withdrew their minds from the simplicity of the Gospel, and increasingly transformed it into a philosophy of religion. The proposition that the Logos had appeared among men had an intoxicating effect, but the enthusiasm and transport which it produced in the soul did not lead with any certainty to the God whom Jesus Christ proclaimed.

The loss of an original element and the gain of a fresh one, namely, the Greek, are insufficient to explain the great change which the Christian religion experienced in the second century. We must bear in mind, thirdly, the great struggle which that religion was then carrying on within its own domain. Parallel with the slow influx of the element of Greek philosophy experiments were being made all along the line in the direction of what may be briefly called "acute Hellenisation". While they offer us a most magnificent historical spectacle, in the period itself they were a terrible danger. More than any before it, the second century is the century of religious fusion, of theocracy. The problem was to bring Christianity into the realm of theocracy, as one element among others, although the chief. The "Hellenism" which made this endeavour had already attracted to itself all the mysteries, all the philosophy of Eastern worship, elements the most sublime and the most absurd, and by the never failing aid of philosophical, that is to say, of allegorical interpretation, had spun them all into a glittering web. It now fell upon—I cannot help so expressing it—the Christian religion. It was impressed by the sublime character of this religion; it did reverence to Jesus Christ as the Saviour of the world; it offered to give up everything that it possessed—all the treasures of its civilisation and its wisdom—to this message, if only the message would suffer them to stand. As though endowed with the right to rule, the message was to make its entry into a ready-made theory of the world and religion, and into mysteries already prepared for it. What a proof of the impression which this message made, and what a temptation! This "Gnosticism"—such is the name which the movement has received—strong and active in the plenitude of its religious experiments, established itself under Christ's name, developed a vigorous and abiding feeling for many Christian ideas, sought to give shape to what was still shapeless, to settle accounts with what was externally incomplete, and to bring the whole stream of the Christian movement into its own channel. The majority of the faithful, led by their bishops, so far from yielding to these enticements, took up the struggle with them in the conviction that they masked a demonic temptation. But struggle in this case meant definition, that is to say, drawing a sharp line of demarcation around what was Christian and declaring everything heathen that would not keep within it. *The struggle with Gnosticism compelled the Church to put its teaching, its worship, and its discipline, into fixed forms and ordinances, and to exclude everyone who would not yield them obedience.* In the conviction that it was everywhere only conserving and honouring what had been handed down, it never for a moment doubted that the obedience which it demanded was anything more than subjection to the divine will itself, and that in the doctrines with which it encountered the enemy it was exhibiting *the impress of religion itself.*

If by "Catholic" we mean the church of doctrine and of law, then the Catholic church had its origin in the struggle with Gnosticism. It had to pay a heavy price for the victory which kept that tendency at bay; we may almost say that the vanquished imposed their terms upon the victor: *Victi victoribus legem dederunt.* It kept Dualism and the acute phase of Hellenism at bay; but by becoming a community with a fully worked out scheme of doctrine, and a definite form of public worship, it was of necessity compelled to take on forms analogous to those which it combated in the Gnostics. To encounter our enemy's theses by setting up others one by one, is to change over to his ground. How much of its original freedom the Church sacrificed! It was now forced to say: You are no Christian, you cannot come into any relation with God at all, unless you have first of all acknowledged these doctrines, yielded obedience to these ordinances, and followed out definite forms of mediation. Nor was anyone to think a religious experience legitimate that had not been sanctioned by sound doctrine and approved by the priests. The Church found no other way and no other means of maintaining itself against Gnosticism, and what was set up as a protection against enemies from without became the palladium, nay, the very foundation, within. This entire development, it is true, would probably have taken place apart from the struggle in question—the two elements which we first discussed would have produced it—but that it took place so rapidly and assumed so positive, nay, so Draconian, a shape, was due to the fact that the struggle was one in which the very existence of the traditional religion was at stake. The superficial view that the personal ambition of certain individuals was at the bottom of the whole system of established ordinance and priesthood is absolutely untenable. The loss of the original, living element is by itself sufficient to explain the phenomena. *La médiocrité fonde l'autorité.* It is the man who knows religion only as usage and obedience that creates the priest, for the purpose of ridding himself of an essential part of the obligations which he feels by loading him with them. He also makes ordinances, for the semi-religious prefer an ordinance to a Gospel.

What is Christianity?
(trans. by T. B. Saunders, ed. 1957), pp. *190–209*

PART VI

AUGUSTE SABATIER

ON A SCIENTIFIC THEOLOGY

1. Conditions of a Scientific Theology

The time has gone by when theology, as a Roman matron her hand-maidens, held all other mental disciplines under its sovereign sway. That time will never return unless humanity, decrepit and senile, falls into a second childhood. To-day the situation is entirely reversed. The present question for theology is whether it may achieve a place in the consecrated choir of modern sciences, or whether it will be shut out for want of any common interest with them.

The scientific consciousness of our time recognises, in fact, no specifically sacred science, no science fallen from heaven and not the fruit of man's travail of mind. From its point of view the most transcendent theology, however saturated with mystery, is still a human thing. To take refuge behind a supernatural authority, that it may thus impose itself from without upon the mind, is in its opinion nothing other than gratuitously to cut itself off from all communion with the scientific labour of modern times. That which was once the dread privilege of theology has to-day become its fatal infirmity. The question is no longer of theology being the queen of the other sciences, but whether they will accept her as their sister.

She can be so accepted only on condition of herself becoming a science, distinct from the others of course, as to subject, but similar to them and of like nature with them as to method.

Two conditions are necessary to the constitution of a science: in the first place it must be competent to set apart from the wide domain of the real a well-defined field, large or small, which properly belongs to itself, that is, it must have a positive and definite object of study; in the second place, in its mode of study it must give up the old method of authority and own allegiance to the method of observation and experiment. Thus one after the other all modern sciences have thrown off the yoke of time-honoured authority and constituted themselves anew. Galileo, Bacon, Descartes, were the great initiators of the new era. Theology must undergo a like revolution if it will take its place as a factor in the encyclopaedic organism of human sciences.

The two conditions just stated are inseparable and mutually self-originating. It is because Catholic theology, far from renouncing the method of authority, has become more than ever subject to it, that it is unable to define its particular object. What is a *summa theologica*? If one subtracts from it that which properly belongs to rational philosophy, there is nothing left but an inorganic series of commentaries, classified by rubric, upon mysteries which are declared inaccessible alike to reason and human experience; so that we arrive at the singular and self-contradictory definition of a science whose object is those things which cannot be known. Whence it results that the object of theological science thus conceived is reduced to formulas that must be correctly repeated and obstinately defended, but which rest upon an obscure vacuum, an unknowable reality, whose purely verbal definition it is impossible to verify. How can such formulas be established except by the method of authority? Thus the dogma of the Trinity rests upon the authority of the bishops of Nicaea and Constantinople, who formulated it, and in the scientific order it has precisely the weight of the scientific competency of its authors. If it is canonised and declared intangible and indisputable, it is so by an authority of the same order as that which to-day in France forbids the discussion of the republican form of government. It is politics; it is not science.

This is why the Catholic church is obliged to have a science apart, separate universities, just as it separates the clergy from the laity and religious society from civil. The method of authority so entirely isolates Catholic theology from the general scientific movement that it is futile to enter into discussion with it, and generally it is set aside by mere preterition.

Entirely different is the history of Protestant theology. Finding a place in national universities by the same title as other humane disciplines, it has necessarily followed their progressive evolution, and like them has gradually freed itself from the method of authority, and taken possession of the restricted but positive domain which is its own.

Schleiermacher, who at the beginning of the last century was the initiator of the new theology, assigned to it the religious phenomenon as its object of study; and more especially the Christian phenomenon, which is only a higher form of the other; at the same time he laid upon it the method of psychological and historical observation. Religious facts, indeed, belong to the domain of consciousness; they can be grasped, verified, and described only by the observation of the religious psychologist or by the historic exegesis of documents in which the religious consciousness of the past has left its imprint. This is why the accurate delimitation of the object of theology brings in its train the substitution of the method of observation and experiment for the old method of authority. One had lost all the ground that the other is gaining, and the measure of the progress of the new method during the century is the measure of the scientific character of the new theology.

But it will still be long before the habits of the method of authority entirely disappear from theology. Far too frequently in discussions between theologians we meet forms of reasoning which bear its indelible mark. Such are the arguments drawn from practical utility, or religious fear. We cite two examples.

The difficulties raised by the question of the authenticity of St John's Gospel are well known. It is a problem of literary history, and should be discussed solely according to the strict method elsewhere used by literary history. How many religious critics have thought to supplement the notorious insufficiency of the traditional proofs by insisting that if this gospel is not the immediate work of the apostle, the son of Zebedee, the Christian religion is undermined! And it is by virtue of such reasoning that they hope to make the apostolicity of this writing an article of faith for the Christian conscience! It is almost as if a chemist should undertake to establish a theory as to the origin of quinine upon the fact that the doctors find it useful for the cure of fever. Science demands greater candour. There are in history certain things which one should be in a condition to affirm; there are also legendary things which must be recognised as such, and doubtful matters concerning which one must be willing to be in doubt until new light shines. We may indeed bring down the scales by throwing in some extrinsic matter, but that both falsifies the weight and shows a lack of scientific probity. If it is not historically demonstrated that the Fourth

Gospel is by the Apostle John, no extra-historical reasoning will make it so.

Another example: A certain school of theology which considers itself very much emancipated hopes to deduce the dogma of the divinity of Christ from the fact of his pre-existence, although there is no necessary connection between the notions of pre-existence and divinity, as is proved by Origen's theory of the pre-existence of human souls. And to command acceptance of the fact of the pre-existence of Jesus of Nazareth they add, as was urged concerning the Gospel of St John, that this is the keystone of the arch of the Christian religion, and that if it should be lost to dogmatics, the Christian faith would go with it. Thus they cut short the scientific study of the progressive formation and development of the notion of pre-existence among the Jews and early Christians, and by a sort of authoritative fiat they give the lie to the scientific character of theology. Theology cannot be a true science until it has been freed from these old tatters of a method which it professes to have abandoned.

The proper object of theology is the study of the religious phenomenon in general and the Christian phenomenon in particular; this is that section of reality which it is the duty of theology to study and make known to others. For however mysterious may be their first cause, and however complex may appear their manifestation, religious phenomena are psychological facts, which everyone discovers first in himself and then in the past. Theology therefore has two sources—psychology and history, and their union must constitute its entire method of observation, direct and indirect. History is psychology going back to the past as far and as fully as the documents permit; psychology is history carried down to the present moment and into the personal experience of the thinker. There is therefore no compromising dualism in the theological method. The more sincerely the method is applied the more serious will be its results. If mental probity is a duty in every order of research, it seems to be more imperatively so in the religious order, in which illusions, being more easy, call for the greater vigilance and disinterestedness. The theologian, knowing no sources of information beyond psychology and history, ought to be the most clear-sighted of psychologists and the most rigorous of critics. He can make his task a scientific work only on these two conditions.

2. Objectivity in Religious and Christian Experience

An invincible character of subjectivity is inherent in all human sciences, because all are in two respects dependent upon the forms of the sensitive faculty and the constitution of the mind. Mathematics is no exception, notwithstanding the realm of pure evidence in which it moves, for if from the formal point of view it is limited to the application of the logical principle of identity, $A = A$, from the material point of view it operates only upon the purely relative idea of size or quantity, and is based upon the notion of space to which we attain by means of abstraction. That which makes the objectivity of the natural sciences is, therefore, not that they find their object outside of the knowledge of it which we already possess, it is simply the unescapable necessity of the laws and conditions which determine knowledge. With regard to these laws and conditions the will of the thinking subject is powerless. He can make an abstraction of them, and the importance of the abstraction in each science remains exactly that of the objectivity of which the science may boast.

But moral sciences, and theology in particular, are subjective to a still higher degree. In fact the very object of their study, that is, the moral and religious life, is the creation of the free determinations of the Me, so that without these determinations of the will moral and religious morality would not even manifest itself to the conscience, and would awaken in us no image nor any idea. What is moral good, virtue, to him whose conscience imposes no obligation upon the will? What is God to him who is totally deprived of the religious sentiment, that is, of the sense of an inner relation with God? Now it is certain that the free will of the subject intervening here, it depends upon the subject whether the religious and moral quality of the life of the spirit is more or less clearly felt and perceived by the conscience. Therefore moral sciences are doubly subjective as compared with physical sciences.

And yet, the law according to which religious and moral phenomena become realised none the less ends in a sort of objectivity which it is necessary to define. The objectivity of the physical sciences if founded, as we have just seen, upon the absolute and constraining necessity imposed upon natural laws by the principle of causality which constitutes them. The moral law has doubtless not the same character, but it is subject to another sort of necessity, which may be described by Kant's expression, *Categorical imperative*. Moral obligation makes appeal to the decision of the Me, and consequently treasures and respects it; but on the other hand, is it not absolute in so far as it may prescribe and prephesy that *which ought to be?* Are not the idea of life and the idea of the good identical? If the law of duty is the immanent law of the life of the spirit, if outside of it life is overwhelmed and lost in animality, if the apostle's word is true, "The wages of sin is death"; if humanity makes no progress, fails to realise its true being or to advance toward its ideal, except by obedience; if necessity is laid upon individuals as upon nations either to make moral growth or become extinct; if this law commands universal evolution, marking its line—does it not become evident that on this side the law of duty shares in the objectivity of cosmic laws themselves, appearing as highest and most sovereign among them all?

Experience confirms this deduction. Morals and religion, issuing from the individualistic sphere of consciousness, become historic potencies, and with philosophy and science are the great creative potencies of civilisation, and the revelatory signs of the true nature of the human spirit. That historic objectivity which observation may grasp may at least not be denied them, and being granted, moral and religious science has at least an equal dignity with philosophy and history, in which it at the same time participates. Theology is in fact historical by the material upon which it works, and philosophical by the method according to which it is constructed.

It is a grave error to imagine, as is sometimes said, that scientific theology has for the object and material of its study only the religious or moral phenomena which take place in the individual conscience, and that it is consequently useless, because there is no good reason for supposing purely individual phenomena to be anything else than the dreams or illusions of the subject who experiences them. The moral and religious life is not only individual, it is collective. It is pre-eminently a social and human fact. It is with the moral as with the physical individual. However independent may be its life, it can develop only in the bosom of the family or the race. It is a drop of water in a river, a link in a chain. In its consciousness are individual phenomena ephemeral as a dream, no doubt, or as a caprice or a perverse passion, but there are also movements which, being repeated from end to end of the human chain, are thus prolonged; there are natural instincts which burst into flower and show their true importance only in the life of the entire species. Just as, in the physical order, the love of one sex for the other, instead of appearing to be an individual fugitive caprice, is the invincible power which preserves and propagates the species, so moral and religious inspiration is the mysterious breath which lifts up the human soul and from generation to generation carries man forward toward humanity.

It is impossible to insist too much upon the organic and indissoluble bond which thus attaches individual experience to historic and collective experience. Scientific theology considers them in their essential unity, and the object of its study lacks neither consistency nor greatness. Its problem is to formulate the theory of the religious and moral life of all humanity.

This programme cannot as yet be entirely filled. The religious archives of the human race have not yet been thoroughly explored, nor is religious psychology as yet sufficiently advanced. The science of religion must therefore be progressive; in common with the other sciences it will gain a new character which will earn for it credit in place of disdain. But if its pathway is undefined its direction is at least marked by two fixed points which experience has furnished. The first is the religious consciousness of savage and primitive man; the second is the religious consciousness of Jesus Christ, which has become the regulating principle of the Christian consciousness of civilised peoples.

To explain the ascending movement by which humanity has passed from one point to the other, to reveal the basis and essence of the Christian consciousness and explain its necessary relations with human consciousness in general and with modern culture in particular, this is the task with which modern theology is now confronted, and which it may undertake with some hope of success. The Christian consciousness is not merely an accidental form or part of the general religious consciousness of humanity, it is a necessary and dominant part of it, to which all the others tend as to their ideal, and in which alone they find their explanation and perfecting. It is with the final term of this evolution as with the summit of a mountain; the summit is a part of the mountain, but it dominates all the other parts in their ascending stages from the depths of the valley to itself, and by that fact it embraces them all and assigns to each its place and rank in the whole.

The line of evolution of all peoples as they press toward the realisation of the true humanity necessarily passes by way of Christianity. This is why scientific theology cannot be anything else than Christian theology.

3. Religion and Theology

It is impossible to grasp religious or moral experience in its pure and isolated condition. It is with it as with life, which nowhere and never manifests itself without matter, although neither its principle nor its power resides in matter. So the religious life cannot exist without belief, although belief is neither it principle nor its source. For this reason in these days men almost invariably, and with reason, distinguish between religion and theology.

This distinction, which forces itself upon the religious consciousness, implies at the outset two elements in piety. The pious emotion, by which I mean the need, the desire, and the impulse which disquiet the entire Me and inclines it toward God, is always accompanied by an intuition, arising from an ideal picture representing to consciousness the object which produces this kind of emotion. In its turn and under the influence of reflection this image is changed, in idea, into doctrine and dogma. Such is the psychological genesis of the religious phenomenon. Pure, abstract logic says that one must know before he can adore, historical psychology shows that in the first instance one desires, prays, adores, and thus comes to know, and that the definition of the object of adoration is drawn from the worship offered to it and the benefits expected from it. If, as it would be the part of widsom to do, we restrict the term faith to the moral act which inclines the soul toward God, we must say, not that belief, an essentially intellectual act, is the cause of faith, but that it is faith which produces belief. In the last analysis, the latter is simply the ideal expression of the former.

It is indeed true that in its turn belief, being preached, provokes faith, that is to say, the religious life; that there is a strong action and reaction between the two during their whole subsequent development. But we must be wary here; the belief which is brought to me from without by one of my brethren awakens the religious life in me only as it finds in me a latent need, a predisposition to faith. Otherwise it remains sterile, and I may even accept it unreservedly without by that becoming religious. Many so-called conversions are only parrot conversions.

God alone is the author of life. It is by good right that Christians say that faith, the earliest manifestation of the life of the soul, comes from the immanent action of God. Man, therefore, receives life, but makes his own belief. And this fact establishes a new and most important difference between the life of faith and the form of belief.

Let us follow it still farther. The propagation of life is not an individual act; it is a social act. The individual does not produce himself, he is produced in a society. An absolute and abstract individualism is false and sterile. Physiology denies it in the physical order, psychology in the moral and religious order. To propose to draw life from one's self like certain philosophers and theologians who hope to deduce their religious faith from a theoretical demonstration, is a dangerous delusion, an idealism which will soon leave them discouraged, sceptical, and powerless. We must place ourselves in the actuality of life. That which takes place for the physical life is precisely repeated in the animal life. The source of an individual's life is not in himself, but in society. The historic source of the religious life is in the religious society.

Without doubt the Spirit of God is its author. But the Spirit does not work by chance, accidentally and from without. The Spirit of life is incarnate and immanent in the religious society which it is continually creating and renewing. Assuredly it blows where it will, but if we may so speak no wind blows apart from the atmosphere; none comes from the azure realms of ether. The wind is found in the agitation of molecules of the air; so the mysterious action of the Spirit of God is found in the agitation of the spirits of men. Thence the vital bond of solidarity which unites the religious man to religious society, the Christian to Christian society. The saying of Cyprian, which Calvin emphatically made his own, is true: "The Church is the mother of all of whom God is the Father." And this is said, not to limit or deny the liberty of God or of man, but to show the organic conditions in which both liberties are invariably exercised.

Such is the order of life; quite other is the order of belief. God gives the first; he does not command the second; but he has bestowed upon man the faculties of imagination and intelligence that he may note the experiences of life, interpret and express them. Without the slightest doubt thoughts come from the heart and ideas are born of experience, but this is by an intellectual elaboration whose character is always and necessarily subjective and contingent. It is with religious ideas as with all others; we cannot cite a single one which came down ready-made from heaven, none which was not formed in a human brain, none whose genesis we cannot trace, and its development through generations. The bread of the spirit has its price equally with that of the body. Whence ensues this consequence: hereditary conceptions which were once individual conceptions are never absolute and may always be indefinitely modified by the travail of mind which created them.

Tempora mutantur, nos et mutamur in illis.

If the religious life implies faith, belief implies theology. In the first the soul is essentially receptive, in the other it is active and productive. And because the elaboration of doctrine is a work of intellectual activity it implies the responsibility of the theologian. Here, as in every other field of labour, man reaps what he has sown. To speak with the apostle, one man brings to this building gold, silver, excellent materials, another brings wood or stubble. The fire of time tests the value of the work of both.

Very different and even morally contradictory appear therefore the attitudes of the believer and the theologian. When, as in the case of the theologian, the same man is obliged to maintain both attitudes, how shall he reconcile them? From God, through the religious society in which he caused me to be born, I receive life, and that I may receive it I must be humble and docile; but my personal thought once thus aroused, I necessarily become the judge of the teaching I have received. Can I stand at the same time in the place of catechumen and critic; can I at once feel the dependence of my individual consciousness upon the collective consciousness apart from which my life must dwindle and die, and at the same time recognise the autonomy of my thought, without which I am no longer I, and cannot even have a personal faith? This problem is the problem of life. I escape from the tyranny of the Church by the intellectual and moral vigour by which I can distinguish between the work of God and the work of men in the very tradition of the Church itself; and I escape from the dangers of an individualism rooted in nothing, by the humility which reminds me that here below I am at school to others, while at the same time I must be the master of myself.

In fact, both these attitudes are imposed upon me by the needs of my nature. Each is justified by the other, and both make progress by mutual conflict. The things that I learn at the school of the past serve to fortify my own personality, and the stronger it grows, the more imperative becomes its duty to find its own place in the social order, and discover in this order its function and employment. To individualise in myself the faith of my fathers, while freeing it from all that was erroneous in that faith, to socialise my personal faith by freeing it from all egotism and gaining for it an ever clearer consciousness of being rooted in the past, and having much in common with the faith of the society of the present, this is my double task, the double rhythm of my inward life, by which I love both the tradition which compels me and the inward liberty which makes my dignity.

To remain loyal to the religious tradition of the past, to enhance its dignity in the present and carry it on into the future, this is the mission of the theologian.

Religions of Authority and Religions of the Spirit, pp. *345–56*

DOGMA

1. Definition

Dogma, in the strictest sense, is one or more doctrinal propositions which, in a religious society, and as a result of the decisions of the competent authority, have become the object of faith, and the rule of belief and practice.

It would not be enough to say that a religious society has dogmas as a political society has laws. For the first, it is a much greater necessity. Moral societies not only need to be governed; they need to define themselves and to explain their *raison d'être*. Now, they can only do this in their dogma.

Dogma therefore is a phenomenon of social life. One cannot conceive either dogma without a Church, or a Church without dogma. The two notions are correlative and inseparable.

There are three elements in dogma: a religious element, which springs from piety; an intellectual or philosophic element, which supposes reflection and discussion; and an element of authority, which comes from the Church. Dogma is a doctrine of which the Church has made a law.

All the peoples of antiquity believed that their legislation came from heaven. In like manner all the Churches have believed, and many of them still believe, that their dogmas, in their official form, have been directly given to them by God himself. The history of evolution, political and religious, has dissipated these illusions. Every law of righteousness and truth should, doubtless, be referred to the mysterious action of the Divine Spirit which works incessantly in the spirits of men; but, in its historical form, it bears, nevertheless, the stamp of the contingent conditions in which it is born. The genius of a people is nowhere more manifest than in its constitution and its laws, nor the soul and the original inspiration of a Church than in its dogmatic creations. The work always bears the moral impress of the workman.

It follows that a Church cannot claim for its dogma more authority than it possesses itself. Only a Church which is infallible can issue immutable dogmas. When Protestantism sets up such a pretension, it falls into a radical contradiction with its own principle, and that contradiction ruins all attempts of this kind.

In Catholicism the theory of the immutability of dogmas is opposed to history; in Protestantism it is opposed to logic. In both cases the affirmation is shown to be illusory. It is with dogmas, so long as they are alive, as it is with all living things; they are in a perpetual state of transformation. They only become immutable when they are dead, and they begin to die when they cease to be studied for their own sakes —that is, to be discussed.

Dogma, therefore, which serves as a law and visible bond to the Church, is neither the principle nor the foundation of religion. It is not primitive; it never appears until late in the history of religious evolution. "There were poets and orators," says Voltaire, "before there was a grammar and a rhetoric." Man chanted before he reasoned. Everywhere the prophet preceded the rabbi, and religion theology. It may be said, no doubt, that dogma is in religion, since it comes out of it; but it is in it as the fruits of Autumn are in the blossoms of Spring. Dogmas and fruits, in order to form and ripen, need long summers and much sunshine. The best way to describe their nature will be to trace their genesis.

2. The Genesis of Dogma

Dogma has its tap-root in religion. In every positive Religion there is an internal and an external element, a soul and a body. The soul is inward piety, the movement of adoration and of prayer, the divine sensibility of the heart; the body consists of external forms, of rites and dogmas, institutions and codes. Life consists in the organic union of these two elements. Without the soul, religion is but an empty form, a mere corpse. Without the body, which is the expression and the instrument of the soul, religion is indiscernible, unconscious, and unrealised.

Which of these two elements is primitive and generative? The answer is not doubtful. Modern psychology has learnt it in a manner never to be forgotten from Schleiermacher, Benjamin Constant, and Alexander Vinet. The principle of all religion is in piety, just as the principle of language is in thought, although it is not possible now to conceive of them as being separate. Consider a moment. That religion which time and custom have transformed, perhaps into a mechanical round of ceremonies, or into a system of abstractions and metaphysical theories, what was it at first? Trace it to its source, and you will find that these cold blocks of lava once came burning hot from an interior fire.

But this is the parting of the ways. This is the point at which religious minds separate into widely different groups.

Regarding religion as a saving institution in the form of a visible organised Church maintained by God and provided with all the means of grace, Catholicism was bound to end in a sort of mechanical psychology, and to explain the sentiment of piety as the inward effect of the outward and supernatural institution. This is done by Bellarmine and de Bonald, the most consistent of the Catholic theologians. Protestantism, on the contrary, which makes of the faith of the heart, of the immediate and personal relation of the soul to God, the very principle of justification, and of all religious life, was bound none the less logically to end, by analysis, in a more profound psychology, and to refer to an inward principle all the forms and manifestations of religion. Religious history thus becomes homogeneous, and runs parallel with that of all the other activities of the human mind.

None the less, this subjectivity of the religious principle frightens many good men. Persons devoted to practice, and unconsciously dominated by the habits and necessities of ecclesiastical government and religious teaching, hesitate to enter upon a road so naturally opened. As, from generation to generation, religion has been taught and propagated externally by the Church, the family, or special agents, it is impossible for them to imagine that it was not always so, and not to trace back to God himself that chain or tradition of external instruction. In which they are certainly right. Their only error, but it is a grave one, is to represent God as an ordinary teacher, the first of a series, who once acted, like the rest of them, upon His pupils from without; whereas God works in all souls, acts and teaches without ceasing through all human masters, and is present throughout the whole religious education of humanity.

Who does not see that to represent things otherwise is to remain in the crudest and least religious of anthropomorphisms? At bottom, these men are afraid of losing revelation, which they rightly judge to be inseparable from the very idea of religion. They object that piety and the awakening of the religious sentiment must have an objective cause, and that that cause can only be a revelation of God himself. Nothing is more true; but this revelation which is effected without, in the events of Nature or of History, is only known within, in and by the human consciousness. This inward inspiration alone enables religious men to interpret Nature and History religiously. Now, this interpretation is made by their intellect and according to the laws and conditions which regulate it. The religious phenomenon therefore has not two moments only, the objective revelation as a cause and the subjective piety as an effect; it has three, which always follow each other in the same order: the inner revelation of God, which produces the subjective piety of man, which, in its turn engenders the historical religious forms, rites, formularies of faith, sacred books, social creations, which we can know and describe as external facts. It will be seen what an error they commit, what a mistake they make, who identify the third term with the first, suppressing the second, which is the necessary link and forms the transition between the other two. Whoever will fathom this little problem in psychology, and reflect upon it with a little attention, will see that all religious revelation of God must necessarily pass through human subjectivity before arriving at historical objectivity.

Passing now from the intellectual interpretation to the intellectual expression of religion, and noting the successive stages through which it must necessarily advance towards dogma, I remark once more that man's first language is that of the imagination. The imagination of the child or of the savage animates, dramatises, and transfigures everything. It spontaneously engenders vivid and poetic images. At the beginning, religion, consisting chiefly of emotions, presentiments, movements of the heart, clothed itself in mythologic forms. . . . But the age of individual reflection comes. The image tends to change into the idea. Men interpret, define, translate it. The religious myth is replaced by the religious doctrine. These are at first entirely personal interpretations. Nevertheless, these opinions desire to propagate themselves, to become general, and, as they are imperfect and diverse, they engender conflicts which threaten to become schisms. Myths, appealing to the imagination merely, and only professing to translate the common emotion, draw souls together and fuse them into a real unity; individual reason, private exegesis, inevitably separates them. But the consciousness of the community, thus menaced, naturally reacts by the instincts of conservation. There is therefore a struggle between the two, and out of this conflict dogma is born.

A new element must intervene. There must be a Church. Now, all religions do not form churches. The phenomenon is only produced in the universalist and moral religions. Strictly speaking, there is no Church except in Christianity; and no dogmas save Christian dogmas. In ancient societies, where religion was confounded either with the State, or with the nationality, the religious unity was maintained and guaranteed by the same means as the political unity. There were no dogmas, because dogmas were of no use. As much may be said of Hebraism and of Islam: in them there were rites, external signs and seals, which sufficed to weld and to maintain the religious bond.

Dogma only arises when the religious society, distinguishing itself from the civil, becomes a moral society, recruiting itself by voluntary adherents. This society, like every other, gives to itself what it needs in order to live, to defend itself, and propagate itself. Doctrine necessarily becomes for it an essential thing; for in its doctrine it expresses its soul, its mission, its faith. It is necessary also that it should carry precision high enough to embrace and to translate all the moments of its religious experience and to eliminate all alien and hostile elements. Controversy springs up and threatens to rend it. The Church then chooses and formulates a definition of the point contested: it enacts it as the adequate expression of its faith, and sanctions it with all its objective authority: dogma is born. From that moment also the two correlative notions of *orthodoxy* and *heresy* are formed. Orthodoxy is official and collective doctrine; heresy is individual doctrine or interpretation. . . .

M

By and by symbols or confessions of faith are formed, and these become the standards of faith and practice in the various churches that adopt them.

This long evolution is fully justified in the eyes of reason. It is a movement of the mind as legitimate as it is necessary. The germ must become a tree, the child grow to manhood, the image be transformed into the idea, and poetry give place to prose. It is possible to be mistaken as to the nature, origin, and value of dogma, but not as to its necessity. The Church may make a different use of it in the future, but it will not be able to dispense with it, for the doctrinal form of religion answers to an imperative need of the epoch of intellectual growth at which we have arrived. No one can either reverse or arrest its development. . . .

The word dogma is anterior to Catholicism. It had two senses in Greek antiquity: a political and authoritarian sense, designating the decrees of popular assemblies and of kings; this is the meaning which dominates and characterises the Catholic notion of dogma. But the word had also in the schools of Greece an essentially philosophical and doctrinal meaning; it designated the characteristic doctrine of each school. The Protestant Churches have inherited this latter sense of the word: it is in perfect harmony with the spirit and the principle of Protestantism. Dogma, in the Protestant sense, means the doctrinal type generally received in a Church, and publicly expressed in its liturgy, its catechisms, its official teaching, and especially in its Confession of Faith.[1]

3. The Religious Value of Dogma

The intolerance of Catholic dogmatism has had consequences so revolting, and, in Protestantism, wherever this dogmatism has revived, it has given rise to conflicts so sterile and so lamentable, that certain minds have gone so far as to deny the utility of dogma in the largest

---

[1] Originally the word dogma signified a command, a precept, and not a truth (Luke ii. *1*, and the Septuagint of Dan. ii. *13*; vi. *8*; Esther iii. *9*; 2 Maccab. x. *8*, etc.). Ignatius of Antioch still uses the word in this sense. It is not until towards the time of Athanasius or of Augustine that it begins to be used of the doctrinal decisions of the Fathers, the Councils, and the Pope. (Cf. also Acts xv. *28, 29*. This is afterwards called a dogma, the only time it is used in the N.T. with reference to a decision of the Church.)

sense of the word, and have wished to suppress all doctrinal definition of the Christian Faith. To call dogma either divine in itself or evil in itself is to go to an unwarrantable extreme. In religious development, whether individual or social, it has an organic place that cannot be taken away from it, and a practical importance that cannot be contested.

Religious faith is a phenomenon of consciousness. God himself is its author and its cause; but it has for psychological factors all the elements of consciousness—feeling, volition, idea. It must never be forgotten that these verbal distinctions are pure abstractions; that these elements co-exist, and are enveloped and implicated with each other in the unity of the ego. In the living reality there has never existed feeling which did not carry within it some embryo of an idea and translate itself into some voluntary movement. . . . As it is impossible for thought not to manifest itself organically by gesture or language, so it is impossible for religion not to express itself in rites and dogmas.

No doubt, in the first period of physical life, sensation dominates, and at the *début* of religious life, feeling and imagination. But as science springs from sensation, so religious doctrine springs from piety. To say that "Christianity is a life, therefore it is not a doctrine" is to reason very badly. We should rather say, "Christianity is a life and therefore it engenders doctrine"; for man cannot live his life without thinking it. The two things are not hostile; they go together. In apostolic times the greatest of missionaries was the greatest of theologians. St Augustine at the end of the old world, Calvin, Luther, Zwingli, at the beginning of the modern world, followed the example of St Paul. When the sap of piety fails, theology withers. Protestant scholasticism corresponds to a decline of religious life. Spener, by re-opening the springs of piety, renewed the streams of theology. Without Pietism Germany would have had no Schleiermacher; without the religious revival at the beginning of this century we should have had neither Samuel Vincent nor Alexander Vinet.

If the life of a Church be compared to that of a plant, doctrine holds in it the place of the seed. Like the seed, doctrine is the last to be formed; it crowns and closes the annual cycle of vegetation; but it is necessary that it should form and ripen; for it carries within it the power of life and the germ of a new development. A Church without dogmas would be a sterile plant. But let not the partisans of dogmatic immutability triumph: let them pursue the comparison to the end: "Except a grain of wheat fall into the ground and *die*," said Jesus, "it bears no fruit." To be fruitful, dogma must be decomposed—that is to say, it must mix itself unceasingly with the evolution of human thought and die in it; it is the condition of perpetual resurrection.

Without being either absolute, or perfect in itself, then, dogma is absolutely necessary to the propagation and edification of the religious life. The Church has a pedagogic mission that could not be fulfilled without it. It bears souls, nourishes them and brings them up. Its rôle is that of a mother. In that educative mission, we may add, the mother finds the principle and aim of her authority, the reason and the limit of her tutelage. In this sense, dogma is never without authority. But this same pedagogic authority is neither absolute nor eternal; it has a double limit, in the nature of the pupil's soul, which it ought to respect, and in the end it would attain, the making of free men, adult Christians, the sons of God in the image of Christ and in immediate relationship to the Father. If dogma is the heritage of the past transmitted by the Church, it is the children's duty first to receive it, and then to add to its value by continually reforming it, since that is the only way to keep it alive and to render it truly useful and fruitful in the moral development of humanity. It is therefore to this idea of necessary dogma, but of dogma necessarily historical and changing, that we must henceforth accustom ourselves; and we shall most easily habituate ourselves to it by tracing its evolution in the past.

Outlines of a Philosophy of Religion
(trans. by T. A. Seed, ed. *1957*), pp. *223–37*

PROTESTANT CHRISTIANITY

It is strangely to mistake the nature of the Protestant Reformation of the sixteenth century to see in it a sort of semi-rationalism, the inconsistent exercise of free examination, or the revolutionary introduction of a foreign philosophical principle into the warp and woof of Christianity. You have only to read the biography of the Reformers and to make a slight analysis of their soul to form an entirely different idea of their work. The first and almost the only question which preoccupies and troubles them is an exclusively religious and practical question: "What must we do in order to be justified before God? How may we attain to peace of soul and to the assurance of pardon and of life eternal?" To find this peace, this pardon and salvation, which the Church could not procure for them, they determined to turn back and quench their thirst at the primitive sources of the Gospel. They went back to the original documents because they were persuaded that Christianity had been corrupted in the course of centuries; they wished to have it in its purity. Their whole reformation was to consist in this restoration of primitive truth.

But history never recommences. This return to the past and this re-reading of the Bible were accompanied by a religious experience and an act of consciousness which made of their enterprise something essentially new and original, and which rendered it immeasurably fruitful. It is unnecessary to seek elsewhere than in psychological experience the germ of Protestantism. It was in the humble cell of a convent at Erfurt and in the soul of a poor monk that the drama was first enacted from which sprang the revolution that has changed the face of the world.

Luther entered the convent with a faith in the authority of the Church and in the efficacy of its rites as serious and entire as that of any monk. "If it was possible," he said afterwards, "to reach Heaven by monkery, I was resolved to reach it by that road." For years he shrank from nothing that might render God propitious; he multiplied his acts of devotion and his works of penance. There is a striking analogy between the experiences of Luther under the monachal régime and those of Saul of Tarsus under the discipline of the Pharisaic Law. The *dénoûment* was the same. For the second time, the system of pious works was found powerless to appease a conscience which roused against itself the rigour of its own ideal. This struggle against an external law could only exasperate the sense of sin to the point of despair. Paul and Luther, in precisely the same manner, experienced the inward emptiness and radical worthlessness of the religious system in which they had been trained. The more they had tried to realise it in its perfection, the more had they found it wanting. Catholicism, considered as a means of salvation, was rejected by the religious and moral consciousness of Luther, before it was condemned by exegesis and by reasoning. To reach this sentence without appeal the Saxon monk had but to maintain inflexible the demands of the divine law and to measure, without illusion, the abyss that separated him from God, and that no human works could fill. It was in this way that he found himself shut up to the essence of the Gospel of Jesus Christ; he found the peace that fled from him in the pure and simple acceptance of the glad tidings of the paternal love of God, in the confidence that he gives gratuitously that which man can never conquer for himself, namely, the remission of sins and the certitude of eternal life. What then is faith? Is it still intellectual adhesion to dogmas or submission to an external authority? No. It is an act of confidence, the act of a childlike heart, which finds with joy the Father whom it knew not, and whom, without presumption, it is happy henceforth to hold with both its hands. That is what Luther found in Paul's great words: "The just shall live by faith." In this radical transformation of the notion of faith restored to its evangelical meaning is to be found the principle of the greatest religious revolution effected in the world since the preaching of Jesus.

Let us therefore here set forth the radical opposition between the Catholic principle and the Protestant principle in order that we may thoroughly understand the internecine war that was henceforth to be waged between them. In vain will eminent men in both camps, with the most generous and conciliatory intentions, arise and endeavour to find some middle ground, and effect a pacific reunion of the two halves of Christendom. All compromises, all diplomatic negotiations, will fail, because each of the two principles can only subsist by the negation of the other. Having attained to salvation, to full communion with God, independently of and in collision with the authority and the discipline of the sacerdotal Church, how could Luther recognise them any longer as divine and submit to them with sincerity and confidence? The ancient edifice had been the more thoroughly ruined, inasmuch as it had become useless and had been replaced. The originality of Luther consisted in this: his religious enfranchisement sprang from his own piety, and he founded his freedom on his sense of sonship, on the sense he had of his quality and titles as a child and heir of God. How could such a consciousness submit itself to the yoke again without denying itself? Catholicism, on the other hand, cannot be less intransigeant. To recognise in any degree whatever that it is possible to a Christian to enjoy pardon and the sense of the divine fatherhood apart from its dogmas and its priesthood, would not this be to abdicate all its pretensions, and to transform itself to the point of destruction?

No doubt, in actual life, this opposition is attenuated by the fact that in all Catholicism there is a latent Protestantism, and in all Protestantism a latent Catholicism. Between Port-Royal and Geneva, between Bossuet and Leibniz, between Leo XIII and the Anglican Church, the distance seems but little. It is an illusion. Like two electricities of the same name, no sooner do they come into contact than they repel each other and separate more widely than before. In Catholicism Christianity tends to realise itself as a theocratic institution; it becomes an external law, a supernatural power, which, from without, imposes itself on individuals and on peoples. In Protestantism, on the contrary, Christianity is brought back from the exterior to the interior; it plants itself in the soul as a principle of subjective inspiration which, acting organically on individual and social life, transforms it and elevates it progressively without denaturalising and doing violence to it. Protestant subjectivity becomes spontaneity and liberty, just as necessarily as Catholic objectivity becomes supernaturalism and clerical tyranny. The religious element is no longer separated from the moral element; it no longer asserts itself as a truth or a morality superior to human truth and human morality. The intensity of the religious life is no longer measured by the number or the fervour of pious works or ritual practices, but by the sincerity and elevation of the life of the spirit. All asceticism is radically suppressed. Science is set free along with conscience; the political life of the peoples, as well as the inner life of the Christian. Man escapes from tutelage, and in all departments comes into possession of himself, into the full and free development of his being, into his majority.

This subjective character of a religion strictly moral stamps itself with energy on all the specific doctrines of Protestantism. It would be superfluous to dwell upon the doctrine of justification by faith; its subjective character is evident. No doubt the term justification has a legal colour and awakens the idea of a tribunal. But it must not be forgotten that this tribunal is nothing but the inner court where man and God meet each other face to face, where man is accused by his own conscience, and where the sentence which absolves him is the inward witness of the Holy Spirit, heard by him alone.

The doctrine of the sovereign authority of Scripture in matters of faith might seem at first sight to set up an external authority. And it is very true that certain Protestants have often understood it in the

Catholic sense, and have employed it to exercise some violence on their own conscience or on the conscience of their brethren. But they never succeed for long; they soon fall into a too flagrant contradiction. The authority of the Bible is never separated in Protestantism from the right of the individual to interpret it freely, and from the personal duty of assimilating the truths he discovers in it. What therefore are those Protestants doing who attempt to set up a confession of faith as absolute and obligatory truth but imposing on their brethren their own subjective interpretation, and, consequently, denying to others the right which they exercise themselves? Nor let it be forgotten, on the other hand, that the obligation laid on each Christian to read the Bible and draw from it his faith is a perpetual and fruitful appeal to the energy of thought and to the autonomy of the inner life. The authority of Scripture, so far from being a menace to Christian liberty, is its invincible rampart. Not only has the Protestant Christian in the name of the Bible triumphed over eighteen centuries of tradition, but it is the Bible, an appeal to the Bible ever better understood, which has saved Protestant theology from scholasticism, which has prevented it from congealing in a confession of faith, and which, leaving the principle of the Gospel in an ideal transcendence in relation to all its historical expressions or realisations, has maintained, and still maintains, the spirit of reform in the Churches of the Reformation.

The doctrines of grace and of predestination, which are at the centre of Calvinism, have no other meaning. Souls religiously inert see in these doctrines nothing but an abuse of blind power, a sort of divine *fatum*, breaking every spring in the human soul. Nothing appears to be more oppressive or more immoral. But this is only an appearance. There is really no predestination for irreligious souls. This doctrine is but the expression of the inner basis of all true piety, which is nothing if it is not the sense, the feeling, of the presence and the sovereign and continuous action of God in each soul and in all the universe. No other sentiment gives so much spring and vigour to the human will, nothing raises it to such a height or makes it so invincible to all assaults from within and without. "If God be for us, who can be against us?" etc. (Rom. viii. *31-9*). How is it that the Calvinistic Puritans of New England were the founders of modern liberty, and the Jesuits, those admirable theorisers on freewill, the precursors of all the servitudes? It is with predestination as it is with religion itself. Conceived as exterior to the life of the soul, it gives birth, no doubt, to a crushing despotism; conceived as an inward inspiration, sustaining the initiative and even the liberty of the individual, it becomes, in the Christian soul, the source of a force which nothing can break or subdue.

But the point at which the antithesis between Protestantism and Catholicism becomes most patent is the doctrine of the natural priesthood of all Christians as opposed to that of the supernatural priesthood of a privileged clergy. The free and perpetual communion of believing souls with the Father is the foundation of the independence of each and of the fraternal equality of all. The tap-root of clericalism is cut. The individual is a priest before the interior altar of his conscience; the father is a priest in his household; the citizen, if so he wills, in the city.

The Catholic notion of dogma vanishes with all the rest. To speak of an immutable and infallible dogma, in Protestantism, is nonsense; that is to say, if we accept the dictionary definition of dogma—the promulgation by the Church of an absolute formula. The decision of a Church cannot have more authority than that Church itself. Now, no Protestant Church holds itself, or can hold itself without denying itself, to be infallible. How then could it communicate to its definitions an infallibility that it did not itself possess? Protestant confessions of faith are always conditioned in time, and can never be definitive; they are always revisable, consequently they are always liable to criticism and to reform. Thus ceases the solidification of traditional dogma. The old ice melts beneath the breath of knowledge and of piety. The river takes again its natural course, and evolution, under the control of a perpetual criticism, becomes the law of religious thought, as of all other human activities.

From these observations and analyses (necessarily abridged) the true nature of Protestantism will have become sufficiently clear. It is not a dogma set up in the face of another dogma, a Church in competition with a rival Church, a purified Catholicism opposed to a traditional Catholicism. It is more and better than a doctrine, it is a method; more and better than a better Church, it is a new form of piety; it is a different spirit, creating a new world and inaugurating for religious souls a new régime. It is equally evident that Protestantism cannot be imprisoned in any definitive form. It leads to variety of formulas, rites, and associations as necessarily as the Catholic principle leads to unity. No limit can be set to its development. Always interior, invisible, ideal, the religious principle that it represents accompanies the life and activity of the spirit into all the paths that man may pursue and in all the progress he may make. Nothing human is alien to it; nor is it alien to anything that is human. It solves the problem of liberty and authority as it is solved by free and ordered governments; it does not suppress either of the terms, but reconciles them by reducing authority to its pedagogic *rôle*, and by making the Christian spirit the soul and inner rule of liberty.

By very reason of its superiority, and of the conditions of general culture that it presupposes, this form of Christianity could only appear after all the others. The spirit can only become self-conscious by distinguishing itself from the body in which at first it seems as if diffused, and by opposing to it an energetic moral protest. "That is not first which is spiritual, but that which is natural; and afterwards that which is spiritual" (*1* Cor. xv. *46*. Cf. Gal. iv. *1–5*). This divine plan, which the apostle discovered in the ancient history of humanity, is repeated in the history of Christianity. The Messianic form corresponds to infancy, to that brief, happy age in which the impatient imagination nourishes itself on dreams and illusions which the experience of life soon dissipates without killing or even enfeebling the immortal hope at the heart of it. The Catholic form, which succeeds it, endures longer and corresponds to the age of adolescence, in which education is painfully prosecuted, and it demands a strict external discipline and masters whose authority must not be questioned or discussed. It was in this way that Catholic discipline and authority conducted the slow, laborious education of the pagan and barbarian world up to the sixteenth century.

But a moment must arrive when the work of education had succeeded, when the leading strings essential to childhood began to be a bondage and a hindrance. The pedagogic mission of the Church, like that of the family itself, had its limit and its term in the very function it fulfilled. That function was to make adult Christians and free men, not men without rule, but Christians having in themselves, in their conscience and their inner life, the supreme rule of their thought and conduct. This new age of autonomy, of firm possession of self, and of internal self-government, is that which Protestantism represents, and it could only commence in modern times—that is to say, with that general movement which, since the end of the Middle Ages, is leading humanity to an ever completer enfranchisement, and rendering it more universally and more individually responsible for its destinies.

It may be remarked that by this evolution, and under its Protestant form, the Christian principle was only returning to its pure essence and its primitive expression. It could only recognise itself, take cognisance of its true nature, separate itself from that which was not itself; it could only disencumber itself of every material, temporary, or local element, of all by which it had become surcharged in the course of ages, and which was neither religious nor moral, by remounting to its source, and by renewing its strength, through reflection and criticism, at its original springs. That is why Protestantism has taken the form of this return to the past, for in it Christianity does not surpass itself; it simply tries to know itself better and to become more faithful to its principle. In the consciousness of Christ, what did we find was the essence of the perfect and eternal piety? Nothing more than moral repentance, confidence in the love of the Father and the filial sense of his immediate, active presence in the heart: the indestructible foundation of our liberty, of our moral dignity, of our security, in face of the enigmas of the universe and the mysteries of death. Is it not to this eternal gospel that we must always return? To finish its course and complete its work, will humanity ever discover another viaticum that will better renew its courage and its hope? *Ibid.*, pp. *203–17*

PART VII

JOHN RÉVILLE

WHAT LIBERAL PROTESTANTISM STANDS FOR

Liberal Protestantism is not a closed religious system, strictly defined in a confession of faith or in an official catechism; it is essentially a personal matter. It is a general conception of religion, particularly of the Christian religion, under the shelter of which a great number of different doctrines may flourish. This is precisely the reason why it is so difficult to give a specific description of Liberal Protestantism, that is to say, to show plainly wherein lies its unity, often hidden from the eyes of the superficial observer beneath its many varieties.

Not so long ago such a statement would have sufficed to discredit Liberal Protestantism at the very outset. The value of a religion was said to be gauged by the unchangeable character of its ordinances and doctrines. To show the variations of Protestantism was then, even for great intellects, tantamount to condemning it irrevocably. A deeper knowledge of the history and a scientific study of modern religions have completely dispelled such an error. No one now, at least no well-instructed person, would write Bossuet's *Histoire des Variations*. For, on the one hand, modern history has shown in a striking manner that the most flourishing and fruitful religions are precisely those which exhibit the greatest number of specific varieties within the unity of their essential principles; on the other hand, the history of the past has taught us that every religion presents variations, clearly marked in proportion to the activity of the religion itself. Even those religions which have most narrowly bound themselves down to the letter of a religious text, or to the decrees of dogmatic authority, succeed, by their varieties of interpretation and of commentaries, in escaping from the dead level of an immutable uniformity. Wherever there is life there is movement, change, organic evolution. Only the dead religions have become for ever petrified in unchangeable forms.

Thus Liberal Protestantism does not attempt to conceal its varieties; on the contrary, it is inclined to see in them a proof of its vitality. But it claims to be more than a congeries of purely individual religious convictions or practices, for it embraces a certain number of essential principles which are common to all its adherents, and to which their individual varieties attach themselves. These are the principles which constitute its moral unity and which distinguish it from the other religious systems of our time.

The first of these principles, and one which may rightly be considered fundamental, is that religion does not consist in an acceptance of a body of metaphysical doctrines or dogmas, but in a religious attitude of the soul, manifested in a corresponding moral life. Hence, in fact, proceed its broad intellectual tolerance and its willingness to welcome different individual opinions. Liberal Protestantism is, first of all, Protestantism opposed to authority, to intellectual servitude in any shape, and to obligatory creeds. For, once grant that what regenerates man and, by rescuing him from spiritual death or preserving him from evil, saves him, is neither acceptance of certain theological doctrines, such as the Trinity, or Predestination, nor the practice of certain rites or sacraments, such as the Mass or Confession, and it becomes evident that there is no longer any reason for imposing these doctrines and other similar ones or making it obligatory to partake of such sacraments. What is needed is to develop in oneself and to spread abroad those principles of religious and moral life which illumine, raise, and strengthen the mind and the will. But moral consent and acceptance of religious faith cannot be obtained by force; they require free persuasion, instruction, spiritual propagandism and the hallowed contagion of the true and the good.

Liberal Protestantism is thus, as its name implies, a religion of spiritual freedom. It arose and has grown with liberalism and tolerance, those exquisite flowers of high mental culture, the noble efflorescence of the human soul, the harbingers of spiritual progress wherever they flourish. If, however, liberalism forbids any coercion in the mental sphere, it does not follow that a liberal is so far indifferent that, for him, all doctrines are equally good. He has preferences; he subscribes to some and rejects others. He believes in the salutary influence of what he looks upon as the truth and in the baleful consequences of error.

Although he does not arrogate to himself the right to impose truth or to persecute error, it is his bounden duty to propagate the one and to combat the other by lawful means.

Liberal Protestantism is not merely *Protestant Liberalism*. A moderately orthodox[1] believer may practise liberalism; he will not thereby become a Liberal Protestant. Use has given to this appellation a more definite meaning. What in French-speaking countries is termed *Liberal Protestantism*, what is named elsewhere *Broad, Modern,* or *Progressive Protestantism*, is not only liberalism in the matter of dogma or of doctrine, it is also a body of convictions, differing from the traditional doctrines of the Protestant Churches, but none the less looked upon by their adherents as the expression, at once more faithful and better suited to the present times, of the primitive spirit both of the Reformation and of the Gospel. The chief characteristic of Liberal Protestants is that they are independent of the authority of tradition in their respective Churches, claiming, nevertheless, to remain faithful to the fundamental principles of the Reformation and of the Christian religion as taught by Jesus Christ, not, indeed, by reproducing these principles in a servile manner and in the historical garb they wore at their first appearance, but by developing and perpetuating them in accordance with the needs of the present evolution of society and civilisation. This is precisely what we have now to elucidate; our contention can only be rightly understood in the light of history. The historical genesis of Liberal Protestantism will help us to understand its *raison d'être*, and to recognise in it the natural and logical outcome of the evolution of Christianity in modern times.

Modern Liberal Protestantism arose out of traditional Protestantism, by virtue of the same causes which, in the sixteenth century, made the Reformation proceed out of the Catholic Church. It is not, as ill-informed judges are sometimes pleased to proclaim, the result of

---

[1] A strictly orthodox believer cannot be liberal without inconsistency. For orthodoxy in every church proclaims itself to be that divine truth which alone is able to ensure salvation. It is impossible to hold such a doctrine and yet to admit the lawfulness of various doctrines within the religious society. The expression (moderately orthodox) is contradictory; a man cannot, on his own authority, make a choice in the body of revealed truths without substituting his own personal authority for that of divine truth. By such a term I mean those who naïvely look upon themselves as orthodox, without accepting dogma in its entirety, and who, in spite of themselves, come under the influence of liberal ideas.

caprice, of the imagination of individuals, or the negations of a few theologians eager for change.

The Reformation of the sixteenth century was the product of the Renaissance. When once the Renaissance had made known the original texts of the oldest Christian writings, and, above all, had introduced new and better methods of reading and interpreting them, the contrast between the teaching and the institutions of the Catholic Church on the one hand, and the teaching and narratives of the Bible on the other, called forth the righteous indignation of those who were both learned and pious. It was in the name of the Bible and primitive Christian truth at last recovered in documents worthy of credit, that they also took up the work of reform, vainly called for during two centuries by the best and most pious theologians and churchmen. To the authority of the Church, the guardian of venerable tradition, they opposed the authority of the Bible, which became henceforward the basis of Protestantism.

When we thus go back to the beginnings of the Reformation, we find that the Bible was for the Reformers, first and foremost an *historical authority*. The Church of the sixteenth century, as voiced by its Bishops, Popes and Councils, claimed to have faithfully preserved Christian truth and the means of grace granted by God in Jesus Christ to sinful humanity. The Reformers answered: "The oldest and most authentic documents which have preserved the teaching of Christ and the Apostles bear witness to the falsity of such a claim. Christian truth and the means of grace are there seen to be quite other than in the Catholic Church. Elementary good sense bids us trust the direct and immediate teaching of Christ and his Apostles rather than that of the Church, separated from its Founder by fifteen centuries. The tradition it embodies is now nothing short of a terrible perversion of true Christianity."

What was new and epoch-marking in this thesis? Not the fact of looking upon the Bible as the depository of divine revelation, the sacred book in which the Christian truths are to be found; the Catholic Church did not deny that. The main position of the Reformers, what ultimately led them to revolt against the Church, was simply this: the witness of the Bible is of more value than the voice of tradition, as heard in the Church, to teach us what manner of salvation Jesus Christ brought to men; in other words, the historical authority of the Bible is superior to that of tradition.

By the force of circumstances Protestants were soon led to carry to its extreme consequences this principle of the authority of the Scriptures. The first Reformers had exercised a certain freedom of judgment in their interpretation of the Bible; they made a distinction between the human elements, coming from the authors who drew up the different parts, and the divine substance of revelation itself. Luther used to say: "The word must be believed for its own sake, not for the sake of the preacher, even were it preached by all the angels," and he himself did not scruple to style the *Epistle of James* "an Epistle of straw." Impelled by Catholic controversialists, the disciples of the Reformers came at last to drop the distinction. The Bible, in its entirety, became in their eyes "The Word of God", a document divinely inspired from beginning to end, and, therefore, infallible. The Bible was not only the immediate witness of revelation, it now became the actual text of that revelation dictated by God, final, complete, delivered once for all, an infallible authority to be set up against the infallible authority of the Church.

But, in institutions as in ideas, there is an inner logic more powerful than the simple formal logic of party-men. The more men strove to magnify the authority of the Bible as against Catholic controversialists, the more they brought into light other fundamental principles of the Reformation, which had inspired the pioneers of Protestantism, although they had had no clear understanding of their true nature and immense import:—the principles of the *freedom of enquiry* and of the *religious supremacy of the individual conscience*. By taking their stand on the Bible in their revolt against Bishops and Popes, they were firmly convinced that they were opposing the authority of God to the authority of men. Yet, by what right had they taken so bold a step? In whose name, by virtue of what principle, had they proclaimed the duty of Christians to break with the accredited representatives of the Christian Church? It was, as stated above, in obedience to the evidence of reason, because their minds, better instructed, could not but recognise that the direct witness of the sacred writings was obviously worthier of credence than the utterances of Popes or Bishops in the sixteenth century as the means of learning the real work and teaching of Jesus Christ. What is Luther's last word, his final argument, when, at the Diet of Worms, he refuses to recant, despite the threats of the Emperor, the Pope's legate and the princes of the Church to compel

N

him? "If you do not convince me by the witness of the Scriptures or by *conclusive arguments*, I cannot and will not in anywise recant; *for it is a perilous thing to act against one's own conscience.*" What was the final sanction of the authority of Holy Scripture for the first French Calvinists? Was it not "the witness and inner working of the Holy Spirit", that is, the intimate and profound harmony of the individual soul with the truth which commands assent?

Doubtless the Reformers with one accord humiliate man's reason and proclaim the powerlessness of the conscience when abandoned to its own resources. They are intimately persuaded that the force of truth and life which impels them does not proceed from themselves; they recognise in it the grace of God and the spirit of Christ acting through the medium of Holy Scripture brought once more to light. But it is none the less *their* reason and *their* conscience which warrant this action, for the only fact they can point to in proof of the divine nature of the truth they are proclaiming is the cogency with which it commends itself to *their* mind and its holiness as felt by *their* conscience. In spite of all their assertions to the contrary, they cannot do otherwise than appeal to the reason and conscience of their contemporaries, to freedom of enquiry.

This imperative necessity becomes still more visible when the disciples of the Reformers are arguing with Catholic controversialists. Holy Scripture is their sole authority; it becomes henceforth the one infallible consignment of divine revelation. But Holy Scripture must be interpreted. The Old Testament is written in Hebrew, the New Testament in Greek. In order that Christians in the sixteenth century may know what it contains, they must have it translated and explained —a difficulty easily overcome! Translations and commentaries soon abound. But what happens now? Translations and commentaries are not at one. We all know that if, to a class of twenty pupils, the teacher dictates the words of a German or French exercise, no two translations out of the twenty will be exactly alike. How much more will this be true in the case of the Bible, the text of which is so extensive, complex, and, in many places, uncertain.

The Bible is infallible. Granted; but still we must ascertain what it teaches in order to know what Christians must do and believe. Who shall decide between the different translations and interpretations? Here the Catholic Church regained all her superiority from the standpoint of faith based on authority. The interpretation of the Scriptures, she asserted, must be warranted by the Church; she only is competent, being, as she is, the guardian of tradition, which alone enables us to understand and to complete the sacred text. The Protestants, to be sure, had little difficulty in showing the absurdity of such a claim, and, further, the inadmissibility of the interpretations given by the Church. But how were they to prove the superiority of their own interpretations, and, above all, how were they to choose between the numerous varieties which presented themselves? It is evident that here again they were forced to appeal to reason in order to solve their difficulties. The only way to establish the merit of a translation or of a commentary is to prove it by philological, grammatical or historical arguments. The Protestants did not neglect this method. Thus, in the last resort, the basis of Christian truth became the knowledge of the translator; this was the only guarantee one could have of possessing a right understanding of divine revelation.

The leading part taken by reason and free enquiry in Protestantism is still further attested by the efforts on the part of Protestants to sum up their beliefs in professions or confessions of faith. In face of the numerous theological and ecclesiastical varieties which had sprung from the Reformation, the political authorities desired to know precisely what were the doctrines held by the leading bodies with which they were conferring; the Churches already formed wished to ascertain under what conditions they might form an alliance. The question was now no longer simply to translate, but to set forth what was essential in God's revelation. Since the Bible is made up of books varying greatly in origin, since, moreover, it is not a book written by one and the same author, but a collection of works originally independent of each other and emanating from many authors, it contains a great number of incompatible doctrines and ideas. Thus there was here ample matter for disagreement among those who desired to reduce its teaching to a certain number of fundamental articles.

Further, it must be remembered that the first Reformers, so bold in their revolt against the institutions and rites of the Roman Church, had proved extremely conservative in the matter of dogma. Most anxious as they were to show that their opposition to the ecclesiastical authorities, now no longer faithful to their mission, was not the work of heretics, they had clung to the orthodox dogmas even more ardently than the Catholic Church of their day. In this they were still in bondage to the authority of that very tradition which they were elsewhere so vigorously casting off; having as yet only an inadequate knowledge of the history of dogma, neither they nor their successors ever doubted that the principal dogmas long ago promulgated by the Œcumenical Councils were the faithful expression of the Christian faith, and that consequently they were in harmony with the teaching of the Bible.

When, therefore, the disciples of the Reformers summarized their beliefs in confessions of faith, they introduced into them the principal dogmas of Œcumenical tradition side by side with the specific doctrines of the Reformation, the whole being placed under the aegis of the authority of the Bible. The more enlightened among them were not long in perceiving that a fair number of these dogmas were either foreign or contrary to the teaching of the Bible. They tried to correct them out of loyalty to the Bible. Dogmatic and Biblical confessions of faith were thus multiplied in the bosom of Protestantism and became the subject of endless controversies intended to establish their respective claims. In all these controversies to what could appeal be made? Once more, to exegesis, dialectics, argumentation, reason. The authority of the confession of faith ultimately rested upon reason. And those very theologians who, in theory, most flouted reason were not the least given to make use of it in practice.

The time arrived at last when, thanks to the advance of the philosophic spirit since Descartes, the more enlightened among Protestants came to understand that this same human reason—the limitations of which were continually being pointed out by the help of arguments which reason alone could furnish, and to which, nevertheless, men were ever appealing to justify themselves—was also one of God's gifts, the faculty which, in his Providence, He had ordained to enlighten men and to enable them to discern truth from error. A first embodiment of Liberal Protestantism came into being in the shape of Rationalism; and the principle of freedom of enquiry, inherent to Protestantism, at last became conscious of its own power.

As yet the notion of the infallibility of the Bible was too deeply rooted in men's minds to disappear at once. The evolution of religious beliefs is always and everywhere a slow process, because these beliefs are concerned with men's most sacred interests. At first Rationalistic Protestants strove to demonstrate that the teaching of the Bible was always in agreement with the requirements of reason. With this end in view most ingenious and, at times, naïve combinations were elaborated. Prodigies of exegesis were wrought in order that all the narratives of the Bible might be made to appear rational. It is easy to smile at them now: it would be more just to acknowledge the important services rendered by Rationalism in preventing the deplorable divorce of religion and reason. The first and most decisive step had now been taken; the authority of reason, even in the domain of religion, was admitted; all else was to follow of necessity.

New spiritual changes were taking place in our occidental world which were soon to find their counterpart in religious thought. The new astronomy completely overthrows the old ideas about the universe, inherited from antiquity, and which till now had held the field. The rising natural sciences, experimental physics and chemistry, substitute for the ignorance of former days a new conception of nature. Philosophical criticism saps the foundation of the older metaphysics, and on its ruins founds the sovereignty of the autonomous conscience. The revolution overthrows the old social order of things and proclaims the rights of man. Lastly, history, bringing back to light the civilisations of antiquity, and discovering the non-Christian races, gives birth to a new conception of humanity.

How could the infallibility of the Bible have withstood such onslaughts? The books of the Bible, written in antiquity, reflect the conceptions which were current in that part of the ancient world in which they were composed. For the Bible the earth is the centre of the universe, and heaven a region situated above the earth; possessing no knowledge of the laws of physics and chemistry, the Bible looks upon the realm of nature as miraculous; only a small portion of the world is familiar to it, and of mankind, outside the limited circle of its own horizon, it knows nothing. Thus it comes that the Bible contains countless errors in science, giving us, in the matter of the creation, the composition of the world, and the history of humanity, accounts which are irreconcilable with the best established conclusions of the natural sciences and with a comprehensive view of history.

When once enlightened Protestants had acknowledged *de jure* the authority of reason as their predecessors had sedulously maintained it *de facto*, the result of such a conflict could not remain doubtful. Just as Luther at Worms had said to the representatives of religious authority:

"I will not recant unless you convince me of error, for it is a perilous thing to act against one's own conscience";—so too every consistent Protestant must needs say to those who were bringing forward the teaching of the Bible as an answer to the sure results of the new sciences: I cannot surrender my convictions, unless you convince me by fair arguments that I am in the wrong; I cannot act in opposition to my conscience.

And, indeed, those who among Protestants still hold to the infallibility of the Bible are daily becoming fewer. Does this imply that Protestants have therefore given up the very principle upon which the Reformers had built? Not in the least. What they have given up is that false and inferred notion of the authority of the Holy Scriptures which the insufficiently informed disciples of the Reformers professed, namely, that the Bible is made up of the literal words of divine revelation, dictated by God, and that it contains no error. They have returned to the original Protestant principle of the authority of Scripture, to its *historical authority*, as legitimate to-day as it was at the beginning of the sixteenth century. To-day, as then, the Protestant justifies his opposition to Roman Catholicism by taking his stand on the Bible, and that because the Bible furnishes us, to-day as then, with the only authoritative record of the teaching and work of the prophets, of Jesus and his first disciples. When we want to know what is really Christian, we refuse, to-day as in the sixteenth century, to subordinate the direct and original testimony of the Biblical writings to the tardy tradition of the Roman Church, represented by her Councils and Popes, and when the two teachings disagree, we unhesitatingly maintain that preference must be given to the Biblical record. It was not otherwise at the dawn of the Reformation.

But, while thus retaining at its basis the principle of the authority of the Bible, as the historical witness to the sayings and life of Christ, modern Protestantism, enlightened by experience, proclaims without reserve *the authority of reason and conscience in the religious and moral life.* And in this Liberal Protestants are persuaded that they are remaining faithful to the true spirit of Protestantism, seeing that, from the beginning, the Reformers were obliged to appeal to the deep and intimate evidence of truth and to the sovereignty of the conscience as the ultimate justification of their work, and that, at all times, Protestants have been found making a loyal use of the weapons of reason to confound their enemies and propagate their own doctrines.

The wide space which we have just devoted to historical statements enables us to see that we are not departing from Protestant tradition when we assert the authority of reason and conscience in the realm of religion and merely proclaim the historical character of the authority of the Scriptures. Nor, in fact, do the great majority of Protestants in these days act otherwise, not even those of them who imagine they profess doctrines in agreement with the old confessions of faith. There are hardly any among them who do not set aside what in the Bible seems to them contrary to reason or what is condemned by their conscience. Now, as soon as the teaching of a religion is rejected at any single point in the name of reason, the authority of that religion becomes subordinated to the authority of reason.

In this legitimate and logical evolution of Protestantism, the chief characteristic of contemporary Liberal Protestantism is its greater consistency in applying the principles which we have just elucidated. If, in their dealings with Catholicism or even Protestant dogmatic orthodoxy, Liberal Protestants continue before all else to lay stress upon the historical authority of the Bible, in order to confound the ever-recurring claims of the Roman Church or of catholicising orthodoxy to represent the only genuine Christianity,—in their own religious and moral life they staunchly uphold the sovereign authority of reason and conscience, and this they profess loyally without feeling the need of taking shelter behind concessions to traditional ideas respecting the supernatural inspiration of the Bible.

Of course their attitude towards the Bible is one of deep veneration and real gratitude, but they can no longer look upon it as a book essentially unique and distinct from all the other literary productions of the past. Just because, in their eyes, the Bible is before all else a historical record, it is, in the full acceptation of the term, a human book, subject, like every other book, to the inexorable conditions of all human works. Passionately desirous to find its true meaning and bearing, they study it with every instrument which modern historical science and historical criticism place at their disposal. And, while they recognise that much is still uncertain or undecided in many of the positions of Biblical criticism, they cannot help accepting those of its conclusions which are well established. The Bible has thus come to be for them a twofold collection of Jewish or Christian books, originally independent of each other, and never meant by their respective writers to be gathered together into a single whole. By the simple fact, these books, going back to very different periods, do not always agree in their teaching or in their statements. A large number of them were re-edited in accordance with the literary habits of antiquity before assuming their final shape in the Canon as we now have it. The majority are not the work of the authors to whom they are attributed. Frequently it is difficult for us to arrive at their real text and true meaning. For a long time the limits of the Biblical collection were uncertain, some Canons including certain books which others definitely rejected. Almost all the narratives of the Bible come from the pen of writers who did not themselves witness the events which they record, but who, only having received them from a more or less faithful tradition, relate the facts in accordance with their own ideas.

In a word, the books of the Bible were subject to the same vicissitudes as the writings of antiquity in general. Nothing distinguishes them in this respect from the other literary works of ancient times, or rather they were even more subject to change than many other classical works, later in date and less exposed to alterations due to current opinion. How then shall we continue to speak of an inspiration peculiar to the Bible, and the exclusive privilege of writers raised, by divine intervention, above the natural conditions of their time and environment?

How, on the other hand, can we still claim to invest these books, so different in origin and so dubiously grouped together, with the character of exclusive channels of divine inspiration to the detriment of all the other historical, religious or moral writings of mankind, of those even in which we find the highest teaching, the loftiest aspirations, the noblest transports of the human soul? Assuredly such claims can no longer be made by thoughtful men who have definitely given up the dogma of the magical inspiration and infallible authority of the Holy Scriptures. Modern Liberal Protestantism, guided by the history of religions no less than by historical criticism, has ceased to claim for the writers of the Bible any exclusive and supernatural inspiration, either general or partial. If there are a great many pages in the Bible penetrated by a breath of the very deepest religious and moral inspiration, this inspiration does not differ in nature from that which, in every age, and in all the societies of the past, has raised thinkers, noble artists, poets, heroes of conscience, or great benefactors of humanity, above the miserable conditions of human mediocrity, and which, in the mystery of its inexplicable origin, is everywhere and at all times the divine agent of the slow ascent of humanity towards a higher life.

Will the Bible, then, be for modern Liberal Protestantism nothing but a historical record, good enough to confound the claims of the Roman Church, adequate, when checked by a discriminating historical criticism, to inform us as to the work and teaching of the prophets and Jesus, but divested of all supernatural attributes and special authority?

Well! even were the Bible nothing else, would not that suffice to ensure for it a position of the very highest importance? For, without it, we should probably not even know that Jesus ever lived, and we should be wholly unacquainted with his sayings and life.

But, again, there is this further consideration. If, in the eyes of modern Liberal Protestantism, the collection of literary productions which we name the Bible is invested with no supernatural halo and is the result of no magical inspiration marking it off from all other literary works, this entirely human Bible, for the very reason that it is truly and deeply human, stands out as one of the most wonderful and precious of productions, because it preserves the record of the noblest and holiest religious experiences which the human race has handed on to us—those, namely, of the prophets of Israel, and more especially of the greatest of them all, Jesus the Christ. This it is which constitutes the value of the Bible for us. It is through the Bible and in its pages alone that we are reached by those splendid minds, those matchless pleaders for justice, those heroes of indomitable hope and moral fortitude, those souls whose piety was so pure and holy that the mere fact of our listening to their exhortations and entering into their thoughts suffices to awaken new energies in our spiritual life.

The Bible is not only for us the record of a history which it is all-important that we should know. It is, further, at least in its best and most beautiful pages, a never-failing source of religious and moral education. According to the fine traditional expression it is the book of "edification"—that is to say, of the building up of our moral being: it strengthens and fosters all that is good and healthy in us.

That is why we continue to found our religious education and that of our children upon the Bible, without thereby excluding any other source of moral or religious life. If the Bible has preserved for us noble spiritual experiences, these are not to do away with the religious experiences passed through elsewhere than in Israel or among the first Christians. Wherever a generous thought is to be gleaned, a great and noble example admired, a precept of wisdom or virtue imbibed, a source of healthy active devotion drawn from, we have at heart to avail ourselves of these benefits, whatever be the race, religion, or philosophy whence they come to us. The only condition required for them to become sources of inspiration to us, is that they be justified by our reason and sanctioned by our conscience; for what is irrational or condemned by our conscience can in nowise be for us an element of religious or moral life. It is not because they are in the Bible that we meditate upon the exhortations of the prophets or the appeals of Christ; we do so because they are supremely beautiful and beneficent. And it is because we find them in the Bible that we turn to it, with the feeling, however, that we are quite free to condemn and reject anything which, in this same Bible, shocks our reason or is repugnant to our conscience.

Liberal Protestants mean to be freethinkers in the full and true acceptation of the term—that is to say, men who think freely, not professed unbelievers. They mean to be free believers—that is to say, men who, in the realm of the moral life and in the vast domain beyond the ken of positive science, found their beliefs on free enquiry and moral experience. They have thus the firm assurance of being the continuators of the Reformation, for the latter was no religious revolution ended once and for all in the sixteenth century, a *terminus ad quem* beyond which it is henceforth forbidden to advance; it is rather the proclamation of a principle which must engender its legitimate consequences, the *terminus a quo* of an evolution, the progress of which must needs be correlated to that of general civilisation. To be a Protestant is not to adhere to the doctrine of Luther, Calvin, or any other founder of the Protestant Churches. It means being inspired by the principles which were the *raison d'être* of their work, independently of their personalities, and which are destined to produce natural fruits in proportion as they become more and more openly displayed, and as those who hold them become more and more clearly imbued with them.

The supremacy of reason and conscience in religious matters as in all other departments of spiritual life, the historical authority of the Bible freely studied with all the resources furnished by science and apart from all sectarian prejudice, such are the fundamental principles of Liberal Protestantism.

Liberal Christianity (trans. by V. Leuliette), pp. *1–37*

PART VIII

JAMES FRANKLIN
BETHUNE-BAKER

JESUS AS HUMAN AND DIVINE[1]

Our subject is Jesus as "both human and divine", or, as I should prefer to put it, "the God-Man". We do not ask the old question, *Cur Deus homo?* nor even "How *can* this be?" But, accepting the fact of the *Deus homo*, we only ask: "How was it, how is it so?" What were the conditions of the synthesis? How is it related to the facts of our experience, and what does it mean to us? To clear the ground I would start with two or three premises, and the first of them is that "orthodoxy", in beginning with God, began at the wrong end.

The personality of Jesus is for religion, and for science properly so-called, a perennial problem. The Christian who consciously looks to him as Redeemer and Lord and Judge can leave the problem alone or acquiesce in the general opinion of his Church, clear-cut in expression but very vague in sense.

All Christian doctrine grows out of the puzzlement felt by the first generation of Christians. They knew he was a man in outward appearance and life, but there was something more which baffled them, and the doctrine that he was God as well as Man was an early result of reflexion on the facts of their actual experience.

In a recent controversy across the water, one of the protagonists said that he recognized the fact that Jesus was Man as well as God, but it didn't interest him: all he cared to know was how he was more than Man.

That was indeed the question which preoccupied the early Church— to such a degree that the manhood more and more receded behind the Godhead. Christian thought tended to begin at the unknown end. It

[1] A paper read at the Conference of Modern Churchmen held at Girton College, Cambridge, August *1923*.

was a Divine Person who had come into the world. God had been born as Man, without ceasing to be what he was before. This point of view presents us with a hopeless tangle of problems. Today, when in every department of investigation we begin with the relatively known and reason from what we find there to the unknown, it is Jesus as Man in his life in the world that we want to take as our starting point once again—as at the outset he was. That is what gives our modern study of Gospels and Gospel history its interest and importance. We know he was human, we believe he was also divine. It is by finding out how he was Man—what he was in his place in the historic process—that we may come to understand in what sense he was and is also God.

Parenthetically I would say: We must absolutely jettison the traditional doctrine that his personality was not human, but divine. To our modern categories of thought such a statement is a denial of the doctrine of the Incarnation. There is for us no such thing as human nature apart from human personality: the distinction that he was Man but not "a" man, while it has deep religious value,[1] has ceased to be tenable. The personality of Jesus is human—he is "whole" man even for Chalcedon: it is also divine for Christian faith and consciousness in all ages.

The question is one, primarily, for historical investigation. In this historical investigation I can make no use of the traditional beliefs in either his miraculous birth or his personal pre-existence. Both beliefs, no doubt, are of high religious value which Christianity must conserve. The former, like all docetic theories, stands for the fact of something "new" in human experience; but we know enough of the order of Nature now to discredit the ancient idea that the new can only come about by a break in the continuity of the order of Nature, and I can only regard this idea of miraculous birth as aetiological and honorific—in

---

[1]What I have in mind as the religious value, the truth, of this old distinction is retained and even enhanced for "modernists" in the modern emphasis on the fullness of our Lord's humanity. For what is meant is that Jesus does not stand alone as "a" man might be thought to stand, isolated from his fellows. He is one of them among them. He is identified with the whole experience of the race, within it, not outside it as an individual by himself. He is a member of the group, the family, of men, not separated and not separable from it. So like Adam he is representative—the one of the old, the other of the new, moral life of mankind. Without breach in continuity or solidarity a new character is given to the race, a new racial unity is established: a new type, to become endemic and spread its contagion through the whole race.

those days as natural and reasonable a way of accounting for a great personality and the experience of which Jesus was the cause and the centre, as it would be unnatural and irrational[1] today. The latter belief, which is itself an inference from belief in his Godhead, suggests to us that what was made manifest in the personality and life of Jesus was a manifestation in space and time of a reality super-temporal, super-historic. I shall return to this point at the end of my paper.

We must first get our basis in the historical conditions of the manifestation itself, the conditions precedent and actual.

The conditions precedent include the facts of the whole of the long life-history of Man, but more particularly the special cultural history of the race to which Jesus κατὰ σάρκα belonged—all his own inheritance of national religion and ideas of psalmists, prophets, and apocalyptists, which formed the *substratum* of his own personal conscious experience. I am quite willing to use the term "subconsciousness" instead of *substratum* if it be understood that this subconsciousness is thoroughly natural and human. He came into the world with this inheritance, or at any rate it fashioned him from the moment of his birth and provided the channels of his thought, even though he might cut some new ones or divert and give a new direction to the old.

If we give full weight to this cultural inheritance as it is known to us today, we find in Jesus a newness and originality of thought which is selective and evolutionary, shewing that he was on a higher plane and carrying us with him, in the manner of the saying attributed to him about the Law, "I am not come to destroy, but to fulfil". By his rejection of some old ideas and the emphasis of his selection, he becomes the creator of something new in the history of religion: a new conception of God and of Man and of the relations existing ("potentially", perhaps, but that is to say for all religion *really* existing) between them, of the essential character of God and the meaning and purpose of human life.

He was conscious of this newness. He was the first man to know God as he really is. To others discoveries have come, conceived by them as

---

[1] The writer of this paper was asked what he meant in this connexion by "irrational", and replied that he should call a belief "irrational" in any age if it could not be related to the generally accepted *Welt-anschauung* of the period or the knowledge or best thought or theory with regard to the matter in question at the particular time. Such a belief might therefore be rational at one time and irrational at another, according to its cultural or scientific *milieu*.

revelations of reality or truth, granted, given: they have heard the authentic voice or seen things as they are. Often they are eager to tell the world, they must "give" to others what has been "given" to them: but the world is dull of hearing, and only a few will listen. Jesus does not stand alone in this respect: he casts a kind of halo on a great company before him and after him. In the history of human thought there are instances of men who have made discoveries that remain for ever associated with their names: through them "truth", the reality of the things in question, was revealed to the world.

Jesus was also conscious of "mission". He had been chosen by God to be the first man to know him and reveal him to others, and manifest in his own person God's character and purpose by the tenour and purpose of his own life. His sense of mission grew through the course of his own experience more specialized. Nothing was to be allowed to interfere with his fulfilment of this mission. This is a high estimate of self—his significance and his life—in relation to God and to Man and the world. He has in his own esteem a unique part to play in the ever-moving Drama of the Ages and a central position in the mind and purpose of God.

Is this consciousness of self other than human? It is to the human environment, the relatively known, that we must look first. *Causae non sunt multiplicandae praeter necessitatem.* Is a really new factor necessary to produce and account for this kind of consciousness?

When Marcion's docetic view of the Redeemer was met by the objection that by those who saw him he was regarded as a man, he is said to have replied, "*satis erat illi conscientia sua*" (Tert. *de carne, 3*)— "his own knowledge of himself was enough for him". Marcion meant he knew he wasn't a man. But even when the docetic theory was excluded, the great exponents of doctrine, and Christians in general, have assumed that he was conscious of himself as divine. He knew that he was God: and our ecclesiastical theory of the Incarnation and interpretation of the Gospels proceeds on this assumption. I do not think it is in any way *either* justified by the evidence *or* required by the logic of the doctrine. I do not for a moment suppose that Jesus ever thought of himself as God. Nor do I think that even the Fourth Gospel so represents him: else, to cite one passage only, it would hardly have admitted the message sent through Mary to his brethren, "I ascend unto my Father and your Father, and my God and your God" (Jn. xx *17*).

Consciousness of being God was not one of the conditions of the *Deus homo*. The whole content of his consciousness is rightly styled "unique", but it is human. There is no saying or act certainly his, and I think none in the Synoptic Gospels (if we except the narratives of the Nature Miracles) that could not come from a man of his lineage and convictions—the convictions themselves being only "unique" in degree.

I think this reading of the facts has won fairly wide recognition among students today, who are no longer hypnotized by orthodox presuppositions. If we are to work with the orthodox theory of the Incarnation, I am sure we can only do so by making use of the conception of *kenosis*[1] to the full extent: the pre-existent Person must have so limited not only his power, but also his consciousness, as to be able to pass through the normal process of human life. He must have put so complete a restraint on memory that it could only act subconsciously without his being aware of his own prehistoric existence and life.

In my own thought on the subject I have occupied this position. . . . But it is undoubtedly exposed to many of the objections brought against all *kenotic* theories, such as are marshalled in massive array in A. B. Bruce's book *The Humiliation of Christ*. And though it represents the utmost concession that orthodoxy can make to modernist demands, or the nearest approximation that tradition strictly interpreted can reach in its always unwilling, but always inevitable, attempt to come to terms with the thought of successive ages, I do not think it can be a permanently satisfying solution of the problem. It can only be a bridge from the past to the present, and we ought perhaps to be content if most of our friends get on to it and stay there safely, refusing to follow the more active among us who are exploring the country beyond: that country which seems to promise us a habitation more permanent and a climate in which we can breathe more freely and win our souls by a venture costly, perhaps, but not to be refused by us. We do not expect a land flowing with milk and honey, and the Jericho whose walls have already fallen is behind us, though some are trying to build them again.

It is not, I am sure, to any theory of depotentiation of God that we can look to give us the conditions under which we can explain Jesus as both human and divine—the fact of the *Deus homo*. Nor could we hope

---

[1] "Self-emptying"—see *The Epistle to the Philippians* ii. 6 f.

O

to justify the theory from the mere facts of his life in the world apart from the experience known to us as the Resurrection and all that followed it. But when we attempt to place him in the light of all our knowledge of what had been before and what has been since, and see exhibited in him the real relations between God and Man and the key to the riddle of reality—and this is what the philosophy of the Incarnation sees in him—then we are able to say what his being both divine and human means.

The primary and fundamental condition is the fact that the being of God and the being of Man are indissolubly interrelated. We are familiar with the idea of the "eternal" generation of the Son (ἀεὶ γεννᾷ τὸν υἱὸν ὁ πατήρ). We have to apply the same conception to what we call the created world of finite intelligences. The Creator is not separated from his creatures: they do not exist apart from him. They have their origin in the will and love of God: they are the counterparts of that will and love, as necessary to the existence of God as he is to theirs. Neither is complete without the other. Language almost fails us, but God is always being actualized, fulfilled, expressed in Man; and Man only comes to full consciousness—the fullness of his potentiality—in God. It is not only that "in him we live and move and have our being", but also, however much bigger his being may be, it is true that "in us he lives and moves and has his being".

Of course we cannot appeal to our Lord's own words for more than hints of such an idea. But assuredly also we cannot for any of the forms the orthodox doctrine of the Incarnation has assumed. What is much more to the point is that it is he and his life—his experience as man in the world, his consciousness of himself so far as we can read it with the new consciousness in us which he created—that suggests it. And though we can quote none of the standard expressions of Catholic doctrine for it, there has been much Christian thought that tends to support the belief that the historic process of human experience—to use modern terms—is in some real sense God's own experience. He is the subject of it as well as we. We do not, I say, get much help from our technical statements of doctrine. Our technical definitions are frankly dualistic. They treat God and Man as two distinct real existences ("substances"), each with its own special characteristics, which are incapable of being blended or fused into one, though in Jesus Christ they are so brought together and intimately related to each other that a "union" of both can be spoken of.

A form of sound words is obtained by placing the centre of union in his person conceived of as prehistoric and divine and possessing a miraculous unifying power of holding together two distinct and disparate realities and becoming the subject of two sets of experiences which yet remain, in themselves, incongruous even while concurrent. This is to say, it is not professed that the experiences themselves are unified. The subject is one, but two distinct spheres of consciousness remain. And the fact that the unity conceived is beyond words and reason is registered by the decision for two wills and the rejection of the idea of one divine-human activity (θεανδρικὴ ἐγέργεια), as conceived by Dionysius the Areopagite and the Severians of the sixth century.

Our popular theology is indeed here in better case, and in this fact lies our better hope for the future. When we put all our traditional documents into their place in the archives of our religion for the use of our students only, to shew them how things have come to be what they are, to help them to get historical perspective: and when we go out into the market-place and speak with the man in the street, we are much more likely to be able to come to terms with him than we are with orthodoxy. Of course he thinks that God and Man are distinct—very properly (the dualism of our definitions is practically sound: the trouble is that they make this practical dualism theoretic): but the man in the street is familiar with the belief that somehow or other Jesus Christ was both God and man, and he knows that he himself has much in common with Jesus as depicted in his life in the world, and is ready to believe that the something in himself of which he is at least dimly conscious as a "not himself"—which he discerns in Jesus raised, as it were, to its highest power—may be at once really himself and God. He is in a position by no means to bring Jesus down to his own level, but to understand that he really has kinship with him even in that something in virtue of which Christians style him "Lord" and "God".

It has always been the life-blood of common Christian religion that union with God was possible for man in and through Jesus, whether thought has rested primarily on what he did for us, or rather on what he was and is; and side by side with the thought of him as Redeemer has run that of Revealer and Consummator. And in spite of the dichotomies of technical theology, some of the great theologians themselves who gave their minds to the question: How could these things be? found the answer in the fact that God was not only the source, but the continuous potency of man's life and being—the ground of his natural life as well as of the new life made possible for him by the Incarnation. The conception remains vague and attention is concentrated on the far-reaching and revolutionary effects of the Incarnation in renewing Man and opening out to him the path to his true destiny from which he had strayed. But when we use modern language and conceive of God as at once immanent and transcendent, and of personality in each of us as conditioned by and a reflection of the reality which is God: when we find the root of our personality in God, the infinite reservoir of consciousness from which our own trickling streams are drawn and fed, reservoir of all that we know as true and beautiful and good in instinct and purpose and achievement: then we recognize kinship with him, kinship of very life and being, whether by his own *fiat*, or the gift of his love, or the eternal necessity of his being. We may go on contrasting our nature and his, and using the distinction between the natural and the supernatural, but in us—in our persons— there is already the supernatural blended with the natural, there is the suggestion of an Incarnation.

Baron Friedrich von Hügel is thinking on these lines. In an address ... published in the *Constructive Quarterly*, December *1922*, under the title, "Christianity and the Supernatural", he was at pains to bring home to his readers belief in "the natural-supernatural character of human experience as a whole", and (as I understand) to suggest that we have in Jesus, the Christ, "the supreme concrete example" of such a natural-supernatural experience, so that apprehending, as we must, that "the supernatural endowment is very unequal amongst men", we find that there exists in this "one particular human mind and will" "one supremely rich, uniquely intimate union with God". "In this genuinely human mind and will, the series of all possible supernatural experience by man ... reaches its implied goal and centre." And he writes of "a reality distinct from the apprehender, and yet a reality sufficiently like the human spirit, when thus supernaturally sustained and sublimated, to be recognized by this human spirit ... as its living source, support, and end."

Or again, "Jesus ... is declared to hold in his human mind and will as much of God, of God pure, as human nature, at its best and when most completely supernaturalized, can be made by God to hold, whilst remaining genuine human nature still. And yet this same Jesus (though in this supremely heightened sense the Christ) remains thus also truly Jesus—that is, a human mind and human will bound to a human body, to sense stimulation, to history and institutions, to succession, time and space. He can thus be our Master and our Model, our Refuge and our Rest". . . .

It is, I think, only from the point of view of the natural and supernatural as already blended in the being and life of Man, that we can attach meaning to the idea and the fact of Jesus Christ as the incarnate Son of God, the supreme example of Man in conscious dependence on and union with the source and stay of his life, finding the fullness of his personal potentialities—the realization of himself—by losing himself in God, by persistent identification of thought, feeling, purpose, activity, with the highest, most pure and beneficent that Man had conceived, and by that very process carrying the achievement of the race a stage farther on, and by his personal attainment creating in the long history of human experience a new type of human personality in which we discern, as we could not otherwise have known it, the fulfilment of a design which aims at not simply throwing up from time to time an individual like him, but producing a world-wide society of human persons fashioned after that type.

Along these lines of thought we have the Catholic and common conviction that Jesus was "perfect man", the actualized ideal of man, man at the end of his evolution, complete; not that the manhood has been deified, nor yet again dehumanized (thoughts so abhorrent to Nestorius), but in virtue of its constitution *capax Dei*. And again, we have the substance of the Pauline thought of the summing up of all things in Christ which the insight of Irenaeus seized on and emphasized before Christian piety had fully recoiled from the plain facts of the Gospel history as to the "limitations" of the manhood.

All these convictions, of course, work with the idea of life as rational, with a purpose in view, an end to be attained, which is pictured as the will of a supreme personal intelligence. They are positive convictions and a complete negation of [Thomas] Hardy's idea of an unconscious will of the universe blindly at work, struggling in the dark, with just a possibility of attaining consciousness of beneficent purpose and goal and means to the end. On the other hand, they do not exclude the idea of a God who, in willing the world and personal intelligences and wills that were to be faint copies of his own, capable of conflicting with each other and with his, willed struggle for himself and them. He "created" difficulties for himself and them.

The idea of a prime Mover himself unmoved, or of a God within whose Being there is nothing analogous to the insurgencies of human affections and emotions, is not Christian, though many Christians have had it.

The one and the many of non-Christian philosophy from the beginning until now meet in the God-Man reality implied in the fact of the Incarnation and the doctrine of the Trinity. Personality is something not in essence singular, but plural. Reality is represented ultimately by the Pauline "All in All" (πάντα ἐν πᾶσιν)—a plural phrase.

I think I have said enough now for the purpose of discussion; but you will expect something more than I have said about the traditional doctrine of the "personal pre-existence" of our Lord. For St Paul, who seems to have believed in an ideal man or Messiah, stored away in the heavens, to be manifested in due season on earth, the conception was a natural, almost unconscious, inference from his belief that Jesus was Messiah. Those categories have no obvious relevance to knowledge and thought today.

Again, to early Christian religiosity, with its background of angels and daemons, its world of physics in which there was nothing that could not happen because no one knew how [or why] anything happened, the idea of the pre-existence of Jesus was an almost inevitable inference from the belief in his Godhead—an inference from an inference. God had sent his Son into the world to save it, and the Son had come of his own free will. "He loved me and gave himself for me": that is the authentic note of Christian faith and experience. And nothing can ever more convincingly commend to us the concept of God as Love than this picture of Father and Son alike and together agreeing in the great redeeming purpose and action. Any doctrine that can claim to be Christian must safeguard the conviction that the activity of redeeming love—the action of sacrifice—is the very centre of reality. . . .

We may drop the category of "substance", under cover of which the old orthodoxy could speak of "ways" or "modes" of existence— one being described as Father, one as Son, and one as Holy Spirit—a "substance" which had these three "personal" and characteristic activities: but we may not as Christians conceive of the personality of God as less capacious and rich in its activities and relationships—less subject of manifold experience of the most profound and intimate order—than our Christian forefathers represented by the philosophical terms and the human analogies in which their convictions and reflection were expressed. It is, however, significant that it is on ethical rather than metaphysical grounds that the theory of "personal pre-existence" is defended today by its only considerable champions[1]—quite a modern line of defence that is congruous with the increasingly ethical tone of ontological speculation and the current philosophy of values. It is argued that the great sacrifice which the belief that God is Love implies, which is manifested in the life of the Incarnate, must belong to the very Being of God. It must be pretemporal, prehistoric. The Son himself is involved in it, must share in it *ab initio*, in person, not only in idea. The relationship Father and Son, as representing the actuality of love and its inherent activity of sacrifice, must be rooted in the Being of God. So the Son must be as eternally existent as the Father. The religious value of the idea is obvious. I do not think we can escape the logic of the argument or entrench ourselves behind the thought of an ideal existence outside Time in contrast with a real one in Time.

But it must be observed that for scientific theology the pre-existence of the Son is not really "personal" in the sense in which popular religion understands the term. By faith in God today we mean the conviction that Power and Love and Purpose are the characteristics of ultimate reality. And the Pauline conception of pre-existence, to which I have referred, may be found to have its true religious and scientific value for us as the expression of the conviction that the personality and life of Jesus was the crowning manifestation of this divine power and love and purpose: that in him regarded as Redeemer was revealed in the fullness of time and actualized—or we might say evolved as the natural resultant in due sequence of the whole course of human experience and history to that moment—the ideal which was in God's mind in the creation of man. Where it is the eternal and inherent creativeness of God that is in action, the highest manifestation of it in human experience and history "always" "was".

---

[1] E.g. H. R. Mackintosh in *The Person of Christ*, pp. 445 f. (as indeed by A. B. Bruce, in *The Humiliation of Christ*, before him).

Or I would put it in another way and say: For love to be there must be subject and object, but there need not be reciprocation. If reality is really God and Man: if a world of finite intelligences is co-eternal with God, whether the world we know or another or many others, and if it is the externalization of himself as it has been conceived as being; then the doctrine of the Incarnation means that the expression of himself (thus externally in time in the world and Man) reached its plenitude in the man Jesus. He is the perfect expression in time and space of the personality of God: no sudden intrusion on the historic process, but its perfect product, the scion of many forefathers to be the firstborn of many brethren.

So, if I may end this long paper with an attempt to say as simply as possible what, on this conception of the conditions of the Incarnation, the Incarnation means, and put it personally, I should say that what my faith in the Godhead of Jesus means to me is that I believe that, in getting to know him, I get to know God: that what he does for me, the at-one-ment of which he makes me conscious, is a divine work. Never does he cease to be man for me: the whole appeal he makes to me is through that which I have in common with him; only when I regard him as Man can I learn anything from him. Yet what I learn from him is God as well as Man. He becomes for me merged, as it were, in God, or identical with God. It is not that love for him "leads me on" to love for the Father he loved, but that in loving him I believe I love the Father. If I am on his side, I am on God's side. If I truly serve him, I am serving God. I am constantly left to my own devices as to ways and means of living in the world as it is on the lines he manifested and reveals. But so far as I can make his ideals and his values of life my own, I am sure I am doing the will of God. God stands to me for the highest values in life, and because I believe those values were actualized in the person and life of Jesus, I must use the title "God" of him.

When I take St Thomas' words, penetrating and personal as they are, and declare Jesus "my Lord and my God", I am conscious that my categories of thought are not the same as those of a Tertullian or the Fathers of Nicaea or of Chalcedon, or of any ecclesiastical definitions down to the present day. I do not know exactly how to describe the *differentia*. It is not quite satisfactory to say that those definitions are conceived on lines of thought that are "physical" and "ontological" when they deal with the relation between Jesus and God; for those were the terms in which they described ultimate reality, and when I call Jesus God I mean to express the same relation between him and reality. I think I mean quite as much as the Fourth Evangelist meant when he created the St Thomas narrative to become the classic expression of faith in the incredible, *credo quia impossibile*, and as he meant by the words he assigns to Jesus himself: "He that hath seen me, hath seen the Father".

When our conception of reality has become essentially ethical, spiritual, personal, then our faith, our religion, must be expressed in terms of our own relation as persons to it: and when I say that the man Jesus is "God", I mean that he is for me the index of my conception of God. I say "he", because I mean not only his teaching, his own ideas about God, but also his life, his personality as a whole, as I learn it, primarily from the impression he made, so far as it can be inferred from the Gospels and the early religious experience of which he was the centre.

It is not from anything that I know beforehand about God that I infer that Jesus is God incarnate. I know almost nothing about God's character apart from Jesus. But I attribute to God the character of Jesus. I say my conception of God is formed by my conception of Jesus. The God I recognize is a supreme "person" like Jesus in all that makes "personality". In thinking of God personally as Jesus did and as we do, I believe that I am, at all events, thinking along the lines of truth, in the right direction. So Jesus is the creator of my God. The relations into which I can enter with Jesus are for me relations with God. I know, of course, that I may be the victim of an illusion; it is my faith that through this estimate of him, of his significance, I am in touch with reality. *The Way of Modernism*, pp. *92–112*

PART IX

CECIL JOHN CADOUX

AUTHORITY AND INFALLIBILITY

We may ... think of the Will of God as the ultimate ground of moral values, in the same way that we think of his Nature as the ground of all cognizable reality. The problem of authority therefore is the question, What is the truth in regard to the Nature and Will of God? And the very fact that we enter into arguments with one another on the subject presupposes a common belief that that Nature and that Will have constituted for us a great objective world of realities and values— a world which, despite its manifoldness, is yet one, a world which is our natural home, into which we fit, and which we are therefore not only disposed by a love of truth to investigate, but which we are capable of progressively discovering and interpreting. God, however, does not offer his ultimate truth to our minds with that quasi-immediacy and unmistakableness with which material objects are presented to our senses: still less can we simply equate human experience and Divine truth. It is necessary therefore to inquire as to the means at our disposal for discovering his Nature and his Will. If and when any authority other than God is accepted by a Christian man, it is accepted only on the ground that it expresses his meaning and can produce and substantiate credentials from him. If and when any such authority is rejected, it is rejected because it is not believed to have his authorization. Hence it may be truly said that "the principle of authority (namely, that of divine revelation) is the natural principle of Christian theology".[1] Men know instinctively that they stand in need of authoritative guidance and of Divine control, however inarticulate that knowledge may often be, and however confused its expression. The recent and rapid loss of faith in a number of previously venerated seats of authority

[1] Julius Kaftan, in *The American Journal of Theology*, Oct. *1900*, p. *680*.

has created something like a panic in the minds of many; and some are consequently disposed to give their support to any authoritative form of religion, so long as it *is*, in men's estimate, authoritative, irrespective of the question whether it is well- or ill-founded in the matter of truth.

To many it seems theoretically unquestionable, and in practice a *sine-quâ-non*, that God should provide us with an absolutely infallible, unmistakable, and objective embodiment of such of his truth and guidance as we need to possess. It is urged by Romanists, for instance, as a piece of cogent reasoning that, if God be believed to have given any revelation at all, he must be supposed to have made it not only obvious but incapable of error. It is urged as an unquestionable practical necessity for the Church that it should have an infallible head, a supreme court beyond which there is no appeal. It may readily be conceded that the desire for such a complete and serviceable, because plain and unerring, authority is a very natural desire for men to feel. That argument, however, is very far from proving that any such authority actually exists. Nor, of course, does the alleged necessity for it in practice (for the settlement of controversies) constitute any proof of its real presence. The question as to whether history gives us any ground for believing that such an authority has in fact been provided, will have to be considered in detail later. It remains here only to consider the argument in so far as it is advanced on grounds of *a priori* probability, namely that, if God has given us any revelation at all, then it must be through the instrumentality of some infallible authority of the kind just described. It is, however, obvious that the argument is purely presumptive, and that it ought not to be made the basis of further inferences unless and until it has been verified *a posteriori* in experience. We may not argue that, because we think it ought to be so, because we should like it to be so, because it would be very convenient in many ways if it were so, therefore it is so. That is clearly a *"non sequitur"*. "Our *a priori* assumptions of the modes in which God *must* have provided for our need of guidance and enablement are very liable to be overturned in the school of daily experience." There is nothing in the Gospels to suggest that God guarantees to protect the Church against error more completely than he protects the individual. And how much support can be found for the theory in the analogy of God's provision for our other needs? We have health and safety, and it is his will that we should have them: but has he provided any means by which we can make perfectly certain of them? Still more urgently do we—and does the Church—need sinlessness of life: still more unquestionably does God will that we and she should have it; and bounteous is the help that he has given for the quest of it. But does he undertake to keep the Church or the individual unfailingly sinless? Obviously not. Why therefore ought we to believe, prior to inquiry into the facts, that God must have acted in quite a different manner as regards our need for sound doctrine? Not only is the theory that there *must* be somewhere an infallible guide at best a plausible assumption void of logical cogency; but every analogy drawn from God's *known methods* of providing for us in other ways tends to show that, plausible or not, it is inherently unlikely to be true.

Catholicism and Christianity, pp. 105–8

THE USE OF CREEDS

That none of the Creeds can be regarded as necessarily and absolutely infallible follows of course from the general fact that they are all partially human productions, and more especially from the fallibility of the Church that fashioned and adopted them. For the purpose of the present discussion it is quite irrelevant to establish a very early date for the Apostles' Creed. Actual Apostolic authorship cannot be proved and is extremely unlikely. It may have been quite right for Bishop Pecock in the fifteenth century to urge that, even if it were not written by Apostles, that would not destroy its value: it is equally necessary to urge that, even if it were written by Apostles, that would not guarantee its infallibility, though it would of course add immensely to its authority and interest. We have seen ... how inevitably men's vision of truth is qualified and limited and at times even somewhat perverted by their personal factor. It is because the personal factor differs in different men that it is impossible to exact from any man *unconditional* assent to the statements of any other man. When we study the personal factor of the Christian fathers who framed the Church's Creeds, we find that it was in many ways special and widely different from our own. Their cosmology was geocentric, their eschatology in origin Jewish, their philosophy Stoic or Platonic: their views of historical evidence, Scriptural authority, and human personality were of necessity such as cannot be adopted by us to-day. Allow for this personal factor, and you will see at once that it puts the infallibility of the Creeds out of the question.

But if it is impossible to guarantee the infallibility of any of the Creeds or of any other definite attempt to state the Christian essentials, there must necessarily be something arbitrary in selecting one to which all must subscribe under pain of exclusion or expulsion. Many reasons may be given why, say, the Apostles' Creed, or the Nicene Creed, possesses special weight: but what exactly are the premises from which it follows that acceptance of the one or the other should be made an absolute condition of entrance into the Church of Christ? Why these Creeds in particular? There have been other unanimous beliefs of the Church (e.g. the expectation of an early and visible return of Christ) which were clearly wrong: and we can all of us think of yet other doctrines, which are not included in our selected creed, but which are yet for us and many of our fellows true and fundamental. In *1629* the Lutheran Calixtus proposed that all Christians might rally round the consent of the fathers of the fifth century; and the position of some of the early Tractarians was very similar. But why the fifth, we ask, rather than the sixth or fourth? The attempt to constitute some exact and definite body of objective teaching not simply a declaratory manifesto of the Church's position, but a touchstone for determining fitness for Church-membership, is thus clearly a mistaken method—mistaken (if for no other reason) because of necessity arbitrary.

But—more seriously still—I plead, as a matter of vital principle, that any Creed, which is to serve as a ground for excluding from the Church of Jesus Christ those who cannot entirely accept it, but who desire to enter and remain within the Church, must be either absolutely and demonstrably infallible or else utterly and disastrously unfit for the purpose. Its fitness is not proved by the usage and precedents of the past, by its wide or even universal acceptance, or by any inherent merits that it may possess. Nothing less than complete and indubitable infallibility can suffice. For if this be lacking, then the margin of uncertainty or arbitrariness or relativity, however narrow it be, may prove to be the very flaw which causes the exclusion of some genuine Christian from that Church within which *as a Christian* he has an indefeasible right to stand. Those who are not prepared to prove their credal test to be infallible must admit, on their own premises, at least the possibility that, where a modern Christian cannot accept some clause in the Creed, he may be right and the clause wrong. But if so, why exclude him from the Church for denying the clause? The Commonwealth-divines appointed by Parliament to draw up a list of the fundamental beliefs comprised in the profession of "faith in God by Jesus Christ" (which was to be the condition of religious liberty) soon found, Baxter tells us, "how ticklish a business the enumeration of fundamentals was". No wonder. Those who undertake to legislate—or to enforce the legislation of others—as to who are to be recognized to belong to the Church, may well feel, like members of the jury in a murder-case, that nothing less than certainty can justify a verdict of "guilty". Just as it is better for the guilty to escape than for the innocent to suffer capital punishment, so it is better for the errorist to be admitted to the Church than for the Lord's disciple to be excluded. No Creed, as we have already argued at length, is possessed of the requisite measure of infallibility: therefore no Christian applicant should be excluded from the Church on the ground of his refusal to subscribe a Creed.

The illegitimacy of requiring subscription to a Creed as a condition of membership in the Church early came to be a characteristic tenet of Congregationalism. It has also been observed—in whole or in part—by certain other bodies. It may however be said hardly to have received as yet, even among Congregationalists, that full explication and defence of which it stands in need. One cannot therefore be altogether surprised that it has been misunderstood. One Anglican writer, for instance, speaks of "the root fallacy of this modern Protestant position (which in its most logical and consistent form involves the rejection, upon grounds of principle, of sacraments and dogmas alike)".[1] But a distinction must in fairness be drawn between rejecting dogmas as tests of fitness for membership, even in the local church (which is what Congregationalists do), and rejecting them as authoritative though not infallible documents (which is what they do not do). Another writes as if "Christian societies which would repudiate the restraint of any creed" desire to use the Bible instead of the Creeds and in the same way in which Anglicans and Catholics use the Creeds, viz: as a sufficient basis for the unity of the Church.[2] But however confused some statements of such societies may be, their real and defensible position is not: The

[1] A. E. J. Rawlinson, in *Foundations*, p. 390.
[2] A. C. Headlam, in *The Doctrine of the Church*, p. 238.

Bible only, and not the Creed; it is rather: Neither Bible nor Creed as infallible and ultimate, but both Bible and Creed and all other true and inspired writings as sources to be learnt from by the light of God's Spirit within us.

The position here defended implies no quarrel with the Church's formulation, publication, and teaching of Creeds as such, or any insensitiveness to the deep and saving truths which the Creeds were intended to express. Although the Creed-makers themselves often regretted the necessity of formulating the faith, although they sometimes tried to be precise in matters where precision was really beyond human reach, and although the desire for an infallible formulation of "the faith" as a means of excluding heretics was due to a certain waning of primitive spirituality, yet the composition and defence of Creeds sprang, in part at least, from the thoroughly healthy and Divinely-implanted instinct which makes man desire to systematize his thought and experience into a tenable philosophy of life. The real trouble arose from—and is to-day widely perpetuated by—the failure to make allowance for the true character and seat of religious authority. Much bitterness and offence might have been avoided by more thorough and searching reflection on the psychological and philosophical aspects of this subject. It would then have been seen that the *ultimate* ground for accepting any credal statement as true is not the authority of the Church that imposes it: to appeal to that is but to push the problem one stage further back, and provoke the question, Why should the Church's judgment in this matter be trusted and obeyed? The only ultimate ground is rather the witness of God's Holy Spirit operating in the will, heart, and mind of the teachable believer. The aid of this witness, when its light is turned on the manifold data of religious history and experience, brings within the reach of men a large body of Divine truth, not all of it equally clear and certain, and not precisely defined or constant as to its limits, but sufficient in amount and reliability for the spiritual and moral needs of the day, and capable of being continually sifted, adjusted, and verified by comparison with the objective reality of things. But the whole process is qualified in each man by the personal factor, which limits and conditions and sometimes even distorts his learning, and does this in a way and measure special to himself, and beyond precise calculation or complete elimination. The operation of this personal factor in all human thinking, *for which the Catholic view of the determination of authoritative doctrine makes no allowance whatever,* does not indeed prevent much reliable learning of truth on the part of one man from the lips of another; but it does effectually debar any one man or any one set of men from defining *unconditionally* for another or others the essentials or fundamentals of Christian truth. Christians are entitled to teach and admonish, and even to warn and rebuke, one another in matters of doctrine: they are not entitled to unchurch one another because they judge differently of the essentials in doctrine. In the nature of the case, though we have the same God and the same Saviour Jesus Christ, yet the apprehensible essentials of Divine truth cannot be the same for us all. "Although the perfection of knowledge in matters of religion is an object of the most worthy ambition to every Christian for himself, something immensely less than the perfection of religious knowledge is all we are entitled to demand from others as the condition of holding with them Christian fellowship."[1] In the open-eyed Christian charity and wisdom which recognizes not only the limitations of all human attempts to understand the ways of God, but also the necessary differences in the attempts of different men, we have the one and sufficient basis for religious toleration.

The Christian Church, from its very nature, cannot therefore be built up into any true unity by demanding from those who desire to enter it any defined minimum standard of attainment either in practical virtue or in belief. Perfection in belief, as in conduct, it is our duty to strive after, and the duty of the Church to assist us to attain. It may even at times become the Church's duty strongly to recommend a suspension of fellowship until penitence has atoned for some grave moral lapse. But just as there can be no exact *definition* of that measure of moral failure which deprives a man, *against his own desire,* of the Christian name, so there can be no exact definition of that measure of doctrinal imperfection which entitles others to exclude him *against his will* from the Church. To fix on some particular Creed for the purpose is, as we have shown, mistaken in principle and calamitous in results. The same could be said of the alternatives sometimes suggested in place of the Creed, such as the Te Deum or the Lord's Prayer. The only condition of mutual recognition which Christians are entitled to exact from Christians, and which the Church is entitled to demand from candidates

---

[1] Isaac Taylor, *Fanaticism (1833),* p. *349.*

P

for membership, is the expressed wish for that membership, public avowal of faith in Jesus Christ, and acceptance of whatever that may be found to involve in the search for truth in belief and for righteousness in life. That, and that only, is the real *"quod semper, quod ubique, quod ab omnibus"*.   *Ibid.*, pp. *242–8*

MIRACLES

When objection is raised to the philosophical presuppositions of the critic, what is generally meant is that he refuses credence to some or all of the biblical miracles. A good deal, though not everything, here depends on how one defines the term. For a miracle is not simply a wonderful and unusual event that surprises us, but is in essence a clear departure from the regular ways of Nature, in so far as these are conceived of as governed by known laws. Could we agree that miracles are brought about by some natural law not yet detected or understood, a considerable step towards agreement would have been taken. But this is precisely what orthodox scholars will not admit. It seems to them necessary to the real initiative of God that such incidents should *not* be instances of unexplored natural laws, but that they (or at least some of them) should be special and unique irruptions of God into Nature *as it really is*. There can be no doubt that it was this sense of the word "miracles" that the Vatican Council had in mind in anathematizing those who deny their occurrence. We are all well aware of the fact that there has prevailed in the past a very widespread prejudice against belief in any "miracle" (in either sense of the word), that the same prejudice exists to-day in certain quarters, but that (owing to revolutionary enlargements of our scientific knowledge of the universe) the dis-inclination to admit the possibility of miracles has recently weakened very considerably indeed. The assumption is often made that biblical higher critics as a class decide in advance that miracles are impossible, and come to the evidence with their minds unreasonably made up to deny them. But this has certainly not been the attitude of the majority of such critics; nor is it at all a necessary element even in the advanced position known as liberal modernism. Critics and modernists do not need to say—and for the most part do not say—"No such thing as a real miracle has ever actually happened". Quite well-attested narratives turn up from time to time describing events for which no scientific explanation is known. The beating of a man's heart is restored after ceasing for three minutes when he is under an anaesthetic. An Egyptian fakir, in a state of catalepsy, is kept for an hour in a coffin under water, and is seen to be alive and well after the experiment. A Bedouin, under the close inspection of witnesses (including an English traveller), thrice licks a red-hot spoon without suffering any sort of harmful effect on his tongue. Such incidents undoubtedly occur, and could certainly be multiplied if one took the trouble to collect and test the evidence. The records of psychical research are particularly rich in them, though not possessing any monopoly. Modern scientific method takes cognizance of the great power of spirit over matter and of our very limited knowledge of the real Laws of Nature, and forbids us to say in advance that anything this is not self-contradictory is impossible. But to admit the possibility of miracles is very far from settling the problem of the historicity of those miracles with which the biblical critic is concerned. The question the critic has to decide is rather this: Given the existence of this or that miraculous narrative, which is the more likely to be true, that the miracle really happened, and was accurately reported, or that the miracle did not happen, but somehow came to be mistakenly believed and reported to have happened? In endeavouring to answer this question rightly, he cannot help feeling that, in view of *all* that we know about Nature and about the minds and habits of men, a miraculous narrative must necessarily labour under a great initial and inherent improbability. With all due concessions as to what is possible on a theistic view of the universe, the presumption is that God's modes of working in the physical world are constant and will remain so. It is only playing with the problem to urge the obvious truths that many familiar things, such as the conception and birth of a child, and the conversion of a soul, are miracles, that at bottom everything in Nature is beyond our powers to explain it, and is in that sense miraculous, and that—in philosophy and theology especially—"*omnia abeunt in mysterium*". The question turns not on ultimate inexplicability, but upon rarity and strangeness, and consists in weighing the trustworthiness of the narrative against its inherent improbability. No student would think twice about admitting this improbability in the case of non-biblical and (especially if he were a Catholic) non-ecclesiastical narratives. The question is entirely one of adequate evidence. "The evidence for miracles," my conservative friend used to tell me, "is

P*

there all right; only you will not accept it." But before I accept it, I must know whether it is sufficient to justify belief: for does not honesty require me to withhold belief from any statement unless there is at least sufficient evidence to make its truth more probable than its untruth? In weighing the evidence, we have to remember the admittedly uniform habit of all other religions, besides Judaism and Christianity to produce untrue miraculous narratives (a tendency shared, as many educated Catholics would be ready to admit, by mediaeval Catholicism); we have to take into consideration how oriental and especially Semitic minds would be likely to work in an unscientific age and under the impulse of strong religious feeling; and we have to make due allowance for the fact that, in Scripture as in other religious narratives, the element of miracle is comparatively rare in documents contemporary with the events, and increases in almost exact proportion with the years that elapse after their occurrence. Is it unreasonable, in the face of facts like these, to hold that the evidence for the biblical miracles—broadly speaking—does not nearly reach that severe standard of strength which we must demand as a condition of credence? Is it not at least a sound principle of study that natural explanations of the data must be exhausted before recourse is had to theories of miraculous or even exceptional providences?

At the bottom of the stubborn defence of the Bible-miracles against liberal criticism is the notion—consciously or unconsciously held—that without them we have no guarantee of the real activity and initiative of God in human affairs. Miracles have stood for the real participation of God in man's life, the means by which he intended to create, or at least to encourage, faith in himself, and frequently in experience the real cause or occasion of that faith. To this it may be replied on behalf of criticism, firstly, that an increasing number of modern religious minds derive no religious help whatever from miracle-narratives as such, have no wish to see their historicity proved, and are only repelled by being required to believe them; secondly, that there is after all no good reason for regarding a miracle as the only really cogent evidence or guarantee of the Divine activity. It is perfectly possible in the abstract, and not rare in experience, to disbelieve all miracles (in the sense of real breaches purposely effected *ad hoc* by God in the order of Nature), to treat all abnormal incidents that are well-attested as due to the operation of as yet unknown natural laws, to think of the natural as including the supernatural within itself, and at the same time to believe in the fullest sense in the Heavenly Father of Jesus Christ.   *Ibid.*, pp. *195–8*

PART X

WILLIAM ADAMS BROWN

THE ESSENCE OF CHRISTIANITY

In order to establish the scientific character of any definition, we have seen that two things are necessary. It must be universal, and it must be definite. That is to say, in the first place, the standard to which appeal is made must be one which is open to men in general, and not simply private or esoteric; and, in the second place, the qualities in which the distinctive character of the object is found must be stated with such clearness and precision as practically to admit the application of the test. If, then, it is a question of defining Christianity we must be able to show, first, that the standard to which we appeal is really one which admits a universal application, and secondly, that our definition is sufficiently clear and unambiguous to enable the test to be made. Is this possible in the present case?

Criticisms of what may be called the dogmatic conception of Christianity[1] are commonly based upon the first of these grounds. It is claimed that the supernatural evidence to which appeal is made is something of which science knows nothing, and which a large proportion of reasonable men reject. On the testimony of its own advocates religion is isolated from the rest of human life, and confined to a transcendent realm to which only the select company of the initiated possess the key. To talk of a scientific definition under such circumstances is to misuse words.

This argument, though plausible, fails to stand the test of serious examination. If universal assent at any particular time be the test of scientific truth, then science in every form is impossible. Not all men are in possession of the evidence, nor are all competent by habit and

---

[1] We use the phrase as a convenient designation for all definitions, whether Catholic or Protestant, which take their departure from the ontological view of the Absolute.

training to judge it even when presented. All that can reasonably be asked is that there should be no inherent obstacle in the way; that the evidence be open to him who is willing to take the trouble to qualify himself to approach it, and that in the case of those best fitted to make the test, actual agreement should have been reached. In the case of a definition of Christianity, therefore, all that needs to be shown is that the evidence is open to all men who choose to fulfil the conditions.

This is, in fact, what the advocates of the dogmatic view claim. The Christian apologist, whether Catholic or Protestant, is well aware that all men do not recognize the force of his evidence. But he maintains that good reasons can be given for their failure. Many causes are responsible, some intellectual, some moral. When these are removed, as through the results of Christian instruction and contact is constantly being done, the expected recognition follows. With the steady growth of the Christian church and the consequent extension of the Christian experience, the number of men who are open to the Christian evidences is continually increasing, and it is only a question of time when the universal assent which science demands shall be reached.

We are not now concerned to inquire whether this hope is well founded. That is a matter which can only be determined by experience. One may take as unfavorable a view as one pleases of what is likely to be the outcome of such an experiment. Our present contention is simply that, so far as universal consent is concerned, there is nothing in the dogmatic conception of Christianity to render a scientific definition *a priori* impossible.[1]

The real difficulty with the dogmatic conception of Christianity lies elsewhere. The trouble is not with the court of appeal, but with the use to be made of it when it is found. Definitions based upon the ontological conception fail because they are unable to express their conception of Christianity in sufficiently clear and unambiguous terms to admit of a scientific test, even before judges of their own choosing. This may seem a curious charge to bring. Indefiniteness is not usually

---

[1] An exception must of course be made in the case of all theories which deny the possibility of a universal Christian experience. If, as in some forms of historic Calvinism, God be thought of as arbitrarily withholding from a part of mankind the knowledge of those facts concerning Himself upon which right thinking depends, it is not possible to appeal to any universally accepted standard, and a scientific definition of Christianity is therefore out of the question.

thought to be the besetting sin of the dogmatist. When he is criticized, it is commonly for over rather than for under definition. Yet the two points are not so inconsistent as a superficial judgment might conclude. Too great detail may be as confusing as too little. It is the disposition, common to Catholic and Protestant alike, to extend the absoluteness of Christianity over the widest possible territory which is the parent of the indefiniteness of which we complain. True Christianity, we are told, is what the church teaches or what the Scriptures reveal. But what does the church teach? How far does the Biblical revelation extend? Here we find differences of opinion. The exegetes agree as little as the doctors. Nor is there anything either in the churchly or in the Biblical principle which of itself enables us to decide between them. That which in theory is claimed as the chief merit of each, its supernatural character, proves in practice its fatal weakness. The Absolute knows no difference of value or of degree. Yet without the recognition of such differences, how is it possible to secure the definiteness which is essential to scientific definition?

No doubt this indefiniteness is more apparent in the former case than in the latter. Here the vastness of the territory opens up a field for misunderstanding which is little less than appalling. It was not a Protestant controversialist, but her own great teacher, who said of the Catholic church that she was a *corpus permixtum*, containing within her capacious bosom both the good and the evil, the false and the true.[1] Strange bed-fellows have found themselves united by the tradition principle. To harmonize all the material which has received Catholic sanction would be an impossible task. If we are bidden to look to the decisions of the church, it is only to be met by new perplexities, for the councils themselves do not agree; or, what comes to the same thing for our present purpose, honest men have not yet been able to discover their agreement. The official definitions themselves need defining. When this has been done, there remains the task of reconciling the new dogma with the old; while still beyond crowds a circle of questions, more or less vital, upon which no decision has been reached. Thus we find that one who takes refuge from the strife of the schools in the bosom of the church Catholic, does not escape from uncertainties.[2] If

[1] Augustine, *De Doctrina Christiana*, iii. *32*.
[2] An excellent illustration is to be found in the often-quoted passage from Cardinal Newman's *Apologia*, in which he describes the state of his mind since

we wish a clear definition of essential Christianity, we must seek our
answer elsewhere.

Nor is it otherwise with the Biblical principle. No doubt Holy
Scripture furnishes a standard at once more definite and more manage-
able than tradition. But when it comes to defining essential Christianity,
we find that its acceptance does not deliver us from uncertainty. The
Bible is a large book. It extends over many centuries, and includes the
most diverse matters. As to the meaning and relative importance of
much that it contains interpreters are not agreed. The Westminster
Confession bids us distinguish, within the teaching of Scripture, between certain weighty matters essential to salvation, and others less
important about which good men may differ without peril.[1] But when
we try to carry out this distinction in practice we find that it is by no
means easy. What is essential, and what is unessential? This is the very
point on which we find the widest difference of opinion. Here the
Biblical principle fails us. For this simply asserts the infallible authority
of all that Scripture contains, leaving each man free to interpret his
authority as best he may. Calvinist and Arminian, churchman and indi-
vidualist, rationalist and mystic, each appeals to the book in support
of his own peculiar view of Christianity, and condemns those who
differ from him as unbiblical. It would seem, then, that if we are to

---

entering the Roman church. The certainty in which he there represents himself
as rejoicing is simply the clear perception that certainty is impossible. It is the
peace which follows the abandonment of a hopeless quest. His answer to those who
object to the doctrines of the church as unbelievable is their removal from the
realm to which rational tests apply. Catholic doctrine, he tells us, deals not with
phenomena but with substance. And substance is "what no one on earth knows
anything about". Armed with this principle of "invincible ignorance", it is easy
for him to accept the most mysterious dogmas, sure that no assault of human
reason can penetrate to the inaccessible fortress within which they have withdrawn themselves for refuge. Does one object that transubstantiation is not true,
since he has seen the bread, and its qualities remain unchanged? The Catholic
doctrine "does not say that the phenomena go; on the contrary, it says that they
remain; nor does it say that the same phenomena are in several places at once.
It deals with what no one on earth knows anything about, the material substances
themselves. And, in like manner, of that majestic article of the Anglican as well as
of the Catholic creed,—the doctrine of the Trinity in Unity. What do I know of
the Essence of the Divine Being? I know that my abstract idea of three is simply
incompatible with my idea of one; but when I come to the question of concrete
fact, I have no means of proving that there is not a sense in which one and three
can equally be predicated of the Incommunicable God."

[1] i. 6, 7.

gain a satisfactory answer to our question some more definite test must be found.

Thus in both its great historic forms the dogmatic position proves itself unsatisfactory. The philosophical basis on which it rests is a realism which antedates the results of modern critical study. Its Absolute suggests problems rather than solves them. Judged on its own merits without prejudice, it is unable to give us a definition which, by reason of its clearness, conciseness, and general acceptance is worthy to be called scientific.[1]

With the other two methods of approaching our problem we may deal more briefly. However different the conclusions to which they come, they move in the same general world of thought, and the question at issue between them admits of being very simply stated. Both the advocates of the mathematical and the psychological views are convinced that if the distinctive character of Christianity is to be found at all, it must be sought in the positive qualities which characterize it as a historic religion, and which are to be determined by the same methods of comparison which science employs in all other departments of research. The question is simply whether or no this inductive method is compatible with the recognition of the absoluteness of Christianity in any sense. Those who hold the mathematical view deny this; those who take the psychological view affirm it. The question, as we shall see, resolves itself into this: whether the conception of the Absolute is purely negative, or whether it has a positive significance which justifies its use in scientific discussion.

To those who take the former view, any attempt to conceive of the Absolute positively involves a contradiction in terms. As the ultimate reality, it lies back of experience, as the unapproachable goal, both of thought and of aspiration. It has its psychological foundation, as a

---

[1] It is hardly necessary to state that in thus criticizing the ontological conception of Christianity, we are far from denying the scientific value of the work done by many of those who have shared this view. The great theologians, Catholic and Protestant alike, have not been content with such general conceptions of Christianity as we have indicated. They have sought to discover on the basis of reason, history, and experience what were the distinctive features of their religion, and have set them forth and defended them with a clearness worthy of all praise. Our present contention is simply that so far as they have been successful in accomplishing their aim, it has been by ignoring the indefinite standards which are all that their philosophy allows, and seeking the definition of Christianity along other and less ambiguous lines.

necessary concept of the mind. And it may even be granted a certain objective reality, in that it is a fact that our finite and limited experience is set in the midst of the great ocean of the infinite. But—so far as we are concerned—the function of this unknown reality is purely negative. It is, as we have already seen, a concept of limitation; the mark of the boundary of our knowledge. So far as the latter advances, it recedes. Nor can any conceivable increase of experience bring man to a positive knowledge of the infinite. Even if we conceive this unfathomed region as the home of some mysterious being upon whom our finite universe depends, we are no whit better off. For of the nature of this mysterious something we can form no conception. The Absolute in all its forms is by definition unknowable.

It is clear that from this point of view an absolute religion is out of the question. On all sides of life, moral, intellectual, aesthetic, religious, man is shut up to the sphere of the relative. From our limited subjective point of view, we may compare things as better or worse, more or less true, more or less beautiful; but the distinctions have only relative validity, and are constantly being superseded and corrected by an enlarging experience. The several religions are natural phenomena in which, under the differing conditions in which he has found himself, and with more or less crudity and imperfection, man has endeavored at once to express and to deepen his sense of the mystery and the wonder of life. So far as they attempt positive interpretation they are all alike superstitious and inadequate; yet this does not hinder them from performing a useful function in human life. They are necessary steps in the evolution of humanity, and form an outlet for natural instincts which cannot but seek expression. To pick out one fro them number of these partial and inadequate religions in order to raise it to a position of absolute supremacy is to be guilty of the greatest inconsistency.

We find those who take this position differing widely in their positive estimate of Christianity. One regards it as a mere superstition, all the more dangerous because of its great age and many-sided associations; an enemy against which all right-minded men ought to unite in making war, and which in time is destined to be utterly overthrown and destroyed, in order to make way for the irreligion which is to be the religion of the future. Another recognizes in it the highest flower of human genius, sees in its doctrines symbols of profound spiritual truth, and cheerfully admits the extraordinary part which it has played in the betterment of society and the elevation of the race. Some even go so far as to bow reverently before its founder as the best and purest of the sons of men, and gladly unite with those who frequent its churches in the worship of that mysterious being whose counsels are unsearchable and his ways past finding out. But whatever may be the particular attitude taken to Christianity, it can never include the element of finality which absoluteness involves. Beautiful and helpful though it may be, Christianity is only a stage in the religious history of humanity, destined in time to be superseded by another, more helpful and more beautiful.

The weakness of this position lies in its exaggeration. It seizes upon one meaning of the term Absolute, and emphasizes it to the exclusion of others equally legitimate. What the advocates of the mathematical view tell us of the part played by the sense of mystery in religion is entirely in place, and no one is more ready to recognize it than the Christian. It is true that God is greater than our thought, and that all our knowledge is set in the midst of a vast ocean of ignorance. Against all dogmatic efforts to stretch our knowledge beyond its proper limits the agnostic protest is in place. We need to be called down from the transcendental realm where theology has often made its home, and to be set to the more fruitful task of studying experience that we may learn what it has to teach us.

But it is a mistake to think that in coming back to experience we take leave of the Absolute. This common opinion rests on a failure to understand the real meaning of the term. By the Absolute we mean the ultimate reality, that in which thought and aspiration rest. This may be a positive conception as well as a negative one. Experience is full of ultimates. Force, law, reason, beauty, duty, personality, love; all of these are general conceptions in which thought may rest, and which, therefore, it is open to man to conceive as absolute. This is the truth for which the psychological view stands.

When, therefore, the advocates of the mathematical view tell us that an absolute religion is a contradiction in terms, we answer that we are not speaking about the same thing. They are thinking of that side of God which by definition can never be known. We are thinking of God, so far as he manifests himself to human thought and experience. The Absolute which we seek to know is that which is absolute for us. We wish to discover, if possible, what that principle is which, so far as human experience goes, is final. To say that this is impossible is to prejudge *a priori* that which can only be determined as a result of experiment. It is to rule out of court with a single stroke of the pen the entire enterprise upon which philosophy has been embarked from the beginning of time.

For what is philosophy, if it be not the search for the Absolute? In all its forms, from Anaxagoras to Hegel, it is the effort to discover what is the ultimate reality in the universe, and to define its nature in the simplest and clearest terms. Prove to men that this attempt is foredoomed to fail, and you cut the nerve of philosophic thought. At the basis of all large speculative endeavor lies a faith in the rationality of the world; and this, when properly understood, is only a different form of stating the knowability of the Absolute. To say that this is a rational world is to say that the ultimate principles by which it is governed lie within the reach of human reason. Even philosophers theoretically the most sceptical show by their practice that they share this faith. Thus Mr Spencer,[1] in the very same breath in which he speaks of the Absolute as unknowable, declares that it is cause and force, and proceeds to set it about all manner of indispensable work in his universe. Even to say that the Absolute is unknowable implies the previous possession of a final standard of knowledge, and, so far forth, a positive acquaintance with the ultimate reality. Let a man try to think at all, and he will find it simply impossible to avoid a conception, more or less positive, of the Absolute. As he studies the universe and is drawn more and more under the spell of its wondrous unity and order, man feels himself in the presence of a single all-comprehending principle, and he cannot but believe that as he penetrates more deeply into the nature and meaning of life, he is at the same time coming to understand the nature of the supreme being who is its cause. Modern philosophy differs from ancient, not in the object of its search, but in its clearer perception of the difficulties in the way, and in its franker recognition of the subjective conditions through conformity to which alone success is possible.

What we have called the psychological conception of the Absolute is simply the new view of God which is the result of this conviction. It is the view which finds God in his world rather than outside of it; and

---

[1] Herbert Spencer (*1820–1903*), to whose *First Principles*, published in *1862*, the author is here alluding. (*Ed.*)

seeks to gain an insight into the nature of the ultimate reality through the discovery of the permanent elements in the experience of man.

Approaching the problem in this spirit, we see at once that the Absolute may have two very different meanings according to our point of view. In the narrower sense, it denotes that principle which is final for the individual man. Each of us has his own standard, more or less clear and definite, his own conception, more or less crude, of the ultimate reality; in a word, his own Absolute. These several standards differ among themselves, and the reconciliation and overcoming of their differences is the problem of philosophy. The philosophic standpoint differs from that of the individual in that it attempts to rise above the various petty and local considerations by which each man's opinion is more or less determined to a region of truly universal judgments. The Absolute of philosophy is won by abstracting from the several judgments of individuals all that is accidental and temporary. It is that principle or standard which is valid for man as man.

Applying these principles to our matter of the absolute religion, we see their bearing at once. By the absolute religion we mean a religion which is valid for man as man; one which meets every essential religious need, and satisfies every permanent religious instinct, and which, because it does this, does not need to be altered or superseded. Such a religion, if it could be found, would realize the idea of the absolute religion. The question of the absoluteness of Christianity in the philosophical sense is the question whether as a matter of fact Christianity can be shown to possess these characteristics.

In endeavoring to answer this question two points need to be considered; first, that of the abstract possibility of such a religion, and secondly, that of the method of its proof.

The first admits of a very short answer. Whatever one may think of the likelihood or unlikelihood of such a religion as a matter of fact, no reasonable man can deny its possibility. Among the various alternatives which the future presents, it is at least conceivable that it may include a religion which, by the richness and many-sidedness with which it meets the religious needs of man in general, shall prove itself, from the human standpoint with which we have here alone to do, ultimate.

Granting the possibility of such a religion, how is its existence to be proved? Here it is evident that the appeal to history must be final. From the point of view of the individual man, his own religious experience may be sufficient. But so long as good men differ there is need of an appeal to some wider standard. Clearly in this case the only way in which the absolute religion could justify its claim would be for it to show itself absolute in fact. If its claim is a valid one, we should expect to find it drawing to itself the good and wise of all ages and races; to see them owning its supremacy, and winning out of its abundance unfailing supply for their deepest needs. Not until this victorious progress had reached its completion, and we beheld all men organized into a great brotherhood under the shelter of a single faith, would it be possible to speak of a proof of the absoluteness of any religion, which should be in the strict sense scientific.

But in the meantime, while the process is incomplete, what then? Are we shut up to uncertainties? Must we wait till the end of time before we make up our minds? Or if, discouraged by the shortness of our life, compared with the vast stage upon which the mighty drama is to be played out, we make a premature choice, must it be at the peril of our scientific standing? This is not the attitude which men take in other departments of life. The student of physical science is not deterred by the fact that his induction is not complete, from making his theory as to the ultimate reality which we call matter. Nor does the fact that his predecessors have made mistakes shake his faith that the problem may ultimately be solved, and that his work may have a share in bringing about the solution. Each new statement, if founded upon honest study of the facts, brings the goal nearer, and narrows the range of inquiry within which the final solution is to be sought. In like manner of the ultimate religious problems. If there be a God, more and more clearly revealing himself in the religious life of man, the effort to understand his revelation, and to determine wherein its distinctive features consist, cannot be hopeless. Especially must this be the case with those men who have found in some particular historic faith the key to the world problem, and the solution of the mystery of the individual human life. Possessed of such convictions, they are constrained to express them with all the clearness of which they are master, to relate them to other forms of thought and life, and to discover, and so far as may be to remove, the difficulties which have thus far kept others of their fellow men from so inspiring and uplifting an insight. Surely, if the absolute religion is ever to win the universal recognition which is its right, it must be through some such process as this.

Upon this problem some of the finest minds of Christendom have been at work for more than a century. Rejecting the dilemma presented to them both by the dogmatist and the agnostic, they have sought to show that on purely scientific grounds it is possible to maintain the finality of Christianity. Various influences have combined to lead them to this conviction. On the intellectual side, there is the belief that the idea of the Absolute is too deeply inwrought into human life and thought to be ignored, together with the resulting desire to gain a conception of it which shall avoid the crass dualism of ordinary dogmatic theology, with its sharp antithesis between the natural and the supernatural. On the religious side, there is the conviction that Christianity stands for truths too lofty, and experiences too precious, to be put on a par with those of any other religion, however worthy, together with the resulting desire to find some way to express this uniqueness, which shall not do violence to the intellectual standards which govern the rest of life. But whatever the special interest which leads to the endeavor, they agree in striving to justify the claim of Christianity to a unique position by calling attention to certain definite characteristics which separate it from all other known religions. Or, to put the matter in another form, they attempt a scientific definition of Christianity which shall include its absoluteness.

This being the case, the subject with which the present essay deals becomes of the highest importance. The history of the attempt to define Christianity scientifically is at the same time the history of the effort to determine what are the permanent elements in historic Christianity which justify its absolute claim. The two things stand or fall together. If we cannot discover what Christianity is, it is hopeless to try to defend it. *The Essence of Christianity*, pp. *26–42*

INDEX OF PERSONS

INDEX OF SUBJECTS